Henry Jones

The Laws and Principles

of whist stated and explained and its practice illustrated on an original system

Henry Jones

The Laws and Principles
of whist stated and explained and its practice illustrated on an original system

ISBN/EAN: 9783337192600

Printed in Europe, USA, Canada, Australia, Japan

Cover: Foto ©Suzi / pixelio.de

More available books at **www.hansebooks.com**

FRONTISPIECE.

RUFF and HONOURS (from the Compleat Gamester 1680)

" Lastly, observe the Women with what grace
They sit, and look their Partners in the face,
Who from their eyes shoot Cupids fiery darts;
Thus make them lose at once their Game and Hearts."

THE

LAWS AND PRINCIPLES

OF

WHIST

STATED AND EXPLAINED

AND ITS

PRACTICE ILLUSTRATED

ON AN ORIGINAL SYSTEM

BY MEANS OF HANDS PLAYED COMPLETELY THROUGH.

BY

"CAVENDISH."

TENTH EDITION,
REVISED AND GREATLY ENLARGED.

LONDON:
THOS. DE LA RUE & CO.
1875.

PRINTED BY
THOMAS DE LA RUE AND CO., BUNHILL ROW
LONDON.

𝔗𝔬 𝔱𝔥𝔢 𝔐𝔢𝔪𝔬𝔯𝔶

OF

JAMES CLAY

PREFACE TO THE FIRST EDITION.

It has often occurred to the Author that there are two principal defects in the existing treatises on the game of Whist—the one that the principles of play are, in general, laid down as so many isolated and arbitrary conventions, the reasons upon which such principles are based being seldom, if at all, and scarcely ever fully, stated; the other, that suitable illustrations, by which alone the principles can be brought forcibly home and fixed in the memory, are almost entirely wanting. The present work is an attempt to supply these deficiencies. With regard to the latter, the Author feels that nothing, in point of illustration of principles, can be so instructive as a selection of hands played completely through, and accompanied by copious explanations. The idea, it is believed, as applied to Whist, is a new one, though a similar plan has long been in use in treatises on Chess.

It has not been deemed necessary to occupy space by detailing the mode of playing and of scoring, as this information can be readily acquired at the table. The reader is, therefore, credited with this elementary knowledge, and is conducted at once to the General Principles, which he is advised to consider carefully before proceeding to the Hands.

PREFACE TO THE EIGHTH EDITION.

SINCE the publication of the previous edition, the Laws of Whist have been revised by the Arlington and Portland Clubs, and the revised laws have been generally adopted. The Author acknowledges with thanks the permission granted him to print the Club Code *verbatim*.

Some cases and decisions are added. These being approved by "J. C." are submitted with confidence to the reader.

The whole of the Part included under the head of "General Principles" has been carefully revised.

The hands have been recast, and diagram cards substituted for the symbols formerly used.

PORTLAND CLUB,
January, 1868.

PREFACE TO THE TENTH EDITION.

THE stereotype plates of the ninth edition being worn out, the Author has once more submitted his work to careful revision. He has also made the following additions :—1. A Historical Sketch of the Game of Whist. 2. A fuller statement of the principles which should guide the discard. 3. Some illustrations of the best known *coups*. 4. A number of fresh Hands (the Hands also have been re-arranged). 5. An Appendix on a new method, suggested by the Author, of leading from suits of more than four cards. And 6. An Appendix on the Management of Trumps when led or called for by the partner.

PORTLAND CLUB,
June 1, 1874.

CONTENTS.

PART I.
GENERAL PRINCIPLES.
THE FIRST HAND OR LEAD.

THE SECOND HAND.

THE THIRD HAND.

THE FOURTH HAND.

TRUMPS.

PART II.

THE LAWS OF WHIST.

BY PERMISSION, *VERBATIM* FROM THE CLUB CODE.

THE FOOT NOTES ARE ADDED BY THE AUTHOR.

———•◇•———

THE RUBBER.

1. The rubber is the best of three games. If the first two games be won by the same players, the third game is not played.

SCORING.

2. A game consists of five points. Each trick, above six, counts one point.

3. Honours, *i.e.*, Ace, King, Queen, and Knave of trumps, are thus reckoned:

If a player and his partner, either separately or conjointly, hold—

    I. The four honours, they score four points.
    II. Any three honours, they score two points.
    III. Only two honours, they do not score.

4. Those players, who, at the commencement of a deal, are at the score of four, cannot score honours.

B

5. The penalty for a revoke[1] takes precedence of all other scores. Tricks score next. Honours last.

6. Honours, unless claimed before the trump card of the following deal is turned up, cannot be scored.

7. To score honours is not sufficient; they must be called at the end of the hand; if so called, they may be scored at any time during the game.

8. The winners gain—

    I. A treble, or game of three points, when their adversaries have not scored.

    II. A double, or game of two points, when their adversaries have scored less than three.

    III. A single, or game of one point, when their adversaries have scored three, or four.

9. The winners of the rubber gain two points (commonly called the rubber points), in addition to the value of their games.

10. Should the rubber have consisted of three games, the value of the losers' game is deducted from the gross number of points gained by their opponents.

11. If an erroneous score be proved, such mistake can be corrected prior to the conclusion of the game in which it occurred, and such game is not concluded until the trump card of the following deal has been turned up.

---

1 *Vide* Law 72.

12. If an erroneous score, affecting the amount of the rubber,[1] be proved, such mistake can be rectified at any time during the rubber.

CUTTING.

13. The ace is the lowest card.

14. In all cases, every one must cut from the same pack.

15. Should a player expose more than one card, he must cut again.

FORMATION OF TABLE.

16. If there are more than four candidates, the players are selected by cutting: those first in the room having the preference. The four who cut the lowest cards play first, and again cut to decide on partners; the two lowest play against the two highest; the lowest is the dealer, who has choice of cards and seats, and, having once made his selection, must abide by it.

17. When there are more than six candidates, those who cut the two next lowest cards belong to the table, which is complete with six players; on the retirement of one of those six players, the candidate who cut the next lowest card has a prior right to any aftercomer to enter the table.

---

[1] *e.g.* If a single is scored by mistake for a double or treble, or *vice versâ.*

CUTTING CARDS OF EQUAL VALUE.

18. Two players cutting cards of equal value,[1] unless such cards are the two highest, cut again; should they be the two lowest, a fresh cut is necessary to decide which of those two deals.[2]

19. Three players cutting cards of equal value cut again; should the fourth (or remaining) card be the highest, the two lowest of the new cut are partners, the lower of those two the dealer; should the fourth card be the lowest, the two highest are partners, the original lowest the dealer.[3]

CUTTING OUT.

20. At the end of a rubber, should admission be claimed by any one, or by two candidates, he who

---

[1] In cutting for partners.

[2] *Example.* A three, two sixes, and a knave are cut. The two sixes cut again, and the lowest plays with the three. Suppose at the second cut, the two sixes cut a king and a queen, the queen plays with the three.

If at the second cut a lower card than the three is cut, the three still retains its privileges as original low, and has the deal and choice of cards and seats.

[3] *Example.* Three aces and a two are cut. The three aces cut again. The two is the original high, and plays with the highest of the next cut.

Suppose at the second cut, two more twos and a king are drawn. The king plays with the original two, and the other pair of twos cut again for deal

Suppose instead, the second cut to consist of an ace and two knaves. The two knaves cut again, and the highest plays with the two.

has, or they who have, played a greater number of consecutive rubbers than the others is, or are, out; but when all have played the same number, they must cut to decide upon the out-goers; the highest are out.

ENTRY AND RE-ENTRY.

21. A candidate wishing to enter a table must declare such intention prior to any of the players having cut a card, either for the purpose of commencing a fresh rubber, or of cutting out.

22. In the formation of fresh tables, those candidates who have neither belonged to nor played at any other table have the prior right of entry; the others decide their right of admission by cutting.

23. Any one quitting a table prior to the conclusion of a rubber, may, with consent of the other three players, appoint a substitute in his absence during that rubber.

24. A player cutting into one table, whilst belonging to another, loses his right[1] of re-entry into that latter, and takes his chance of cutting in, as if he were a fresh candidate.[2]

25. If any one break up a table, the remaining players have the prior right to him of entry into any other, and should there not be sufficient vacancies at such other table to admit all those candidates, they settle their precedence by cutting.

---

[1] i.e. his prior right.
[2] And last in the room (vide Law 16).

SHUFFLING.

26. The pack must neither be shuffled below the table nor so that the face of any card be seen.

27. The pack must not be shuffled during the play of the hand.

28. A pack, having been played with, must neither be shuffled, by dealing it into packets, nor across the table.

29. Each player has a right to shuffle, once only, except as provided by Rule 32, prior to a deal, after a false cut,[1] or when a new deal[2] has occurred.

30. The dealer's partner must collect the cards for the ensuing deal, and has the first right to shuffle that pack.

31. Each player, after shuffling, must place the cards, properly collected and face downwards, to the left of the player about to deal.

32. The dealer has always the right to shuffle last; but should a card or cards be seen during his shuffling or whilst giving the pack to be cut, he may be compelled to re-shuffle.

THE DEAL.

33. Each player deals in his turn; the right of dealing goes to the left.

34. The player on the dealer's right cuts the pack, and in dividing it, must not leave fewer than four cards in either packet; if in cutting, or in replacing

---

[1] *Vide* Law 34.   [2] *Vide* Law 37.

one of the **two** packets on the other, **a** card be exposed,[1] or if there be any confusion of the cards, or a doubt as to the exact place in which the pack was divided, there must be a fresh cut.

35. When a player, whose duty it **is to** cut, has once separated the pack, he cannot alter his intention; he can neither re-shuffle nor **re-cut the cards.**

36. When the pack is cut, should the dealer shuffle the cards, he loses his deal.

A NEW DEAL.

37. There must be a new deal[2]—

    I. **If, during a** deal, or **during the** play of a hand, **the pack** be proved incorrect or imperfect.
    II. If any card, **excepting the last, be faced in the** pack.

38. **If, whilst** dealing, a card be exposed **by** the dealer **or his** partner, should neither of the adversaries have touched the cards, the latter can claim a new deal; **a card** exposed by either adversary gives that claim to the dealer, provided that his partner has not touched a card; if a **new** deal does not take place, the exposed card cannot be called.

39. **If,** during dealing, a player touch any of his **cards,** the adversaries may do the same, without losing their privilege of claiming a **new** deal, should chance give them such option.

---

[1] After the two packets have **been** re-united, Law 38 comes into operation.

[2] i.e., the same dealer must deal again. *Vide* also Laws 47 and 50.

40. If, in dealing, one of the last cards be exposed, and the dealer turn up the trump before there is reasonable time for his adversaries to decide as to a fresh deal, they do not thereby lose their privilege.

41. If a player, whilst dealing, look at the trump card, his adversaries have a right to see it, and may exact a new deal.

42. If a player take into the hand dealt to him a card belonging to the other pack, the adversaries, on discovery of the error, may decide whether they will have a fresh deal or not.

A MISDEAL.

43. A misdeal loses the deal.[1]

44. It is a misdeal[2]—

    I. Unless the cards are dealt into four packets, one at a time in regular rotation, beginning with the player to the dealer's left.

    II. Should the dealer place the last (*i.e.*, the trump) card, face downwards, on his own, or any other pack.

    III. Should the trump card not come in its regular order to the dealer; but he does not lose his deal if the pack be proved imperfect.

    IV. Should a player have fourteen[3] cards, and either of the other three less than thirteen.[4]

    V. Should the dealer, under an impression that he has made a mistake, either count the cards on the table, or the remainder of the pack.

---

[1] Except as provided in Laws 45 and **50**.

[2] *Vide* also Law 36.

[3] Or more.

[4] The pack being perfect. *Vide* Law 47.

VI. Should the dealer deal two cards at once, or two cards to the same hand, and then deal a third; but if, prior to dealing that third card, the dealer can, by altering the position of one card only, rectify such error, he may do so, except as provided by the second paragraph of this Law.

VII. Should the dealer omit to have the pack cut to him, and the adversaries discover the error, prior to the trump card being turned up, and before looking at their cards, but not after having done so.

45. A misdeal does not lose the deal if, during the dealing, either of the adversaries touch the cards prior to the dealer's partner having done so, but should the latter have first interfered with the cards, notwithstanding either or both of the adversaries have subsequently done the same, the deal is lost.

46. Should three players have their right number of cards—the fourth have less than thirteen, and not discover such deficiency until he has played any of his cards,[1] the deal stands good; should he have played, he is as answerable for any revoke he may have made as if the missing card, or cards, had been in his hand;[2] he may search the other pack for it, or them.

47. If a pack, during or after a rubber, be proved incorrect or imperfect, such proof does not alter any past score, game, or rubber; that hand in which the imperfection was detected is null and void; the dealer deals again.

[1] *i.e*, until after he has played to the first trick.
[2] *Vide* also Law 70, and Law 44, paragraph iv.

48. Any one dealing out of turn, or with the adversary's cards, may be stopped before the trump card is turned up, after which the game must proceed as if no mistake had been made.

49. A player can neither shuffle, cut, nor deal for his partner, without the permission of his opponents.

50. If the adversaries interrupt a dealer whilst dealing, either by questioning the score or asserting that it is not his deal, and fail to establish such claim, should a misdeal occur, he may deal again.

51. Should a player take his partner's deal, and misdeal, the latter is liable to the usual penalty, and the adversary next in rotation to the player who ought to have dealt then deals.

THE TRUMP CARD.

52. The dealer, when it is his turn to play to the first trick, should take the trump card into his hand; if left on the table after the first trick be turned and quitted, it is liable to be called;[1] his partner may at any time remind him of the liability.

53. After the dealer has taken the trump card into his hand, it cannot be asked for;[2] a player naming it at any time during the play of that hand is liable to have his highest or lowest trump called.[3]

54. If the dealer take the trump card into his hand before it is his turn to play, he may be desired to lay

---

[1] It is not usual to call the trump card if left on the table.

[2] Any one may inquire what the trump suit is, at any time.

[3] In the manner described in Law 55.

it on the table; should he show a wrong card, this card may be called, as also a second, a third, &c., until the trump card be produced.

55. If the dealer declare himself unable to recollect the trump card, his highest or lowest trump may be called at any time during that hand, and, unless it cause him to revoke, must be played; the call may be repeated, but not changed, *i.e.*, from highest to lowest, or *vice versâ*, until such card is played.

CARDS LIABLE TO BE CALLED.

56. All exposed cards are liable to be called, and must be left[1] on the table; but a card is not an exposed card when dropped on the floor, or elsewhere below the table.

The following are exposed[2] cards : —

    I. Two or more cards played at once.[3]
    II. Any card dropped with its face upwards, or in any way exposed on or above the table, even though snatched up so quickly that no one can name it.

57. If any one play to an imperfect trick the best card on the table,[4] or lead one which is a winning card

---

[1] Face upwards.

[2] Detached cards (*i.e.*, cards taken out of the hand but not dropped) are not liable to be called unless named; *vide* Law 60. It is important to distinguish between exposed and detached cards.

[3] If two or more cards are played at once, the adversaries have a right to call which they please to the trick in course of play, and afterwards to call the others.

[4] And then lead without waiting for his partner to play.

as against his adversaries, and then lead again,[1] or play several such winning cards, one after the other, without waiting for his partner to play, the latter may be called on to win, if he can, the first or any other of those tricks, and the other cards thus improperly played are exposed cards.

58. If a player, or players, under the impression that the game is lost—or won—or for other reasons—throw his or their cards on the table face upwards, such cards are exposed, and liable to be called, each player's by the adversary; but should one player alone retain his hand, he cannot be forced to abandon it.

59. If all four players throw their cards on the table face upwards, the hands are abandoned; and no one can again take up his cards. Should this general exhibition show that the game might have been saved, or won, neither claim can be entertained, unless a revoke be established. The revoking players are then liable to the following penalties : they cannot under any circumstances win the game by the result of that hand, and the adversaries may add three to their score, or deduct three from that of the revoking players.

60. A card detached from the rest of the hand so as to be named is liable to be called ; but should the adversary name a wrong card, he is liable to have a suit called when he or his partner have the lead.[2]

61. If a player, who has rendered himself liable to

---

[1] Without waiting for his partner to play.

[2] i.e., the first time that side obtains the lead.

have the highest or lowest of a suit called, fail to play as desired, or if when called on to lead one suit, lead another, having in his hand one or more cards of that suit demanded, he incurs the penalty of a revoke.

62. If any player lead out of turn, his adversaries may either call the card erroneously led—or may call a suit from him or his partner when it is next the turn of either of them[1] to lead.

63. If any player lead out of turn, and the other three have followed him, the trick is complete, and the error cannot be rectified; but if only the second, or the second and third, have played to the false lead, their cards, on discovery of the mistake, are taken back; there is no penalty against any one, excepting the original offender, whose card may be called—or he, or his partner, when either of them[2] has next the lead, may be compelled to play any suit demanded by the adversaries.

64. In no case can a player be compelled to play a card which would oblige him to revoke.

65. The call of a card may be repeated[3] until such card has been played.

66. If a player called on to lead a suit have none of it, the penalty is paid.

---

[1] i.e., the penalty of calling a suit must be exacted from whichever of them next first obtains the lead. It follows that if the player who leads out of turn is the partner of the person who ought to have led, and a suit is called, it must be called at once from the right leader. If he is allowed to play as he pleases, the only penalty that remains is to call the card erroneously led.

[2] i.e., whichever of them next first has the lead.

[3] At every trick.

CARDS PLAYED IN ERROR, OR NOT PLAYED TO A TRICK.

67. If the third hand play before the second, the fourth hand may play before his partner.

68. Should the third hand not have played, and the fourth play before his partner, the latter may be called on to win, or not to win the trick.

69. If any one omit playing to a former trick, and such error be not discovered until he has played to the next, the adversaries may claim a new deal; should they decide that the deal stand good, the surplus card at the end of the hand is considered to have been played to the imperfect trick, but does not constitute a revoke therein.

70. If any one play two cards to the same trick, or mix his trump, or other card, with a trick to which it does not properly belong, and the mistake be not discovered until the hand is played out, he is answerable for all consequent revokes he may have made.[1]   If, during the play of the hand, the error be detected, the tricks may be counted face downwards, in order to ascertain whether there be among them a card too many : should this be the case they may be searched, and the card restored; the player is, however, liable for all revokes which he may have meanwhile made.

THE REVOKE.

71. Is when a player, holding one or more cards of the suit led, plays a card of a different suit.[2]

[1] *Vide* also Law 46.   [2] *Vide* also Law 61.

72. The penalty for a revoke :—

    I. Is at the option of the adversaries, who, at the end of the hand, may either take three tricks from the revoking player[1]—or deduct three points from his score—or add three to their own score ;

    II. Can be claimed for as many revokes as occur during the hand ;

    III. Is applicable only to the score of the game in which it occurs ;

    IV. Cannot be divided, *i.e.*, a player cannot add one or two to his own score and deduct one or two from the revoking player ;

    V. Takes precedence of every other score, *e.g.*,— The claimants two—their opponents nothing —the former add three to their score—and thereby win a treble game, even should the latter have made thirteen tricks, and held four honours.

73. A revoke is established, if the trick in which it occur be turned and quitted, *i.e.*, the hand removed from that trick after it has been turned face downwards on the table—or if either the revoking player or his partner, whether in his right turn or otherwise, lead or play to the following trick.

74. A player may ask his partner whether he has not a card of the suit which he has renounced ; should the question be asked before the trick is turned and quitted, subsequent turning and quitting does not establish the revoke, and the error may be corrected, unless the question be answered in the negative, or unless the revoking player or his partner have led or played to the following trick.

[1] And add them to their own.

75. At the end of the hand, the claimants of a revoke may search all the tricks.[1]

76. If a player discover his mistake in time to save a revoke, the adversaries, whenever they think fit, may call the card thus played in error, or may require him to play his highest or lowest card to that trick in which he has renounced;—any player or players who have played after him may withdraw their cards and substitute others: the cards withdrawn are not liable to be called.

77. If a revoke be claimed, and the accused player or his partner mix the cards before they have been sufficiently examined by the adversaries, the revoke is established. The mixing of the cards only renders the proof of a revoke difficult, but does not prevent the claim, and possible establishment, of the penalty.

78. A revoke cannot be claimed after the cards have been cut for the following deal.

79. The revoking player and his partner may, under all circumstances, require the hand in which the revoke has been detected to be played out.

80. If a revoke occur, be claimed and proved, bets on the odd trick, or on amount of score, must be decided by the actual state of the latter, after the penalty is paid.

81. Should the players on both sides subject themselves to the penalty of one or more revokes, neither can win the game; each is punished at the discretion of his adversary.[2]

[1] *Vide* Law 77.   [2] In the manner prescribed in Law 72.

82. In whatever way the penalty be enforced, under no circumstances can a player win the game by the result of the hand during which he has revoked; he cannot score more than four. (*Vide* Rule 61.)

CALLING FOR NEW CARDS.

83. Any player (on paying for them) before, but not after, the pack be cut for the deal, may call for fresh cards. He must call for two new packs, of which the dealer takes his choice.

GENERAL RULES.

84. Where a player and his partner have an option of exacting from their adversaries one of two penalties, they should agree who is to make the election, but must not consult with one another which of the two penalties it is advisable to exact; if they do so consult they lose their right;[1] and if either of them, with or without consent of his partner, demand a penalty to which he is entitled, such decision is final.

This rule does not apply in exacting the penalties for a revoke; partners have then a right to consult.

85. Any one during the play of a trick, or after the four cards are played, and before, but not after, they are touched for the purpose of gathering them together, may demand that the cards be placed before their respective players.

[1] To demand any penalty.

C

86. If any one, prior to his partner playing, should call attention to the trick—either by saying that it is his, or by naming his card, or, without being required so to do, by drawing it towards him—the adversaries may require that opponent's partner to play the highest or lowest of the suit then led, or to win or lose[1] the trick.

87. In all cases where a penalty has been incurred, the offender is bound to give reasonable time for the decision of his adversaries.

88. If a bystander make any remark which calls the attention of a player or players to an oversight affecting the score, he is liable to be called on, by the players only, to pay the stakes and all bets on that game or rubber.

89. A bystander, by agreement among the players, may decide any question.

90. A card or cards torn or marked must be either replaced by agreement, or new cards called at the expense of the table.

91. Any player may demand to see the last trick turned, and no more. Under no circumstances can more than eight cards be seen during the play of the hand, viz.: the four cards on the table which have not been turned and quitted, and the last trick turned.

---

[1] i.e., refrain from winning.

ETIQUETTE OF WHIST.

The following rules belong to the established Etiquette of Whist. They are not called laws, as it is difficult—in some cases impossible—to apply any penalty to their infraction, and the only remedy is to cease to play with players who habitually disregard them.

Two packs of cards are invariably used at Clubs: if possible this should be adhered to.

Any one, having the lead and several winning cards to play, should not draw a second card out of his hand until his partner has played to the first trick, such act being a distinct intimation that the former has played a winning card.

No intimation whatever, by word or gesture, should be given by a player as to the state of his hand, or of the game.[1]

A player who desires the cards to be placed, or who demands to see the last trick,[2] should do it for his own information only, and not in order to invite the attention of his partner.

No player should object to refer to a bystander who professes himself uninterested in the game, and able to decide any disputed question of facts; as to who

[1] The question "Who dealt?" is irregular, and if asked should not be answered.

[2] Or who asks what the trump suit is.

played any particular card—whether honours were claimed though not scored, or *vice versâ*—etc., etc.

It is unfair to revoke purposely; having made a revoke, a player is not justified in making a second in order to conceal the first.

Until the players have made such bets as they wish, bets should not be made with bystanders.

Bystanders should make no remark, neither should they by word or gesture give any intimation of the state of the game until concluded and scored, nor should they walk round the table to look at the different hands.

No one should look over the hand of a player against whom he is betting.

DUMMY

Is played by three players.

One hand, called Dummy's, lies exposed on the table.

The laws are the same as those of Whist, with the following exceptions :—

    I. Dummy deals at the commencement of each rubber.

    II. Dummy is not liable to the penalty for a revoke, as his adversaries see his cards: should he[1] revoke and the error not be discovered until the trick is turned and quitted, it stands good.[2]

---

[1] *i. e.* Dummy's hand. **If Dummy's partner revokes, he is liable to the** usual penalties.

[2] And the hand proceeds as though the revoke had not been discovered.

III. Dummy being blind and deaf, his Partner is not liable to any penalty for an error whence he can gain no advantage. Thus, he may expose some, or all of his cards, or may declare that he has the game, or trick, &c., without incurring any penalty; if, however, he lead from Dummy's hand when he should lead from his own, or *vice versâ*, a suit may be called from the hand which ought to have led.

DOUBLE DUMMY

Is played by two players, each having a Dummy or exposed hand for his partner. The laws of the game do not differ from Dummy Whist, except in the following special law: There is no misdeal, as the deal is a disadvantage.

CASES AND DECISIONS.

Card laws are intended to effect two objects : 1. To preserve the harmony and determine the ordering of the table. Such, for example, are the laws in the previous code, which regulate scoring, cutting, shuffling, &c. and the miscellaneous rules included under the head of Etiquette. 2. To prevent any player from obtaining an unfair advantage.

The word "unfair" must be taken in a restricted sense. It does not mean intentional unfairness. This is not to be dealt with by laws, but by exclusion from the card table. In deciding cases of card law, the offender should be credited with *bona fides*. It follows from this, that offences should not be judged by the intention of the player, but by the amount of injury which his irregularity may inflict on the opponents.

In a perfect code, there should be a penalty for all errors or irregularities, by which the player committing them, or his side, *might* profit; and on the other hand there should be no penalty for errors by which he who commits them, *cannot possibly* gain an advantage.

Penalties should be proportioned as closely as possible to the gain which might ensue to the offender. For instance : if the third hand has not played and the fourth plays before his partner, the second hand is informed whether or not his partner is likely to win the trick. The law, therefore, provides that the adversaries shall be entitled to call on the second player either to win the trick, or not to win it, whichever they please. Say, the fourth hand plays an ace out of turn. The second hand may be required to win the trick. If he has none of the suit he must trump it. In the opposite case, if the fourth hand plays a small card, and the second is called on not to win the trick, he must play a small card also. In this manner, the second player is prevented from benefiting by the irregular information afforded him. Other offences are legislated against in a similar way, the point kept in view throughout being, that no player shall be allowed to profit by his own wrong doing.

However carefully a code is drawn up, it will not unfrequently happen in practice, that cases occur which are but imperfectly provided for. Such cases should be referred for decision to some arbitrator. The arbitrator will find himself materially assisted by keeping well before him the two great objects with which the laws have been framed.

The following general rules will also be found useful in guiding him to just decisions :

Where two or more players are in fault, it should be considered with whom the first fault lies, and how far it induced or invited the subsequent error of the adversary.

Questions of fact should be settled before the case is referred, either by a majority of the players, or, if they are divided in opinion, by an onlooker agreed to by both parties, the decision of this referee being final.

When the facts are agreed to they should be written down, and the written statement submitted to the judge, who should return a written answer.

Should it so happen that a case is referred, wherein the players are divided in opinion as to the facts, the arbitrator will do well to decline to give a decision. The disputants, however, may be reminded that the player whom it is proposed to punish is entitled to the benefit of reasonable doubt.

Questions of interpretation of law should be decided liberally, in accordance with the spirit rather than the letter of the law. On the other hand, the arbitrator should bear in mind the great inconvenience of a lax interpretation of card laws, and, having made up his mind as to the intention of the law, should decide all cases with the utmost strictness.

The following cases, with decisions, selected from a large number which have been brought under the author's notice as having occurred in actual play, are given in exemplification of the foregoing remarks.

CASE I.

The play of the hand shows that AB (partners) hold no honour. The hand is therefore abandoned and the adversaries (YZ) score the game. It is then discovered that Y has only twelve cards, and one of

the honours is found on the floor. AB then object
to the score on the ground that YZ only "held"
three honours (*vide* Law 3).

Decision—YZ are entitled to score four by honours
Y is not obliged to play with his cards in his hand.
Besides, the game having been abandoned, Law 59
comes into operation. The penalty for playing with
twelve cards is laid down in Law 46. Y is liable for
any revoke he may have made.

CASE II.

AB claim "the game" and score it. After the
trump card of the following deal is turned up, YZ
object that AB have not claimed honours (*vide* Laws
6 and 7).

Decision—The honours were claimed within the
meaning of the law. The objection to the score, if
made really in ignorance of how it accrued, should
have been taken at once. YZ should not wait the
completion of the deal, so as to entrap AB on a mere
technicality.

Note. This is a good instance of interpretation
in accordance with the spirit of the law. Laws
should never be so construed as to inflict a wholly
unnecessary wrong, as would happen in this case
were the law insisted on literally. The intention of
Law 7 is to require AB to draw attention to the
claim; and this is sufficiently done by the claim of
"the game."

CASE III.

Y throws down his hand and claims "the game." B (Y's adversary) thinking that Y is referring only to the tricks, says, "You are not game." Y then marks four. After the trump card of the following deal is turned up, A remarks, "if Y had scored his honours, he would have been game." Y then claims the game, on the ground that he made the claim in time, and only withdrew it in consequence of B's contradiction. Is Y entitled to score the game?

Decision—No. Y's claim of "the game" is irregular. He is bound to state in what way he wins it (*vide* Law 6). There is no evidence that Y was referring to his honours when he claimed the game, but rather the contrary, as he afterwards withdrew his claim and said nothing about honours.

Note. This is an example of two players being in fault. It seems hard on Y that he should suffer through B's mistake; but it must be borne in mind that the confusion was introduced by Y's own irregularity, and that the omission to score honours was due to his subsequent forgetfulness.

Compare with Case II.

CASE IV.

At the conclusion of the deal the trump card comes to the hand on the dealer's left. The dealer requests the players to count their cards. The player to the dealer's left appropriates a packet of cards lying a little to his own right hand, between himself and the dealer, and finds twelve cards in it. The other hands each contain thirteen. The dealer now claims the hand with twelve cards in it as his hand. Must the players accept the hands thus given to them, or is it a misdeal?

Decision—It is a misdeal. The fault is entirely with the dealer. If he deals so carelessly that there is any doubt as to the ownership of the hands, he must apportion them, and having once done so, he must not shift the hands about, so as to make a hand with twelve cards in it fall to himself.

CASE V.

Y throws down his cards, remarking, "We have lost the game." On this, A and B (Y's adversaries) throw down their cards. Z retains his hand. AB plead that they were misled by Y and that therefore they are not liable to Law 58.

Decision—A's, Y's, and B's hands are exposed, and must be left on the table to be called, each player's by the adversary. Z is not bound to abandon the game because his partner chooses to do so. Consequently, Y's remark does not bind Z. A and B ought to keep up their cards, until they have ascertained that both adversaries have abandoned the game.

Note. The written law is sufficient to decide this case (*vide* Law 58); but inasmuch as the irregularity in question is a fertile source of disputes, the case has been deemed worthy of insertion.

CASE VI.

When it comes to the last trick of a hand, it appears that the player who has to lead has no card. What is to be done?

Decision—(*a*) If either of the other players remains with two cards, it is a misdeal (*vide* Law 44, paragraph iv). (*b*) If the other players have their right number of cards, the missing card should be searched for (*vide* Law 70) and when found assigned to the leader, who is liable to Law 46. (*c*) If the missing card cannot be found, the tricks may be searched to find what card is wanting, and the absent card assumed to have belonged to the player who had but twelve cards.

Note. It may seem that decision *c* is severe on a player playing *bonâ fide* with an imperfect pack. But each player is bound to count his hand before he plays. His playing to the first trick signifies his acceptance of the hand. If he accepts an imperfect one he must take the consequences.

CASE VII.

Towards the end of a hand a spade is led. The third hand, when it comes to his turn to play, lays down the ace of trumps (hearts) and says " There's the game." He then throws his hand on the table. The hand contains several spades. Is it a revoke?

Decision—It is a question of fact. If the card was exposed in order to save time it is not a revoke. But

if the ace of trumps was played to the trick it is a
revoke, the subsequent throwing down of the cards
being an act of play, equivalent to playing to the
following trick (*vide* **Law 73**).

CASE VIII.

The adversary cuts the pack to the dealer, but
without his consent, *i.e.*, without the dealer's present-
ing it to be cut. Is it too late to claim a revoke in
the previous hand ? (*vide* Law 78).

Decision—It is too late for the player who cut or
for his partner to claim a revoke, but not too late for
the adversaries.

CASE IX.

A player revokes, and on discovering the revoke
before the hand is played out, says in explanation, " I
never saw the card ; it was hidden behind my king of
diamonds"—the king of diamonds being still in his
hand.

Decision—The king of diamonds is constructively an
exposed card, and the adversaries may require that it
be laid on the table to be called.

CASE X.

Y leads out of turn. B (Y's adversary) says to his
partner, " Shall we call a suit or not ? " B's partner
gives no answer. Is the asking the question a consultation within the meaning of Law 84, although no
answer is made to it ?

Decision—Yes. It is the very question Law 84 is framed to prevent. B by the question shows that he is in doubt as to the policy of calling a suit, and thus affords information he has no right to give. Further than this, a reply by word of mouth is not necessary to constitute a consultation. Silence is an answer. The knowledge that a partner is indifferent may convey information that B has no right to extract.

Note. The usual formula is "Will you exact the penalty, or shall I?" This question does not bring the player under the operation of Law 84.

CASE XI.

A leads and the other three players follow suit. A plays another card (it not being his lead) and proceeds to gather the five cards into one trick. On being told of it, A explains that his attention had been diverted, and that he thought he had not played to the trick. The adversaries claim to be entitled to the penalties for leading out of turn, on the ground that the penalty should depend, not on the actual intention of the player, but on his possible intention.

Decision—A has not led out of turn; he has merely exposed a card. The abstract principle pleaded by the adversaries is quite sound, but it does not apply to this case. There can be no doubt of A's intention, as he proceeds to gather the trick.

WHIST.

HISTORICAL.

The early history of Whist is involved in obscurity. All games of high character become perfected by degrees; and Whist, following this rule, has been formed by gradual development. As early as the beginning of the sixteenth century, a card game called *triumph* or *trump* was commonly played both in England and on the continent. This game in its chief feature, viz., the predominance of one particular suit, and in its general construction, was so similar to Whist, that it may be assumed to have been the game from which Whist afterwards developed.

Trump was played in more than one way; or, rather, there were two distinct games called trump. *Triomphe* or *French ruff* was a game very like écarté, only there was no score for the king; Trump or *English ruff-and-honours* was a game closely resembling Whist.

The earliest mention of trump the author has been able to discover is in Berni's " *Capitolo del Gioco della Primera* " (chapter on the game of primero) published at Rome in 1526. In this book several card games are enumerated, and among them "*trionfi*" a game played by the peasants. It seems probable that *trionfi* is the same game as trump.

Under the name of *la triomphe* trump is included by Rabelais in the long list of some two hundred and thirty games that Gargantua played. The famous history was finished about 1545; a portion of it was published before this date.

Douce, in his "Illustrations of Shakespeare," concludes from finding trump in this list that we derived the game from a French source. But it is more probable that the game referred to by Berni and Rabelais was French ruff, and that trump as played in this country was purely of English origin.

How and when trump or English ruff-and-honours originated cannot now be ascertained. It was played at least as early as the time of Henry VIII., for it was taken by Latimer to illustrate his text, in a sermon "On the Card," preached by him at St. Edmund's Church, Cambridge, the Sunday before Christmas, 1529. He mentions the game under its original and corrupted appellations, and clearly alludes to its characteristic feature, as the following extracts will show.

"And where you are wont to celebrate Christmass in playing at Cards, I intend, by God's Grace, to deal unto you Christ's Cards, wherein you shall perceive Christ's Rule. The game that we play at shall be called the Triumph, which, if it be well played at, he that dealeth shall win; the Players shall likewise win; and the standers and lookers upon shall do the same. * * * You must mark

also, that the Triumph must apply to fetch home unto him
all the other Cards, whatever suit they be of. ✳ ✳ ✳ Then
further we must say to ourselves, What requireth Christ of
a Christian man? Now turn up your Trump, your Heart
(Hearts is Trump, as I said before), and cast your Trump,
your Heart, on this card."

Later on in the sixteenth century the game of
trump is not unfrequently referred to, especially in old
plays. In "Gammer Gurton's Needle" (1551),
written by Bishop Still, and said to be the first piece
performed in England under the name of a Comedy,
Old Dame Chat thus invites some friends to a game
at triumph :

"CHAT. What Diccon? Come nere, ye be no stranger ;
    We be set fast at trump, man, hard by the fyre.
    Thou shalt set on the king, if thou come a little
        nyer.
    ✳   ✳   ✳   ✳   ✳   ✳   ✳
    Come hither, Dol ; Dol, sit downe and play this
        game,
    And as thou sawest me do, see thou do even the
        same ;
    There is five trumps besides the queene, the hind-
        most thou shalt find her ;
    Take hede of Sim Glover's wife, she hath an eie
        behind her."

In Decker's or Dekkar's "Belman of London"
(*circa* 1550) it is stated that "Deceipts [are] practised
even in the fayrest and most civill companies, at
primero, sant [piquet], maw [spoil-five], trump, and
such like games."

In Eliot's "Fruits for the French" (1593), trump
is called " a verie common alehouse game," and Rice,

in his " Invective against Vices " (printed before
1600), observes that " renouncing the trompe and
comming in againe " (*i.e.*, revoking intentionally), is a
common sharper's trick.

The game of trump is also mentioned by Shakespeare in " Antony and Cleopatra," Act iv., scene 12
(first published 1623).

"ANT. My good *knave*, Eros, now thy Captain is
 Even such a body ; here am I Antony ;
 Yet cannot hold this visible shape, my *knave*.
 I made these wars for Egypt ; and the *Queen*,—
 Whose *heart* I thought I had, for she had mine ;
 Which, whilst it was mine, had annex'd unto 't
 A million more, now lost,—she, Eros, has
 Packed cards with Cæsar, and *false-played* my glory
 Unto an enemy's *triumph*."

The repeated punning allusions to card-playing in
this passage leave no doubt as to the reference
in the last word. Douce (" Illustrations ") pointed
out its real meaning, and also ridiculed Ben Jonson's
derivation of the word trump from *tromper*.

There is abundant evidence to show that trump is a
corruption of the word triumph. In addition to the
instances already given, the following may be quoted :
In Cotgrave's " French and English Dictionary "
(1611), *Triomphe* is explained as " the Card-game
called ruffe or trump." Seymour, in his " Court
Gamester" (*circa* 1720), says—"The term trump comes
from a corruption of a word triumph ; for wherever
they are they are attended with conquest."

The derivation of the word *ruff* or *ruffe* has caused

much speculation, and has never been satisfactorily settled. Ruffe seems to have been used as a synonym for trump early in the seventeenth century, as appears from the extract from Cotgrave's "Dictionary." Nares, in his " Glossary," says—" Ruff meant a trump card, *charta dominatrix ;*" even at the present day, many Whist players speak of ruffing, *i.e.*, trumping; and, in the expression a cross-ruff, the word ruff is preserved to the exclusion of the word trump.

The game of *ruff-and-honours,* if not the same as trump or ruff, was probably the same game, with the addition of certain advantages to the four highest cards of the trump suit. Rabelais includes in his list a game called " *les Honeurs,*" but whether it had any affinity to ruff-and-honours is doubtful.

It is remarkable that though trump and ruff are often found in early seventeenth century books, honours (so far as the author knows), are never mentioned until 1674. It is possible, therefore, that trump was originally played without honours; though, as no description of the game is known to exist, this is only conjectural. In 1674, Charles Cotton, the poet, published a description of ruff-and-honours in " The Compleat Gamester : or Instructions how to play at Billiards, Trucks, Bowls, and Chess. Together with all manner of usual and most Gentile GAMES, either on Cards or Dice." Cotton gives a drawing of the game of " English Ruff and Honours," (see frontispiece) and thus describes it :—

" At Ruff and Honours, by some called Slamm, you have in the Pack all the Deuces, and the reason is, because four

playing having dealt twelve a-piece, there are four left for
the Stock, the uppermost whereof is turn'd up, and that
is Trumps, he that hath the Ace of that Ruffs ; that is, he
takes in those four Cards, and lays out four others in their
lieu ; the four Honours are the Ace, King, Queen, and
knave ; he that hath three Honours in his own hand, his
partner not having the fourth, sets up Eight by Cards,
that is two tricks; if he hath all four, then Sixteen, that
is four tricks; it is all one if two Partners make them
three or four between them, as if one had them. If the
Honours are eqully divided among the Gamesters of each
side, then they say Honours are split. If either side are
at Eight Groats he hath the benefit of calling Can-ye, if he
hath two Honours in his hand, and if the other answers
one, the game is up, which is nine in all, but if he hath
more than two he shows them, and then it is all one and
the same thing ; but if he forgets to call after playing a
trick, he loseth the advantage of Can-ye for that deal.

" All Cards are of value as they are superiour one to
another, as a Ten wins a nine if not Trumps, so a Queen
a Knave, in like manner ; but the least Trump will win
the highest Card of every other Card [suit] ; where note
the Ace is the highest."

This game was clearly Whist in an imperfect form.
Whist is not mentioned by Shakespeare, nor by any
writer (it is believed) of the Elizabethan era. The
introduction of the name *whist* or *whisk* would appear
to have taken place early in the seventeenth century.

The meaning of the word is unknown. It has been
suggested, and the suggestion is worthy of consideration, that whisk is derived by substitution from ruff,
for both of them signify a piece of lawn used as an
ornament to the dress. The commonly received
opinion is that whist means *silence*. But this loses
sight of the fact that the original appellation was

whisk. The first known appearance of the word in print is in the "Motto" of Taylor, the Water Poet (1621). Taylor spells the word whisk. Speaking of the prodigal, he says :—

"The prodigall's estate, like to a flux,
    The mercer, draper, and the silkman suckes;
    *   *   *   *   *   *   *
    He flings his money free with carelessnesse.
    At novum, mumchance, mischance (chuse ye which).
    At one and thirty. or at poore and rich,
    Ruffe, slam, trump, nody, whisk, hole, sant, new cut."

The word continued to be spelt whisk for about forty years, when the earliest known use of the present spelling obtained, in a passage quoted by Johnson, from the second part of Hudibras (spurious) published in 1663 :

"But what was this? A game at Whist
    Unto our Plowden-Canonist."

After this, the word is spelt indifferently, whisk or whist. In the first edition of "The Compleat Gamester," already referred to, Whist is not named : but in the second edition (1680), Cotton, who never uses or alludes to the earlier name whisk, says, "Ruff and Honours (*alias* Slamm) and Whist, are Games so commonly known in *England*, in all parts thereof, that every Child almost of Eight Years old, hath a competent knowledge in that recreation."

After describing ruff-and-honours as in the first edition, Cotton adds, "Whist is a Game not much differing from this, only they put out the Deuces and

take in no stock ; and is called Whist from the silence
that is to be observed in the play : they deal as before,
playing four, two of a side * * * to each Twelve
a-piece, and the Trump is the bottom Card.   The
manner of crafty playing, the number of the Game
Nine, Honours, and dignity of other Cards, are all
alike, and he that wins most tricks is most forward to
win the set."

Cotton's work was afterwards incorporated with
Seymour's Court Gamester (first published 1719).
The earlier editions contain no Whist, but after the
two books were united (about 1734), Seymour says,
" Whist, vulgarly called whisk.   The original de-
nomination of this game is Whist, [here Seymour is
mistaken] or the silent game at cards."   And again,
" Talking is not allowed at Whist; the very word
implies ' Hold your Tongue.' "

Dr. Johnson does not positively derive Whist from
the *interjectio silentium imperans;* he cautiously explains Whist to be " a game at cards, requiring close
attention and silence."   Nares, in his Glossary, has
" Whist, an interjection commanding silence ;" and he
adds, " That the name of the game of Whist is derived
from this, is known, I presume, to all who play or do
not play."   He, however, in his preface, well remarks
that he knows "the extreme fallaciousness of the science
of etymology when based on mere similarity of sound ;"
but in the case of Whist, he has allowed similarity of
sound to master his judgment.   Looking to the early
spelling, whisk, it appears to the author that the whist-
silence theory has been taken for granted too hastily.

While Whist was undergoing these changes of name and of character, there was for a time associated with it another title, viz., swabbers or swobbers. Fielding, in his "History of the life of the late Mr. Jonathan Wild, the Great," records that when the ingenious Count La Ruse was domiciled with Mr. Geoffrey Snap, in 1682, or, in other words, was in a spunging-house, the Count beguiled the tedium of his in-door existence by playing at Whisk-and-Swabbers, "the game then in the chief vogue." Swift also, in his "Essay on the Fates of Clergymen" (1728), ridicules Archbishop Tenison for not understanding the meaning of swabbers. It appears that a clergyman was recommended to the Archbishop for preferment, when His Grace said, "he had heard that the clergyman used to play at Whist and swobbers; that as to playing now and then a sober game at Whist, it might be pardoned; but he could not digest those wicked swobbers." Johnson defines swobbers as "four privileged cards used incidentally in betting at Whist." It has been conjectured by later writers that swabbers were identical with the honours; but this is an error. In Captain Francis Grose's "Classical Dictionary of the Vulgar Tongue" (1785), swabbers are said to be "The ace of hearts, knave of clubs, ace and duce of trumps at Whist." The Hon. Daines Barrington (writing in 1787), says, that at the beginning of the century, whisk was "played with what were called swabbers, which were possibly so termed, because they who had certain cards in their hand were entitled to take up a share of the stake, independent of the general event of

the game." This was probably the true office of the
swabbers. They, however, soon went out of general
use, but the author has heard that they still linger in
some local coteries. Mr. R. B. Wormald writes thus
respecting them in 1873 :—Being driven by stress of
weather to take shelter in a sequestered hostelry on
the Berkshire bank of the Thames, he found four
persons immersed in the game of Whist : " In the
middle of the hand, one of the players, with a grin that
almost amounted to a chuckle, and a vast display of
moistened thumb, spread out upon the table the ace of
trumps ; whereupon the other three deliberately laid
down their hands, and forthwith severally handed
over the sum of one penny to the fortunate holder of
the card in question: On enquiry, we were informed
that the process was technically known as a 'swap'
(qy. swab or swabber), and was *de rigueur* in all
properly constituted whist circles."

After the swabbers were dropped (and it is probable
that they were not in general use in the eighteenth
century), our national card game became known simply
as Whist, though still occasionally spelt whisk. The
Hon. Daines Barrington (Archæologia, Vol. viii.) says,
that Whist in its infancy was chiefly confined to the
servants' hall. That the game had not yet become
fashionable is evident from the disparaging way in
which it is referred to by writers of the period. In
Farquhar's comedy of the " Beaux's Stratagem "
(1707), Mrs. Sullen, a fine lady from London, speaks
in a contemptuous vein of the "rural accomplishments
of drinking fat ale, playing at whisk, and smoaking

tobacco." Pope also classes Whist as a country squire's game, in his "Epistle to Mrs. Teresa Blount" (1715)—

> "Some Squire, perhaps, you take delight to rack,
> Whose game is Whisk, whose treat a toast in sack."

Thomson, in his "Autumn" (1730), describes how after a heavy hunt dinner—

> "Whist awhile,
> Walks his dull round beneath a cloud of smoke,
> Wreath'd fragrant from the pipe."

Early in the century the points of the game rose from nine to ten (" nine in all," Cotton, 1709 ; " ten in all," Cotton, 1721 ; " nine in all," Cotton, 1725 ; " ten in all," Seymour, 1734, " rectified according to the present standard of play "). Every subsequent edition of Seymour (with which Cotton was incorporated) makes the game ten up. It seems likely that, simultaneously with this change, or closely following it, the practice of playing with the entire pack instead of with but forty-eight cards obtained. This improvement introduced the *odd trick*, an element of the greatest interest in modern Whist.

At this period (early part of the eighteenth century) there was a mania for card playing in all parts of Europe, and in all classes of society, but Whist had not as yet found favour in the highest circles. Piquet, and Ombre, and Quadrille, were the principal games of the fashionable world. But about 1728, the game rose out of its comparative obscurity.

A party of gentlemen (according to Daines Barrington), of whom the first Lord Folkestone was one, used
at this date to frequent the Crown Coffee-house, in
Bedford Row, where they studied Whist scientifically.
They must have made considerable progress in the
game, to judge by the following rules which they laid
down :—" Lead from the strong suit; study your
partner's hand ; and attend to the score."

Shortly after this, the celebrated EDMOND HOYLE,
the father of the game, published his " Short Treatise "
(1742-3).   About Hoyle's antecedents, but little is
known.   He was born in 1672 ; it is said he was
educated for the bar.   It has been stated that he was
born in Yorkshire, but this is doubtful.   At all events,
the author, by personal enquiry, has positively ascertained that he did not belong to the family of Yorkshire Hoyles, who acquired estates near Halifax *temp*
Edward III.   It has also been stated that Hoyle was
appointed registrar of the prerogative court at Dublin,
in 1742.   This, however, is unlikely.   At that time,
Hoyle was probably living at Bath, at least his
treatise was published there, and he afterwards resided
in Queen Square, London.   Hoyle was engaged in
writing on games, and in giving lessons on Whist, at
the time he is supposed to have held the appointment
in question.   The fact is, the name Edmund or Edmond
is common in both the Yorkshire and Irish families of
Hoyle ; and probably one Hoyle has been mistaken for
another.

Hoyle became famous as soon as he avowed the
authorship of the " Short Treatise."   It was originally

published anonymously. It seems probable that
Hoyle originally drew up some notes for the use of the
pupils to whom he gave lessons in Whist, as his
original edition speaks of " purchasers of the *Treatise*
in Manuscript disposed of the last winter," and also
that there was "a Treatise on the Game at *Whist*
lately dispersed among a *few* Hands at a *Guinea*
Price," and further, that the author of it " has fram'd
an *Artificial Memory* which takes not off your Attention from your Game ; and, if required, he is ready to
communicate it upon Payment of one Guinea. And
also, He will explain any *Cases* in the Book, upon
Payment of one Guinea more."

The value of the " Short Treatise," and its rapid
success, caused surreptitious copies to be circulated.
To secure his property, Hoyle printed the manuscript,
and registered it at Stationers' Hall in November, 1742.
It is said that the treatise ran through five editions in
one year, and that Hoyle received a large sum for the
copyright. This last statement, however, requires
verification ; at all events, Hoyle continued for years
to sign every copy personally, as the proprietor of the
copyright. This was done in order to protect the
property from further piracy, as the address to the
reader shows.

The following is a fac-simile of Hoyle's signature,
taken from the fourth edition :—

In the fifteenth edition the signature is impressed
from a wood block, and in the seventeenth it was
announced that Mr. Hoyle was dead.   He died in
Welbank (qy. Welbeck) Street, Cavendish Square, on
August 27th, 1769, aged 97.

One effect of Hoyle's publication was to draw forth
a witty skit, entitled "The Humours of Whist.   A
Dramatic Satire, as acted every day at White's and
other Coffee-Houses and Assemblies" (1743).   The
pamphlet commences with an advertisement mimicking
Hoyle's address to the reader.   The prologue to the
play is supposed to be spoken by a waiter at White's.

> " Who will believe that Man could e'er exist,
>   Who spent near half an Age in studying *Whist ?*
>   Grew gray with Calculation—Labour hard !
>   As if Life's Business center'd in a Card ?
>   That such there is, let me to those appeal,
>   Who with such liberal Hands reward his Zeal.
>   Lo ! *Whist* he makes a science, and our Peers
>   Deign to turn *School Boys* in their riper Years."

The principal characters are Professor Whiston
(Hoyle), who gives lessons in the game of Whist ; Sir
Calculation Puzzle, a passionate admirer of Whist,
who imagines himself a good player, yet always loses ;
Sharpers, Pupils of the Professor, and Cocao, Master
of the Chocolate-house.   The sharpers are disgusted
at the appearance of the book.

> " LURCHUM. Thou knowest we have the Honour to be
> admitted into the best Company, which neither our Birth
> nor Fortunes entitle us to, merely for our Reputation as
> good *Whist*-Players.
>   SHUFFLE. Very well !

LURCH. But if this damn'd **Book** of the Professor's answers, as he pretends, to put Players more upon a Par, what will avail our superior Skill in the Game? We are undone to all Intents and Purposes. * * * We must bid adieu to White's, George's, Brown's, and all the polite Assemblies about Town, and that's enough to make a Man mad instead of thoughtful.

SHUF. Damn him, I say,—Could he find no other Employment for forty Years together, than to study how to circumvent younger Brothers, and such as us, who live by our Wits? A Man that discovers the Secrets of any Profession deserves to be sacrificed, and I would be the first, LURCHUM, to cut the Professor's Throat for what he has done, but that I think I have pretty well defeated the malevolent Effect of his fine spun Calculations.

LURCH. As how, dear SHUFFLE? Thou revivest me.

SHUF. I must confess the Publication of his Treatise gave me at first some slight Alarm; but I did net. like thee, LURCHUM, indulge in melancholy desponding Thoughts: On the contrary, I called up my Indignation to my Assistance, and have ever since been working upon a private Treatise on *Signs* at *Whist*, by way of counter Treatise to his, and which, if I mistake not, totally overthrows his System."

On the other hand, the gentlemen are in raptures.

"SIR CALCULATION PUZZLE. The Progress your Lordship has made for the time you have study'd under the Professor is wonderful.—Pray, has your Lordship seen the dear Man to-day?

LORD SLIM. O yes.—His Grace sate him down at my House, and I have just lent him my Chariot into the City. —How do you like the last edition of his Treatise with the Appendix,[1] Sir CALCULATION? I mean that sign'd with his Name.[2]

---

[1] "The author of this treatise did promise if it met with approbation, to make an addition to it by way of Appendix, which he has done accordingly."—*Hoyle.*

[2] Authorised as revised and corrected under his own hand.—*Hoyle.*

SIR CAL. O Gad, my Lord, there never was so excellent
a Book printed.—I'm quite in Raptures with it—I will
eat with it—sleep with it—go to Court with it—go to
Parliament with it—go to Church with it. I pronounce
it the Gospel of Whist-Players; and the Laws of the
Game ought to be wrote in golden Letters, and hung up
in Coffee-houses, as much as the Ten Commandments in
Parish Churches.

SIR JOHN MEDIUM. Ha! Ha! Ha! you speak of the
Book with the Zeal of a primitive Father.

SIR CAL. Not half enough, Sir JOHN—the Calculations[1]
are so exact! * * * his Observations[2] are quite masterly!
his Rules[3] so comprehensive! his Cautions[4] so judicious!
There are such Variety of Cases[5] in his Treatise, and the
Principles are so new, I want Words to express the
Author, and can look on him in no other Light than as a
second *Newton*."

The way in which Sir Calculation introduces Hoyle's
Calculations of Chances is very amusing.

"SIR JOHN. 'Twas by some such laudable Practices, I
suppose, that you suffered in your last Affair with
LURCHUM.

SIR CAL. O Gad, No, Sir JOHN—Never any thing was
fairer, nor was ever any thing so critical.—We were
nine all. The adverse Party had 3, and we 4 Tricks.
All the Trumps were out. I had Queen and two small
Clubs, with the Lead. Let me see—It was about 222 and

---

[1] "Calculations for those who will bet the odds on any points of the
score," &c.—"Calculations directing with moral certainty, how to play
well any hand or game," &c.—*Hoyle*.

[2] "Games to be played with certain observations," &c.—*Hoyle*.

[3] "Some general rules to be observed," &c.—"Some particular rules to
be observed," &c.—*Hoyle*.

[4] "A caution not to part with the command of your adversaries' great
suit," &c.—*Hoyle*.

[5] "With a variety of Cases added in the Appendix."—*Hoyle*.

3 Halves to—'gad, I forgot how many—that my Partner had the Ace and King—let me recollect—ay—that he had one only was about 31 to 26. That he had not both of them 17 to 2,—and that he had not one, or both, or neither, some 25 to 32. So I, according to the Judgment of the Game, led a Club, my Partner takes it with the King. Then it was exactly 481 for *us* to 222 against *them*. He returns the same Suit ; I win it with my Queen, and return it again ; but the Devil take that LURCHUM, by passing his Ace twice, he took the Trick, and having 2 more Clubs and a 13th Card, I gad, all was over.—But they both allow'd I play'd admirably well for all that."

The following passage from the same pamphlet mentions the Crown—probably the Crown Coffee-house—and it has been inferred from this that Hoyle himself might have been one of Lord Folkestone's party.

"YOUNG JOBBER [A pupil of the Professor's]. Dear, Mr. PROFESSOR, I can never repay you. You have given me such an Insight by this Visit, I am quite another Thing.—I find I knew nothing of the Game before ; tho' I can assure you, I have been reckoned a First-rate Player in the City a good while—nay, for that Matter, I make no bad Figure at the *Crown*—and don't despair, by your Assistance, but to make one at *White's* soon."

Hoyle is also spoken of in his professional capacity in the "Rambler" of May 8, 1750. A lady writes, "As for play, I do think I may indulge in that, now I am my own mistress. Papa made me drudge at Whist till I was tired of it ; and far from wanting a head, Mr. Hoyle, when he had not given me above forty lessons, said I was one of his best scholars."

Again, in "The Gentleman's Magazine" for

February, 1755, a writer, professing to give the auto-
biography of a fashionable physician, says, "Hoyle
tutored me in several games at cards, and under the
name of guarding me from being cheated, insensibly
gave me a taste for sharping."

In the middle of the eighteenth century, Whist was
regularly played in fashionable society. In "Tom
Jones," Lady Bellaston, Lord Fellamar, and others,
are represented as indulging in a rubber. Hoyle also
comes in for notice in the following passage in the
same work : " I happened to come home several hours
before my usual time, when I found four gentlemen of
the cloth at Whist by my fire ;—and my Hoyle, sir,—
my best Hoyle, which cost me a guinea, lying open on
the table, with a quantity of porter spilled on one of
the most material leaves of the whole book. This,
you will allow, was provoking ; but I said nothing
till the rest of the honest company were gone, and
then gave the fellow a gentle rebuke ; who, instead
of expressing any concern, made me a pert answer,
' That servants must have their diversions as well as
other people ; that he was sorry for the accident which
had happened to the book, but that several of his
acquaintance had bought the same for a shilling ; and
that I might stop as much in his wages, if I pleased.' "

In an epic poem on "Whist," by Alexander Thomson,
which appeared in 1791, Hoyle was thus invoked—

> " WHIST, then, delightful WHIST, my theme shall be,
> And first I'll try to trace its pedigree,
> And shew what sage and comprehensive mind
> Gave to the world a pleasure so refin'd :

Then shall the verse its various charms display,
Which bear from ev'ry game the palm away;
And, last of all, those rules and maxims tell,
Which give the envied pow'r to play it well.

But first (for such the mode) some tuneful shade
Must be invok'd, the vent'rous Muse to aid.
Cremona's poet shall I first address,
Who paints with skill the mimic war of chess,
And India's art in Roman accents sings;
Or him who soars on far sublimer wings,
Belinda's bard, who taught his liquid lay
At Ombre's studious game so well to play?

But why thus vainly hesitates the Muse,
In idle doubt, what guardian pow'r to chuse?
What pow'r so well can aid her daring toil,
As the bright spirit of immortal Hoyle?
By whose enlighten'd efforts Whist became
A sober, serious, scientific game;
To whose unwearied pains, while here below,
The great, th' important privilege we owe,
That random strokes disgrace our play no more,
But skill presides, where all was chance before.

Come then, my friend, my teacher, and my guide,
Where'er thy shadowy ghost may now reside;
Perhaps (for Nature ev'ry change defies,
Nor ev'n with death our ruling passion dies)
With fond regret it hovers still, unseen,
Around the tempting boards array'd in green;
Still with delight its fav'rite game regards,
And tho' it plays no more o'erlooks the cards.

Come then, thou glory of Britannia's isle,
On this attempt propitious deign to smile;
Let all thy skill th' unerring page inspire,
And all thy zeal my raptur'd bosom fire."

Hoyle's name also finds a place in Don Juan.
Byron, in saying that Troy owes to Homer what
Whist owes to Hoyle, scarcely does justice to Hoyle,

E

who was rather the founder than the historian of Whist.

The "Short Treatise" appeared just in the nick of time, when Whist was rising in repute, and when card playing was the rage. The work became the authority almost from the date of its appearance.

In 1760, the laws of the game were revised by the members of White's and Saunder's Chocolate-houses, then the head quarters of fashionable play. These revised laws (nearly all Hoyle) are given in every edition of Hoyle from this date. Hoyle's laws, as they were called, guided all Whist coteries for a hundred and four years; when the Arlington (now Turf) and Portland Clubs, re-revised the code of the Chocolate-houses. The laws adopted by these Clubs in 1864, which have by this time (1874) found their way into all Whist circles, deposed Hoyle, and are now the standard by which disputed points are determined.

One of the chief seats of card playing, and consequently, of Whist playing, during the eighteenth century, was Bath. Even Mr. Pickwick is depicted playing Whist there with Miss Bolo, Mr. Bantam, M.C., and the Dowager Lady Snuffanuff, in a passage too well known to require quotation, though Mr. Pickwick's visit was at a date when the chief glories of Bath had departed. Hoyle's first edition, it will be remembered, was published at Bath, as also was Thomas Mat[t]hews' "Advice to the Young Whist Player" (about 1805)—a sound and useful contribution to Whist literature.

Early in this century, the points of the game were altered from ten to five, and the call at eight was abolished. It is doubtful whether this change was for the better. In the author's opinion Long Whist (ten up) is a far finer game than Short Whist, (five up); Short Whist, however, has taken such a hold, that there is no chance of our reverting to the former game. According to Mr. Clay, the alteration took place under the following circumstances : " Some sixty or seventy years back (1804—1814), Lord Peterborough having one night lost a large sum of money, the friends with whom he was playing proposed to make the game five points instead of ten, in order to give the loser a chance, at a quicker game, of recovering his loss. The late Mr. Hoare, of Bath, a very good Whist player, and without a superior at Piquet, was one of the party, and has more than once told me the story. The new game was found to be so lively, and money changed hands with such increased rapidity, that these gentlemen and their friends, all of them members of the leading Clubs of the day, continued to play it. It became general in the Clubs,—thence was introduced to private houses,—travelled into the country,—went to Paris,—and has long since entirely superseded the Whist of Hoyle's day."

Long Whist had long been known in France, but it was not a popular game in that country. Hoyle has been several times translated into French. Whist was played by Louis XV., and under the first Empire was a favorite game with Josephine and Marie Louise. It is on record ("Diaries of a Lady of Quality," 2nd Ed.

E 2

p. 128), that Napoleon used to play Whist at Würtemburg, but not for money, and that he played ill and inattentively. One evening, when the Queen Dowager was playing against him with her husband and his daughter (the Queen of Westphalia, the wife of Jerome), the King stopped Napoleon, who was taking up a trick that did not belong to him, saying, " Sire, on ne joue pas ici en conquérant." After the restoration, Whist was taken up in France more enthusiastically. " The Nobles," says a French writer, " had gone to England to learn to Think, and they brought back the thinking game with them." Talleyrand was a Whist player, and his *mot* to the youngster who boasted his ignorance of the game is well known, " Vous ne savez pas donc le Whiste, jeune homme? Quelle triste vieillesse vous vous préparez!" Charles X. is reported to have been playing Whist at St. Cloud, on July 29, 1830, when the tricolor was waving on the Tuileries, and he had lost his throne.

It is remarkable that the " finest Whist player" who ever lived should have been, according to Mr. Clay, a Frenchman, M. Deschapelles (born 1780, died 1847). He published in 1839 a fragment of a "Traité du Whiste," which treats mainly of the laws, and is of but little value to the Whist player.

Before leaving this historical sketch, a few words may be added respecting the modern literature of the game. So far as the present work is concerned, its *raison d'étre* is explained in the preface to the first edition. How far it has fulfilled the conditions of its

being, it is not for the author to say. It was followed,
however, by two remarkable books, which call for a
short notice.

In 1864, appeared "Short Whist," by James Clay.
Mr. Clay's work is an able dissertation on the game,
by the most brilliant player of his day. He was
Chairman of the Committee appointed to revise the
Laws of Whist in 1863. He sat in Parliament for
many years, being M.P. for Hull at the time of his
death, in 1873.

In 1865, William Pole, F.R.S., Mus. Doc., Oxon,
published "The Theory of the Modern Scientific
Game of Whist," a work which contains a lucid
explanation of the fundamental principles of scientific
play, addressed especially to novices, but of considerable value to players of all grades.

These books exhibit the game both theoretically and
practically, in the perfect state at which it has arrived
during the two centuries that have elapsed since
Whist assumed a definite shape and took its present
name.

PART I.
GENERAL PRINCIPLES.

———◆◆———

INTRODUCTORY REMARKS.

Before entering on an analysis of the general principles of the Game of Whist, it is advisable to explain shortly on what foundation these principles rest; for it might be supposed that a demonstration of the propositions contained in these pages is about to be offered; that the chances for and against all possible systems of play have been calculated; and that the one here upheld can be proved to be certainly right, and all others certainly wrong. Such a view would be altogether erroneous. The problem is far too intricate to admit of being treated with mathematical precision. The conclusion that the chances are in favour of a certain line of play is not arrived at by abstract calculation, but by general reasoning, confirmed by the accumulated experience of practised players. The student must not, therefore, expect absolute proof. He must frequently be satisfied if the reasons given appear weighty in themselves, and none weightier can be suggested on the other side; and also with the assurance that the method of play recommended in this work is for the most part that which, having stood the test of time, is generally adopted.

THE FIRST HAND OR LEAD.

The considerations that determine the most advantageous card to lead at the commencement of a hand differ from those which regulate the lead at other periods ; for, at starting, the Doctrine of Probabilities is the only guide ; while, as the hand advances, each player is able, with more or less certainty, to draw inferences as to the position of some of the remaining cards. The number of the inferences, and the certainty with which they can be drawn from the previous play, constantly increase ; so that it not unfrequently happens that, towards the termination of a hand, the position of every material card is known.

In treating of the lead, it will be most convenient to begin by examining the principles which govern the original lead. The application of these principles will require to be somewhat modified in the case of trumps, as will appear hereafter.

I. LEAD ORIGINALLY FROM YOUR STRONGEST SUIT.

The first question that arises is, Which is the strongest suit ? A suit may be strong in two distinct ways. 1. It may contain more than its proportion of *high* cards. For example, it may contain two or more

honours—one honour in each suit being the average
for each hand. 2. It may consist of more than the
average *number* of cards, in which case it is a
numerically strong or long suit. Thus a suit of four
cards has numerical strength; a suit of five cards
great numerical strength. On the other hand a suit
of three cards is numerically weak.

In selecting a suit for the lead, numerical strength
is the principal point to look to; for it must be borne
in mind that aces and kings are not the only cards
which make tricks; twos and threes may become
quite as valuable when the suit is *established*—
i.e., when the higher cards of the suit are exhausted.
To obtain for your own small cards a value that does
not intrinsically belong to them, and to prevent the
adversary from obtaining it for his, is evidently an
advantage. Both these ends are advanced by choosing
for your original lead the suit in which you have the
greatest numerical strength; for you may establish a
suit of this description, while, owing to your strength,
it is precisely the suit which the adversary has the
smallest chance of establishing against you. A suit
that is numerically weak, though otherwise strong, is
far less eligible.

Suppose, for example, you have five cards headed
by (say) a ten in one suit, and ace, king, and one
other (say the two) in another suit. If you lead from
the ace, king, two suit, all your power is exhausted as
soon as you have parted with the ace and king, and
you have given the holder of numerical strength a
capital chance of establishing the suit. It is true that

this fortunate **person** *may* be your partner; but it is twice **as likely that** he is your adversary, since you **have two adversaries** and only one partner. On the other hand, **if** you lead from the five suit, though **your** chance of establishing it is slight, you, at all events, avoid assisting your adversary to establish **his;** the **ace and king of** your **three suit,** still remaining in your hand, enable you to prevent the establishment of that **suit,** and may procure you the lead at an advanced period of the hand. This we shall find as we proceed **is a** great advantage, especially if, in the course **of play,** you are **left** with all the unplayed **cards, or** *long cards,* of your five suit.

The best suit of all to lead from is, of course, one which combines both elements of strength.

In opening a suit, there is always the danger of finding your **partner very weak,** or of leading up to a **tenace** (*i.e.,* **the best and third best cards,** or the second best **guarded)** in the **hand of** the fourth player. If you lead from a very **strong** suit, these dangers are **more** than compensated **for by** the advantages just explained; **if** your best **suit is** only moderately strong, the lead is not profitable, **but** rather the reverse. If all your suits are weak, the lead is very disadvantageous. **The hand, however weak,** must hold one suit of four **at least, and this, if only** headed by a ten or a nine, **should generally be chosen.** Being unable to strike the adversary, you take the **best chance of** not assisting him.

It follows that a suit consisting of a single card is a very disadvantageous one to lead from; yet no lead is

more common, even among players of some experience.
The reason assigned in favour of this lead is the possibility of making small trumps. But it is important to
observe, that you stand very nearly as good a chance of
making trumps by waiting for some one else to open
the suit. If the suit is opened by the strong hand,
your barrenness will not be suspected; you will be
able, if necessary, to win the second round, while you
will be free from the guilt of having sacrificed any high
card your partner may have possessed in the suit, or of
having assisted in establishing a suit for the adversary.
Again, your partner, if strong in trumps, will very
likely draw yours, and then return your lead, imagining
you led from strength. If, indeed, he is a shrewd
player, he will, after being taken in once or twice,
accommodate his game to yours; but he can never be
sure of the character of your lead, and may often miss
a great game by not being able to depend upon you.
If you have great numerical strength in trumps, the
evils of a single-card lead are lessened; but in this
case, as will hereafter be shown, it is generally right
to lead trumps. In the opinion of the author, it may
be laid down as an axiom, that in plain suits (*i.e.*, in
suits not trumps) an original lead from a single card
is in no case defensible.

Many players will not lead from a strong suit if
headed by a tenace; preferring, for instance, to lead
from ten, nine, three, to ace, queen, four, two. They
argue, that by holding up the ace, queen suit, they
stand a better chance of catching the king. So far
they are right; but they purchase this advantage too

dearly; for the probable loss from leading the weak suit may be taken as greater than the probable gain from holding up the tenace.

Which card of the strong suit should be led originally?—The key to this problem is furnished by the remark, that it conduces to the ultimate establishment of a suit to keep the high or commanding cards of it in the hand that has numerical strength. In the suit of your own choosing, you are presumably stronger than your partner; it is therefore undesirable at once to part with your high cards. Hence it is best, in general, to lead the smallest (but *see* Appendix A, p. 257). Your partner, actuated by a desire to assist in establishing your strong suit, will play his highest card to your lead (*see* Play of Third Hand, p. 84), and, if he fails to win the trick, will, at all events, force a higher card from the fourth player, and so clear the suit for you. Another reason in favour of leading the lowest is, that it increases your chance of making tricks in the first two rounds. For in the first round of a suit the second hand generally puts on his smallest card, as will be seen hereafter. If, therefore, you originally lead the smallest, holding ace and others, the first trick will, in all probability, lie between your partner and the last player; and since there is no reason why the fourth player should hold a better card than the third, it is an even chance that your partner wins the trick. It is certain (bar trumping) that you win the second round; therefore it is an even chance, if the suit is led this way, that you make two tricks in the first two rounds. But if you lead out the ace first, it is two to one against your making the second trick, for the adversaries have two hands against your partner's one, and either may hold the king. A third reason for leading the lowest of your suit is, that your partner may prove utterly weak in it; and in this case it is important that you keep a commanding card, to stop the adversary from establishing it.

It follows, when you lead a small card originally, that your partner should conclude you have led from numerical strength.

There are two exceptions to the rule of originally leading the lowest of a strong suit.—1. When you lead from ace with four or more small ones. In this case it is considered best to begin with the ace, lest it should be trumped in the second round. 2. When your suit contains a strong sequence, it is best to lead one of the sequence, in order to prevent the adversaries from winning the first trick with a very small card.

When you intend to lead from a sequence, the card to be selected depends on the nature of the sequence, namely, whether it is a *head* sequence or an *under* sequence. By a head sequence is meant a sequence of the highest cards of your suit, *i.e.*, of the cards heading your suit; thus, such a suit as queen, knave, ten, six, contains a head sequence of queen, knave, ten. Sequences that do not head your suit are under sequences; thus ace, queen, knave, ten, is an example of an under sequence of queen, knave, ten. You should—

2. LEAD THE HIGHEST OF A HEAD SEQUENCE.

For, otherwise, your partner is uncertain where the highest lies, and you and he **may** play two winning cards **where** one would have **sufficed.** For instance, if, with queen, **knave,** ten, you lead the ten, your partner may put the king on it, but he certainly would not on the queen. In addition to this, if there is any *finessing* to be done in the suit, it can only be by your partner. By finessing is meant playing an inferior card though holding a higher one of the suit, not in sequence with the card played. Thus, to continue the illustration of the sequence of queen, knave, ten. You lead the queen. Your partner has the ace and others. He will not put it on, but will finesse by playing his smallest card ; and if the king lies to your left, that card is completely hemmed in. ₒHad you led the ten, your partner would have put on the ace, and the king have been freed.

On the other hand, if you lead from an under sequence, you should lead the lowest, the reason being that, in this case, you wish your partner to put on his highest card. For example, with king, ten, nine, eight, you should lead the eight and not the ten, as, if your partner's highest card is the knave, you wish **him to** put **it** on, that he may not afterwards block **your suit by** retaining a commanding card of it. Or, suppose your partner's **best** card is the queen, the lead **of** the ten would probably induce him to finesse, and thus give the adversary a chance of making the knave **the** first round, and of retaining the ace in hand, although you and your partner hold two honours in the suit. If your partner puts on the queen, you are still able to finesse the nine when the suit is returned, and this is much more advantageous than your partner's passing the ten. In the first place, the finesse is postponed to the second round, when, more cards having been played, you have more data to guide you as to the policy of making the finesse; and, in the next place, if you have a choice as to whether you or your partner shall finesse in your strong suit, it is, as a rule, more advantageous for you to do it. For, as already explained, it conduces to the establishment of a suit for the strong hand to retain the command of it, and for the presumably weak hand to play his highest cards.

With sequences neither at the top nor bottom of a suit (*intermediate* sequences), the best card to lead is the smallest of the intermediate sequence. From the combination of king, knave, ten, nine, and one or more small cards, containing an intermediate sequence of knave, ten, nine, it is agreed that the nine should be led, and not the smallest of the suit; also from king, knave, ten, and one or more small cards, the ten is the common lead. But with smaller under sequences, as, for example, king, ten, nine, eight, and a small one, say the two, the lowest card of the suit, the two, is frequently led, and not the lowest of the intermediate sequence, the eight. In the opinion of the writer, the eight is the best card to choose where the suit is led originally. This mode of leading is now in course of adoption by advanced players. (For a full explanation of it, and an examination of its advantages, *see* Appendix A, p. 257.)

ANALYSIS OF LEADS IN DETAIL.

[The following analysis should be familiarly known by every player, not only that he himself may follow it, but also that he may, with but little effort, form a correct idea of the cards the other players hold, by observing what they lead.]

Ace, king, and others, lead king. This is an exception to leading the highest of a sequence. If your partner has none of the suit, he should not trump the king, for if you have not the ace, you want the adversary to play it, that he may not hold the winning card of your suit. If your king wins, and you are obliged to change the suit, your partner is pretty sure where the ace is; but if you lead the ace, he can know nothing about the king, unless it is your practice to lead king from ace, king, when he would be sure that the king is against you. An exception to this rule is, if you lead from an ace, king suit after having trumped another suit. You should then lead the ace first, as, if you begin with the king, and your partner happens to have none of the suit, he might trump the king, in order to lead again the suit you are trumping. If you hold *ace, king, and queen,* follow king with queen, and still keep up the ace: and act similarly if intermediate cards drop, and you are left with ace and the next best. With a bad partner all this is useless; he will not be informed by it, and may possibly trump your winning card. *In trumps*, with *ace, king, and five small ones*, lead in the same way, as you are sure to be left with the numerical command of trumps; but with *less than seven trumps*, lead the smallest. Your ace and king must make; you give your partner an even chance of winning the first trick, and you retain the command. With *ace, king, queen, &c., of trumps*, begin with the lowest of the sequence.

Ace, king, knave, &c., generally lead out king and ace, and if queen does not drop, continue with the smallest. If you lead king, and change the suit, your partner should understand that you hold the ace, knave, and are waiting to finesse on the return of the lead. This is generally right *in trumps*, unless there is an object in immediately getting out two rounds. With *more than five trumps* it is, as a rule, better to lead out king and ace, and to take the chance that the queen falls. It is obviously useless to wait for the finesse if queen is turned up to your left.

Ace, queen, knave, &c., lead ace and queen. If king is against you, he wins the queen, and you remain with the best.

Ace, queen, ten, nine, lead the nine. With *more than four*, the ace *in plain suits*, but *in trumps*, the lowest of the ten, nine sequence. With *ace, queen, ten, &c.*, and knave turned up to your right, lead queen.

Ace, knave, ten, nine, lead nine. Some players lead ace and knave. *In trumps*, the nine, *unless queen is turned up to your left*, when lead ace and knave.

In all other suits headed by ace, lead the smallest, except with *four or more small ones*, when lead ace; *in trumps*, the smallest, *unless you have seven trumps*.

King, queen, knave, ten, lead ten. The ace will probably not be played second hand, on the ten, and you thus get an increased chance of two rounds, and so of clearing your suit; also, if your partner has the ace, he will play it on the ten, and leave you with the command.

King, queen, knave, and one small one, lead king; continue with queen, and then, if ace does not fall, with the small one, on the presumption that partner has the ace. You must not presume this because king goes round, the ace being sometimes held up. With *king, queen, knave, and more than one small one*, lead knave. You are so strong that if your partner holds ace you can afford to let him put it on, and so leave you with the command of your suit, even at the expense of winning the trick twice over.

King, queen, and small ones, lead king; *in trumps* the smallest, *unless you hold seven trumps*, or *king, queen, ten, &c.* If king goes round, continue with the smallest. Some players, with ace, knave, &c., will not win the king, in order to keep the command of your suit. You must submit to that contingency. It is seldom good play.

King, knave, and others, lead the lowest. With *ten also* lead the ten; with others in sequence, as *king, knave, ten, nine*, the lowest of the sequence.

F

With *king, knave, nine, &c., and ten turned up to your right*, lead knave.

In other numerically strong suits headed by king, lead the lowest (but *see* Appendix A, p. 257).

Queen, knave, ten, &c., lead queen; and, if it wins, follow with knave.

Queen, knave, nine, &c., lead the smallest, *unless you have six or more of the suit*, when lead queen. *In trumps, if ten is turned up to your right*, lead queen.

Queen, knave, and two or more small ones, lead the lowest. You have numerical strength, and your object is not to take the chance of catching the king, but to establish the suit.

In other suits of four at least, headed by queen, lead the lowest (but *see* Appendix A, p. 257).

Knave, ten, nine, &c., lead knave. From *knave, ten, eight, &c.*, the smallest, except *in trumps, if nine is turned up to your right*, when lead knave.

In all other strong suits headed by knave, lead the lowest (but *see* Appendix A, p. 257).

In all suits of four cards, or more, without an honour, lead the lowest (but *see* Appendix A, p. 257), except with *ten, nine, eight, &c.*, when lead ten *in trumps*, the lowest *in plain suits*.

In the *second round of a suit*, if you have the *winning card*, generally lead it; if you have the *second and third best*, generally lead the second best, *in other cases* generally the lowest.

3. LEAD THE HIGHEST OF A NUMERICALLY WEAK SUIT.

When it is your fate to open a numerically weak suit, your object should be to do as little harm as possible. You cannot expect to win many tricks, so you must do all you can to assist or *strengthen* your partner by leading high or strengthening cards; for, by leading the highest of a suit numerically weak, you take the best chance of keeping the strength in your partner's hand, should he happen to hold it.

It will not often happen that you are driven to open a weak suit originally, as one of your suits must contain as many as four cards. But it may so turn out that your four-card suit is composed of very small cards indeed, in which case you might prefer to open a suit containing better cards, though numerically weaker. Every one can see that ace, king, queen, is a better suit to open than five, four, three, two; but, as you descend in one scale and ascend in the other, there comes a point where the two descriptions of strength nearly or quite balance. With hands containing only a suit of four small cards—say none higher than the eight or nine, and suits of three cards of higher value—the choice is sometimes difficult. As a rule, when you are in doubt, stick to the general principle, and lead from your four-card suit; but if you have such a suit as queen, knave, and another, or knave, ten, and another, you will generally do less harm by opening that.

There is another combination of cards with which
you may be forced to open a numerically weak suit at
starting, viz., when your only four-card suit is the
trump suit. You might then open one of the other
suits, as a smaller evil than leading a trump. No
positive rule can be laid down for such hands as
these.

Whenever you decide on opening a suit of but
three cards, choose, if possible, one in which you hold
a sequence which may be of benefit to your partner.
as queen, knave, ten; queen, knave, and one small
one; knave, ten, and one other, and so on, and lead
the highest. If you have no sequence, lead from
your strongest weak suit. Thus, two honours not in
sequence, and one small one, is a better lead than ace
and two small ones, or king and two small ones.
These, again, should be chosen in preference to queen
and two small ones. When leading from a numerically
weak suit that contains ace, king, or queen, but no
sequence, if you have any indication from the previous
play that your partner is strong in the suit (as will be
explained in Section 4), lead the highest. But having
no guide as to his strength lead the lowest. You run
the risk of making your partner think you have led
from numerical strength; but, on the other hand, by
leading out the high card, you at once give up the
command of the suit, and, unless your partner has
strength in it (the chances being against this), you
leave yourself at the mercy of the opponents.

The case is different with numerically weak suits
headed by a knave or a lower card. Of these suits

you should lead the highest; by retaining such a card
as the knave you would scarcely ever be able to stop
the adversaries from establishing the suit, should they
be strong in it; and, by leading out the high card,
you do all you can to aid your partner, should he
have strength.

Ace and one other, king and one other, or queen
and one other, are very bad suits to lead from. By
holding them up you and your partner stand a better
chance of making tricks on the suit; and if it should
be the adversaries' suit (the chances being two to one
that it is) you keep the power of obstructing it and of
obtaining the lead at advanced periods of the hand.

It follows that when you lead a high card in the
first round of a suit, and in the next drop a lower one
(subject to the rules respecting leads from sequences
and the lead from suits of five cards), your partner
should infer that you have led from a weak suit.
Thus, suppose you lead a nine, which is called an
equivocal card, as it comes from both strong and
weak suits. If in the second round your partner
can infer that you hold a higher card, he knows you
have led from strength. But if in the second round
you play the eight, your partner is equally certain that
your first card was the highest of your weak suit.

4. AVOID CHANGING SUITS,

*When you obtain the lead after one or more tricks
have been played, the question arises whether or not you
should open a fresh suit.* If you have had the lead

before, it is generally advisable to pursue your original lead, for you thus take the best chance of establishing the suit, and you open a fresh suit to a disadvantage.

The fall of the cards in the previous rounds may cause you to alter your game. Thus, the previous play may have already established your suit, or may have so nearly established it as to justify you in leading trumps, as hereafter explained; or your partner may have shown a very strong suit, or a strong trump hand, which may modify your game. Again, your partner may prove utterly weak in your suit; you would then often discontinue it, unless holding the winning cards or a strong sequence, because, with these exceptions, your continuing it gives the adversary the opportunity of finessing against you, and of cutting up your suit; or you may sometimes discontinue a suit if you suspect it will be trumped (as will be further explained in Sections 13-16); but, failing such indications, it is best, as a rule, to pursue the original lead,

If you have not had the lead before, it is in most cases advisable to open your strong suit, when you possess *great* strength in any suit, for you open such suit to advantage; but with weak or only moderately strong suits, which you open to a disadvantage, you would, as a rule, do better to return your partner's original lead, or to lead up to the weak suit of your right-hand adversary, or through the strong suit of your left-hand adversary.

If your partner has had a lead, and you are thoroughly conversant with the system of leading

developed in Sections 2 and 3, and with the Analysis
of Leads (pp. 63-66), you know by the value of the
card he has led whether he is strong or weak in that
suit, unless he has led an equivocal card, which is led
from both strong and weak suits. In this case, if
you have no evidence from your own hand, or from
the fall of the cards, you presume, with a good
partner, that he has led from strength. But you
mostly have some evidence; for instance, if he leads
a ten originally, he has led from king, queen, knave,
ten; from king, knave, ten; or the highest of his
suit. If you hold—or either adversary plays—king
or knave, you know that your partner has led the
highest of his suit. But, in the absence of these
cards, and especially if the ten wins the first round,
or falls to the ace or queen, you may conclude that
your partner's lead was from strength, and you would
do perfectly right to return it.

When you have won the first trick in your partner's
lead cheaply, you must be cautious in returning it, as
the strength must be between your partner and your
right-hand adversary. For example, say A, Y, B, Z,
are the four players, and that they sit in this order
round the table, so that A leads and Z is last player.
If A leads a small card of a plain suit, Y plays a
small one, and B (third player) puts on his best card,
the queen, which wins the trick, it is clear that Z can
have neither ace nor king; A cannot have them both,
or he would have led one, therefore Y must have one of
them at least; and, if B returns the lead, he leads up
to Y's strength, and may cut up his partner's suit.

By observing the **card** led by either adversary, you can similarly tell whether he has led from strength or weakness; so also you can judge from the card played **third** hand by the adversary whether he is weak, it being presumed that the third player puts on his best. It is advantageous to lead up to a weak suit, because you compel the second hand to put **on a** high card, or give your partner the opportunity of finessing. It is generally less advantageous to **lead** through a strong suit, unless **you arc sure that** the second hand is not *very* strong, and that the fourth hand is weak. Otherwise, by continuing the suit, you may be establishing it for the adversary, and getting rid of the command of **it from your** partner's hand.

In discussing leads from weak suits it was supposed, for the sake of convenience, that the leader had no indication from **the play** to guide him. But in practice, in by far the greater number of cases, weak suits are **opened late in a hand** when inference from previous play has given an insight into the strength or weakness of the several players. Thus, you commence with your strong suit; your partner fails to show **any** strength in it. After several other tricks are played you get the lead again, **remaining with** (say) king and **two** others of your first lead. You do not wish to take one of the guards from your king, and you do not deem it advisable to lead a card which **your** partner may be obliged to **trump. You therefore try** another **suit.** By this time you **know,** either by the adversaries' leads what their strong suits are, or by the players' discards (*i.e.*, by the cards they throw away when not able to follow suit,) what their weak suits are, as will be explained under discarding. Guided by these indications, you make choice of a suit for your second lead in which your partner is probably strong, and under such circumstances you would, as a rule, lead the highest of the suit of your second choosing, if numerically weak in it.

When you have led a strengthening card, and it wins the trick, you can rarely do better than continue with your next highest. For example: from queen, knave, and three you lead the queen, which goes round. It hardly requires to be stated that you make the best use of your suit by continuing with the knave. When your strengthening card does not win, the course of the play is the only guide as to whether you should continue the suit. The application of the considerations advanced in this Section will generally inform you where the strong and weak suits lie, and you will act accordingly, giving your partner his strong suit, or, if he has not shown one, leading up to the weak suit of the right-hand adversary, or through the strong suit of the left-hand adversary.

It has several times been assumed that it is advantageous to have the lead at advanced periods of a hand; we now see one principal reason why it is so. The leader knows by observation where the strong and the weak suits lie, and he will generally be able to make use of this knowledge

in assisting his partner, or in obstructing his opponents.

The principles explained in the preceding pages
refer in their integrity to the original lead, or to leads
early in a hand.   They apply also to leads generally;
but, at advanced periods of the hand, and towards
its close, their application is frequently modified by
inferences from the previous play, and by the state
of the score.   Examples of departure from the rules
here laid down will be presented in the illustrative
hands.

In the second round of a suit—

5.   RETURN THE LOWEST OF A STRONG SUIT, THE HIGHEST OF A WEAK SUIT.

When you return your partner's lead, the card you
should choose to lead the second round depends on
the number of cards of the suit you have remaining.
Thus, if you remain with three cards, you must have
had four at first.   You therefore had strength in the
suit, and you should return the smallest of the three
remaining cards, agreeably to the principle that with
strength it is to your advantage to retain the command
in your own hand.   If you remain with two cards
only, you should return the best, to strengthen your
partner; and, similarly, if you have discarded one of
a four-suit, and are left with two only *at the time you
return it,* you have destroyed the numerical power of
your suit, and should therefore treat it as a weak suit,
and return the highest.

The advantages of this principle are numerous. In the case that you and your partner are both numerically strong, the return of the lowest prevents him from finessing in a suit which must be trumped third round. Further, if your hand is weak, you naturally return a suit in which you infer that your partner is strong. You then return a strengthening card to get a high card of your partner's strong suit out of his way, and you enable him to finesse if he thinks proper, and so to keep the command of his suit in his own hand.

It is true that with two small cards only (say the five and the six) you do not strengthen your partner by returning the six. But there is a collateral advantage in keeping to the rule even with small cards— *you enable a good partner to calculate how many you have left of the suit*, and often where the remainder of it lies. Thus, your partner leads a small card of a suit of which you have king, three, and two. You, as third player, put on the king. If you return the suit, you return the three, and not the two, when it ought to be inferred, either that you have returned the smallest of a suit of four or more, or that you have no more of the suit left, or the two only. When your two comes down in the third round it ought to be certain that you have no more. If your partner has confidence in you, he can often calculate what you have left before the third round is played; thus, in the above instance, your partner, not having the two himself, and seeing that it does not drop from the adversaries, concludes, with tolerable certainty, that you remain, after the second round, with the two and no more.

There are two exceptions to the rule of play above stated: 1. When you hold the winning card you return it, whatever number of cards you hold, lest it should be trumped the third round, or, your partner, imagining it to be against him, should finesse; and 2. When you hold the second and third best, in plain suits, you return the highest. Thus, suppose you have queen, knave, ten, and one small one of a suit of which your partner leads a small one, you (third hand) put on the ten, which is won by (say) the ace. If you afterwards return the suit, you should return the queen, for you not only force out the king, if against you, but you also do not block your partner's suit, should he have led from great numerical strength, say five cards to the nine, an advantage which you lose by returning the small one.

It should also be observed that, occasionally, when you return your adversary's strong lead, you do not lead your highest of two remaining cards, especially if you hold the second best guarded. For example, you are A, Y is your left-hand adversary. Y has led a king, which was won by the ace, leaving Y with the queen and others. You remain with knave and one small one. If you are driven to return this suit, you should return the small one. The queen will probably be put on second hand, and you will remain with the best.

THE SECOND HAND.

In the first round of a suit, you should generally,

6. PLAY YOUR LOWEST CARD SECOND HAND.

You presume that the first hand has led from strength, and, if you have a high card in his suit, you lie over him when it is led again; whereas, if you play your high card second hand, you get rid of a commanding card of the adversary's suit, and, when it is returned, the original leader finesses against you. Besides this, the third player will put on his highest card, and, if it is better than yours, you have wasted power to no purpose.

If, however, you have a sequence of high cards, you should put on one of the sequence second hand, for, if you pass the trick altogether, the third hand may win with a very low card, or, with his low card, may force a high one from your partner. The chief objection to playing an unsupported high card does not apply, as the leader cannot successfully finesse against you in the next round.

With a moderate sequence, such as queen, knave— knave, ten—ten, nine—you cover if you are numeri- cally weak; but, with more than three cards of the suit, you pass a small card led, agreeably to the principle already discussed—that in weak suits you play to strengthen your partner, but in strong ones you leave him to help you. For instance: the leader (A) has king, ten, nine, eight, seven of a suit; the second player (Y) has queen, knave, and one small one; the fourth player (Z) has ace and two small ones. A leads the small card; Y should cover with the knave; if he does not, the card led forces Z's ace. It is true that this happens also if Y passes with queen, knave, and two small ones; but Y, in this case, has a guard to his queen and knave, and is left with the two best cards after the second round of the suit.

With a sequence lower than ten, nine, the advantage of covering is very small, and there is some fear of its being taken to indicate a desire for a trump lead—as will be explained in Section 13.

7. PLAY THE LOWEST OF A SEQUENCE.

When you do not head a trick, you throw away your lowest card to economise your strength. Thus, with queen and two small ones, you would not throw the queen to king led. It is an error to suppose that it is of no consequence which card you play when you hold only small cards or cards in sequence. It is not of much consequence as regards merely the chance of making tricks; but it is of great importance in affording information to partner.

Thus, suppose the players to be as before, A, Y, B,

Z. A leads the three of a suit, Y plays the five, B the four. It ought to be certain that B has no more of the suit, it being presumed that he, not being able to head the trick, throws away his smallest. If he afterwards plays the two, and it turns out that he previously played the four *through carelessness*, his partner loses confidence, and gives up all hopes of drawing correct inferences from his play.

The principle applies equally to cards in sequence. Thus, say knave is led, and you (second hand) hold ace and king; if you put on the king, your partner gains the very important information that you have the ace also. For knave is not led from ace, knave, &c. (*see* Analysis of Leads, p. 64), so the leader cannot have the ace; the third hand cannot have it, or he would win the king; and the fourth, not having it himself, infers that you have it. If you put on the ace, not only could he not tell that you have the king, but would presume that it lay with the adversary. The principle, though stated for the sake of convenience in respect of the second hand, applies to the third and fourth hands also. (For a fuller examination of this point *see* Section 12.)

ANALYSIS OF PLAY OF SECOND HAND IN DETAIL.

(See Note on Analysis of Leads, p. 63.)

Ace, king, &c., put on king; *in trumps* it is often right to leave the chance of the first trick to partner. With *queen also*, you are so strong that you should not pass the trick even in trumps.

Ace, king, knave, play king. If the second round comes from the original leader, you will then know whether his lead was from strength or weakness, and will finesse or not accordingly.

Ace, queen, knave, play knave; with *ten also*, or others belonging to the sequence, the lowest of it. *If, in trumps, king is turned up to your left*, of course ace should be put on; obvious alterations on account of the trump card will not be mentioned in future.

Ace, queen, ten, put on queen, as you thus make certain of two tricks, unless you are led through twice, and both king and knave lie over you. *In trumps*, the ten. With *ace, queen, and small ones*, the smallest, *unless knave is led* by a good player, when put on ace; it is useless to cover knave with queen, as the leader cannot have king (*see* Analysis of Leads). This requires modification towards the close of a hand, for then the leader might have the king. With *ace, queen, and three or more small ones*, put on queen if weak in trumps, a small one if strong.

Ace, knave, ten, and one or more small ones, play the smallest; *in trumps*, the ten. For from king, queen, &c., in trumps, a small one is generally led; but, in plain suits, the king is led. If, then, in a plain suit, a small one is led, either king or queen must be in the third or fourth hand, and no good is got by covering. With *ace, knave, and one or more small ones*, it is useless to put on the knave, second hand, in any suit.

With *ace and four small ones* generally pass the first trick, unless the game is in a critical state, and you are weak in trumps; if you suspect a single card lead, it is often right to put on ace.

King, queen, and others, play queen. *In trumps*, the smallest, unless you have *ten also*, or only *three in suit*.

King, knave, ten, &c., the lowest of the knave sequence.

With *queen, knave, &c.—knave, ten, &c.—ten, nine, &c.*—play as directed at pp. 77, 78.

If a small card is led, and you hold an honour and one small card, pass the trick, as a rule; for, by putting on the honour, you expose your weakness, and enable the original leader to finesse in the second round. The principal exception is when the circumstances of a hand cause you to seize any chance of getting the lead—as, when you want to stop a lead of trumps, or want to lead trumps yourself—when it is often right, with ace, or king, or queen, and one small

G

card, to put on the honour second hand. *In trumps,
if king or queen is turned up, and it is only singly
guarded* (*i.e.*, if you have only one other trump), it is
generally best to put on the turn-up second hand. *If
you hold king or queen singly guarded, and a superior
honour is turned up to your right*, you gain an advantage by putting on your king or queen; *if the
superior honour is turned up to your left*, the reverse.
With *queen and another, your partner having turned up
ace or king*, put on the small one second hand.

If a ten is led, and you hold queen and one other,
cover with the queen. With *queen and two others*
pass the ten. *If a ten is led, and you hold knave
and one or more small ones*, you should play a small
one.

*If an honour is led, and you have a higher honour and
numerical weakness*, cover it. With *one honour and
numerical strength* you pass an *honour led*, except you
have the ace, when put it on. Some players pass
queen led if they hold ace, ten, &c., or king, ten, &c.;
but, in the opinion of the writer, it is better to cover.
When you have a fourchette, cover of course; thus,
if knave is led, and you have queen, ten, &c., put on
the queen.

*In the second round of a suit, if you have the winning
card*, you should—in plain suits—generally put it on
second hand; but *in trumps* there are many cases in
which you should not, especially if you have numerical
strength in trumps and a good hand besides. Your
winning trump must make, and, by passing the second
round, you perhaps enable your partner to make a

third best trump—or even a smaller one—yourself retaining the command.

If, when led through in the second round of a suit, you conjecture from previous play that *the second best card is to your right,* it is sometimes advisable to put on the third best. You thus save your partner's hand if he holds the best. For instance : if knave is led in the first round, and your partner (then second player) puts on king, which wins the trick, it is clear (if the ten is your best) that your partner has the ace, for the third player could not win the king, and the leader could not have led from knave, ace. If your right-hand adversary afterwards returns the suit through you, you should put on the ten, in order to save your partner's ace.

THE THIRD HAND.

In the first round of a suit, you should generally

8. PLAY YOUR HIGHEST CARD THIRD HAND.

In order to strengthen your partner. You presume
that he leads from his strong suit, and wants to get
the winning cards of it out of his way; you, therefore,
do not finesse, but play your highest, remembering
that you play the lowest of a sequence (7).

With ace, queen (and, of course, ace, queen, knave,
&c., in sequence) you do finesse, for, in this case, the
finesse cannot be left to your partner. In trumps you
may finesse ace, knave, if an honour is turned up to
your right. Some players finesse knave with king,
knave, &c.; but it is contrary to principle to finesse in
your partner's strong suit.

If your partner leads a strengthening card, the case
is different. If it is an equivocal card, and you have
no indication as to its being from strength or weakness,
you presume it is from strength, and do not finesse.
But, if it is probable that your partner has led from a
weak suit, then you may finesse king, knave, &c., or
pass his card altogether, so as not to give up the entire
command of the suit.

For instance: you would not put ace on your
partner's queen, for you thus part with ace and queen

for one trick, and leave the winning card against you; also, with ace, knave, &c., if ten is led originally, you would pass it: and so on. If ten is led, and your only honour is the ace, put it on. The lead is most probably from king, knave, ten, &c., and you should leave the finesse to your partner. If ten is led, and your only honour is the queen, pass it. If the lead is from king, knave, ten, you gain nothing by putting on the queen; and, if the ten is a strengthening card, you give up the entire command of the suit by covering. If you have considerable strength in a suit, in which a strengthening card is led to you, you must be guided as to the finesse by your strength in trumps; thus, if your partner leads knave of a suit in which you hold ace, king, and small ones—if you have an average hand and four trumps you may pass the knave, but with only three trumps you should not.

In the second round of a suit, if you (third player) hold the best and third-best cards, and you have no indication as to the position of the intermediate card, you should generally finesse if strong in trumps, but not if weak. If you hold second and fourth best, you may nearly always finesse; for you conclude that the winning card is over you in the fourth hand, since your partner has not led it, and the second player has not put it on. If the third best lies over you also, you cannot prevent the tenace from making, and your only chance therefore is to finesse. Thus, if you lead a small card from queen, ten, and two small ones, your partner wins the first trick with the king, and returns a small one. The ace is certainly to your left, you therefore finesse the ten, for if your left-hand adversary holds ace and knave he must make them both; but, otherwise, your ten forces the ace, and you are left with the best. In trumps the winning card is often held up by the adversary, but you must submit to this contingency, and generally finesse.

It is of no use to finesse against your right-hand adversary in a suit in which he has shown weakness. For instance, if the second hand has none of the suit led, and does not trump it, you (third hand) should not finesse a major tenace (*i.e.*, the best and third best cards). This often occurs in the second or third round of a suit; also, if your partner (third player) has won a trick very cheaply, and the suit is returned, it is rarely of any use to finesse if you have the winning card.

In some few positions, however, it is necessary to finesse, even if the second player holds nothing. Thus, your partner leads a knave, and the second hand renounces (*i.e.*, does not follow suit); if you (third player) hold king, it is useless to cover, as ace, queen in the fourth hand must make. Again, you have king and two small trumps; your partner leads a small one; the second hand renounces. If you want one trick to win or save the game, you (third player) play a small trump, when the fourth player will be obliged to lead up to your king guarded.

The state of the game and of the score will often direct as to a finesse late in a hand. Thus, if you hold a winning card, and want one trick to save or

win the game, of course you should not run any risk.
A finesse against even one card is generally wrong, if,
by playing otherwise, you prevent the adversary from
scoring three or five. A finesse is almost always bad,
if, by not finessing, you insure the odd trick, as that
makes a difference of two to the score. In the
opposite case, of course, a finesse is generally right
(sometimes even against more than one card), if its
success gives you the odd trick, or puts you at the
score of three or five.

The considerations as to finessing and the course of
play generally, that come in as the hand proceeds, are
so complicated, and depend so much on inferences
from previous play, and on the state of the score, that
one can scarcely do more than to state a few broad
rules, and to add some examples. Exemplifications
of the conduct of the hand at advanced periods will
be found in Sections 17 and 18 (pp. 113-134), and
more in the illustrative hands.

THE FOURTH HAND.

The fourth player having, with a few exceptions, merely to win the trick, if against him, his play involves no further development of general principles.

The exceptional cases, where the fourth hand should not win the trick though he can, or should win his partner's trick in order to get the lead, depend so much on the previous fall of the cards, that they can best be illustrated in the hands.

THE COMMAND OF SUITS.

In the foregoing chapters it has often been incidentally stated that you should

9. KEEP THE COMMAND **OF YOUR** ADVERSARY'S SUIT: AND

10. GET **RID OF** THE COMMAND OF YOUR PARTNER'S SUIT.

The reasons will be obvious to those who are familiar with the principles in the previous pages; in the first case, you obstruct the adversaries suits, and prevent their establishing them; in the second case, you assist in clearing the suit for your partner.

Thus, with ace and queen only of a suit led by your partner, if you win with the queen, play out the ace at once; but, if the suit is led by your adversary, keep the ace in your hand. If you play out the winning card of the opponent's suit in hopes of trumping the next round, which is often done by those who play a trumping game, you do just what the adversaries want; for the lead of the ace gives them valuable assistance towards bringing in their suit when trumps are out.

In order to get rid, at the proper moment, of the command of suits in which your partner has strength, you need to pay exact attention to the cards previously played, and often to argue ingeniously from them. For example:—1. From ace, queen, and two small cards, you lead the smallest; the second hand renounces; your partner plays the nine; the fourth hand wins with the king, which shows that he has neither ten nor knave. If the fourth hand returns the suit, you (then second player) should play the queen, and not the small one, for your partner must have, at least, ten and knave, and, if he originally had five of the suit, you get out of his way. 2. Your hand contains four cards, viz., ace and one small spade (spades not having been led), and two losing diamonds; your partner has nothing but spades, of which he leads the king. If you pass it you cannot make more than two tricks, for the winning diamonds are against you in one hand; but, if you win your partner's king, and return the small one, and your partner has led from king, queen, you still win two tricks, and get a chance of making three or four.

You help your partner to get rid of the command of your suit by leading the lowest of a sequence, notwithstanding that it heads your suit, when you want him to win your card if he can. For this reason you lead ten from king, queen, knave, ten. Again, suppose you are left with knave, ten, and others of a suit, of which your partner can only have king and another (ace and queen being out), though it is uncertain whether he does hold the king. You would cause him to get rid of the king by leading the ten; whereas, if you led the knave, he probably would not part with the king.

Experienced players frequently endeavour to steal a trick, or to obtain the entire command of a suit (*i.e.*, to keep a sufficient number of winning or commanding cards in it to make every trick), by *underplaying*. Underplay is keeping up the winning card, generally in the second round of a suit, by leading a low card, though holding the best.

Thus, suppose a small trump is led, and you (fourth player) hold ace, knave, and two small ones, and you win with one of the small ones. If you return a small trump, you will very likely cause your left-hand adversary to believe that your partner has the ace; consequently, if your left-hand adversary has the king, he may not put it on; your partner will win the second round with the queen, and you will retain the command of the trump suit.

Underplay is an extempore stratagem depending on observation of the previous fall of the cards, and, therefore, best capable of explanation by examples.

Here is a somewhat complicated one : A, finding his partner strong in trumps, leads the seven. The king is put on by Y (second hand), which B (third hand) wins, holding ace, queen, ten, nine, eight. It is evident to B that A's seven was his highest trump, as the only higher one in is the knave, and A would never lead the seven from knave, seven. The king having been put on second hand, B concludes that Y, in all probability, holds at most one small trump more. The knave is, to a moral certainty, in Z's hand. B, by leading the eight in the second round, will probably win the trick, and, unless Z had four trumps originally, will catch the knave with the queen in the third round. (Further examples of underplay occur in the Hands.)

Players should be on their guard against this manœuvre, particularly when second hand in the second round of a suit they hold the second best card guarded, and the adversary has been playing a strong game (as by leading trumps), and is left with the long trump, or is certain to be able to obtain the lead again. Then it is often right for the second hand to stick on a singly-guarded second best card, especially if that is the only chance of making it. Thus, in the case stated in the previous paragraph, Z's only chance of making the knave, if singly guarded, is to put it on second hand. For, if the queen with small ones is in A's hand, A is sure to finesse on the return of the suit by his partner. Again, take this case : A leads the six of diamonds ; Y, with knave, ten, and a small one, puts on the ten ; B plays the king, and Z wins it with the ace. Presently, A obtains the lead again, and leads the eight of diamonds. A, having led the lowest of his suit in the first round, may be inferred to have led from a strong suit—headed in this case by the queen—and is underplaying with, probably, queen and nine in his hand. Y should observe this, and in the second round should win the eight with the knave.

Refusing to play the winning card in the first and second rounds of a suit—commonly called *holding up*—is, in fact, a species of underplay. For example :— 1. Trumps are led by the player to your left; the third player wins with the ace, and returns the suit through your hand. If you are left with king and one or more small ones, you should play a small one, unless the circumstances of the hand are such that you deem it advantageous to stop the trump lead. The original trump leader, not knowing but that the king is in your partner's hand, will probably finesse. and your partner thus has a chance of making the third best trump, even though unguarded. If your partner has neither second nor third best trump, no harm is done, as you will then probably make but one trick in the suit, however you play. 2. Again, ten tricks are played, and each player is left with three cards of a suit not opened. If the second player puts on the queen (from which it may be inferred that he holds the king also), the third hand should not cover with the ace. For, by winning the trick, he must lead up to king guarded ; but, by passing it, he leaves the lead with the second player, and takes the best chance of making two tricks. 3. One more example will

suffice: A has the last trump, and ace and four small
cards of a suit not led. The adversary now leads the
king, and follows with the queen of that suit. A
should pass them both; by so doing he will probably
make three tricks in the suit if the cards are equally
divided.

DISCARDING.

When you cannot follow suit, you should

11. DISCARD FROM YOUR WEAKEST SUIT.

You weaken a suit by discarding from it, and lessen
the number of long cards you might otherwise establish and bring in (*i.e.*, make tricks with if trumps are
out, and you obtain the lead after the establishment
of your suit). On the other hand, you do but little
harm by throwing from a suit in which you are
already weak. Your partner should understand that
your first or *original discard* is from your *weakest suit*,
just as he understands that your original lead is from
your strongest suit.

But, just as in the case of leads, you are sometimes
obliged to lead from a weak suit, or to make a forced
lead, so sometimes you have to make a *forced discard*.
Forced discards require much more careful consideration than they generally receive.

It is clear that if the opponents declare great strength in trumps (by leading trumps or asking for them, as will be fully explained in Section 13), that your chance of bringing in a suit is practically *nil*. You should therefore, in such cases, abandon the tactics you would otherwise adopt, and play to guard your weaker suits, by discarding from your best protected suit, which is generally your longest suit. You must, in fact, play a defensive game.

If this system of discarding is comprehended by the two players who are partners, it follows, as a matter of course, that *when trumps are not declared against you, your partner will assume you are weak in the suit you first discard;* but, *when trumps are declared against you, he will give you credit for strength in the suit from which you originally throw away.* This is most important, as it affects his subsequent leads. In the first case, he will refrain from leading the suit from which you have discarded; in the second, he will, unless he has a very strong suit of his own, select for his lead the suit in which you have shown strength by your discard.

It must be borne in mind that it is only your original discard which is directive. Having once discarded, you cannot undo your work by any number of discards from another suit.

It is dangerous to unguard an honour, or to blank an ace; and, also, to discard a single card when the game is in an undeveloped stage, as it exposes your weakness almost as soon as the suit is led. But, when you see that there is a probability of strength in trumps on your side, direct your partner to your strong suit by all the means in your power, and unhesitatingly unguard an honour, or throw a single card. Of course, if strength in trumps is against you, these are the very last cards you should think of throwing away.

When your left-hand adversary will have the lead next round, if you discard from a suit in which you hold a tenace, you may possibly induce him to lead that suit up to you. You must be on your guard against this ruse, and not necessarily lead up to the discard of your right-hand opponent.

The same principle applies to trumping as to discarding. The weaker you are in trumps the better it is for you to make a little one by trumping, as will be further explained in Section 14.

THE CONVERSATION OF THE GAME.

12. AFFORD INFORMATION BY YOUR PLAY.

It has several times been assumed in the preceding pages that you should convey information by your play. The question naturally arises, *How is it that a player gains any advantage by publishing information to the table?* It is often argued, and with much show of reason, that as almost every revelation concerning your hand must be given to the whole table, and that as you have two adversaries and only one partner, you publish information at a disadvantage. No doubt this argument would have considerable force if you were compelled to expose the whole of your hand. But you possess the power, to a great extent, of selecting what facts shall be announced and what concealed.

Experienced players are unanimous in admitting that it is an advantage to inform your partner of strength in your own suits, though some advise concealment of strength in suits in which the adversaries have shown strength. Thus, with ace, king, second hand, the usual play is to put on the king. The third hand does not win the king, and hence the leader is able to infer that the ace of his strong suit is against him. But, if you put on the ace second hand, you prevent the leader from discovering where the king of his suit lies. It is, however, found that two honours in the adversary's suit constitute sufficient strength to make it advantageous in the long run to proclaim your force; while, with less strength, it is not easy to mystify the opponents prejudicially; so that, on the whole, it seldom happens that a balance of gain results from the adoption of deceptive play.

It is in most cases unquestionably disadvantageous to you that the whole table should be aware of your being very weak in a particular suit, and, consequently, information of weakness should be withheld as long as possible. If you are led up to fourth hand in such a suit, or if your partner opens the suit with a small card, of course the disclosure is inevitable; but until one of these events happens your poverty can generally be kept out of sight. It may happen that you are occasionally forced to lead a weak suit yourself; and in this event the least disadvantage is to tell the truth at once, by first leading the highest of it. Your partner apprised of the state of your hand by the fall of your smaller card in the subsequent round will probably deem it prudent to strive by defensive tactics to avert total defeat in that suit, rather than to contend single-handed against the combined strength of the opponents. Indeed, at critical points of the game, when you have exhibited weakness in one or more suits, your partner would frequently be justified in playing a false card. He is driven to rely solely on himself, and he is entitled to adopt every artifice his ingenuity can suggest in order to perplex the other side. The consideration that he may mislead you will no longer influence him if he knows you to be powerless for good or for evil.

You inform your partner by following the recognised practice of the game, as by leading from your strong suit originally, by leading the highest of a sequence, by following suit with the lowest of a sequence and so forth. If you adhere to this you will soon acquire a reputation for playing a straightforward intelligible game; and this character alone will counterbalance the disadvantage which will sometimes attach to the fact that you have enabled the adversaries to read your hand. If your partner knows that you play at random and without method, he will be in a state of constant uncertainty; and you almost preclude him from executing any of the finer strokes of play, the opportunities for

H

which generally arise from being able to infer with
confidence the position of particular cards. The
extreme case of two skilled players against two un-
skilled ones amounts almost to this, that towards
the close of a hand the former have the same
advantage as though they had seen each other's
cards, while the latter have not.

It follows that when you are unfortunately tied to
an untaught partner, especially if at the same time you
are pitted against observant adversaries, you should
expose your hand as little as possible, particularly in
respect of minor details.

It will become apparent, on consideration, that the
question of the advisability of affording information is
more or less intimately connected with every card that
is played. It is, therefore, of extreme importance to
ascertain whether the practice is advantageous or the
reverse. The arguments just adduced are doubtless
in favour of the practice of affording information by
the play; but it must be admitted that by far the
strongest authority for it is that experienced players,
by their settled opinions, reject the opposite course.

The instructed player frequently selects one card in
preference to another with the *sole* object of affording
information. When the principle is carried thus far,
the play becomes purely conventional. For example:
you naturally win a trick as cheaply as possible; if,
fourth hand, you could win with a ten you would not
waste an ace. But suppose you held knave and ten,
which card should then be played? The knave and
ten in one hand are of equal value, and therefore to

win with the knave would be no unnecessary sacrifice of strength. Nevertheless, you extend to such cases the rule of winning as cheaply as possible, and you play the ten for the mere purpose of conveying information. This is a simple instance of a pure convention. Though a convention, it is in accordance with, and is suggested by, principle. Indeed, all the established conventions of the game are so chosen as to harmonize with play that would naturally be adopted independently of convention. The aggregation of the recognised rules of play, including the established conventions, constitute what in practice is called the Conversation of the Game of Whist.

It must not be overlooked that unsound players often deceive unintentionally, and all players sometimes with intention. It is, therefore, necessary to be on your guard against drawing inferences too rigidly.

There are some ways of conveying information which have not been explained. One is to keep the turn-up card in hand as long as possible; thus, having turned up the five and holding the six, trump with the six in preference. An exception to this rule is when you are weak in trumps, and the adversaries have shown strength in them, because then, if the adversaries know you have the turn-up card in your hand, they will draw it, whereas, if you play it, they may be uncertain as to your holding another. By leading the lowest of a head sequence of winning trumps you convey information; thus, with ace, king, queen, knave, lead knave and queen, and, when they win,

your partner will see that you have four by honours;
but did you lead out king and queen, as in plain suits,
he could tell nothing about the knave.   So also, if all
the honours are out, and you lead, *e.g.*, from ten,
nine, lead the nine.   You may pursue the same
method in plain suits when your partner has no more
trumps, and with any head sequence when you want
him to win it, or are sure he cannot, and also when
the fourth hand has already renounced in the suit led.
For instance, you have queen, knave, ten, and a small
trump, and your partner turns up the nine; you lead
the small one, and your partner's nine forces the king.
It is now clear that your partner has not the ace, as
he would never finesse ace, nine.   If you next lead
the ten, and it forces the ace from the second hand,
your partner is informed that you hold queen and
knave, which he could not have told if you had continued with the queen.

If you have the complete command of a suit, you
can publish the fact by discarding the highest of it;
the presumption being that you would never throw
away a winning card with a losing one in your hand.
If you discard a second-best card, you ought to have
no more of the suit, for with the best also you would
discard that, and with a smaller one you would discard
that.   By winning with the highest, and returning the
lowest of a sequence (more especially fourth hand),
you show that you have the intermediate cards. Thus,
with ace, king, queen, fourth hand, if you desire to
continue the suit, you would win with the ace and
return the queen.

TRUMPS.

THE MANAGEMENT OF TRUMPS.

The Management of Trumps is, perhaps, the most difficult—certainly the most important—of all points at Whist. Before discussing the special uses of trumps, it may be observed that in some few hands trumps are led like plain suits, because they are your strongest suit, and you prefer leading them to opening a weak suit. The principles already discussed, which guide us to the most favourable chances for making tricks in a suit, apply to trumps equally with other suits. The privilege, however, enjoyed by the trump suit of winning every other, causes some modifications of detail (noticed at pp. 63-66, and at pp. 80-83); for, since the winning trumps *must* make tricks, you play a more backward game in the trump suit. Thus, with ace, king, and small trumps, you lead a small one, by which you obtain an increased chance of making tricks in the suit, and you keep the command of it, and must have the lead after the third round, the advantage of which will be presently explained. Even if your partner is so weak in trumps that the opponent wins the first trick very cheaply, but little (if any) harm accrues; for the opponent then has to open a suit up to you or your partner.

In the great majority of hands, trumps are applied to their special uses, viz.: 1. To disarm the opponents,

and to prevent their trumping your winning cards;
and 2. To trump the winning cards of the adversaries.
In order to comprehend when trumps may be most
profitably applied to the first, and when to the second,
of these uses, we must first clearly perceive the objects
aimed at throughout the hand, viz.: to establish a suit,
to exhaust the adversaries' trumps, and to retain the
long trump, or a certain winning card with which to
get the lead again, for the purpose of bringing in the
suit; also to endeavour to obstruct similar designs of
the opponents.   It follows that you should

13. LEAD TRUMPS WHEN VERY STRONG IN THEM.

It cannot be too strongly impressed that *the primary
use of strength in trumps is to draw the adversaries'
trumps for the bringing in of your own or your partner's
long suit*. With great strength in trumps (five or more),
you may proceed at once to disarm the opponents, and
lead trumps without waiting to establish a suit.   For,
with five trumps or more, the chance of your succeeding
in drawing the other trumps, and of being left with
the long trumps is so considerable, that you may then
almost always lead trumps, whatever your other cards.
This point is much misunderstood even by pretty
good players.   It is often said, " Strength in trumps
is no reason for leading them, unless you have a good
suit as well."   If both you and your partner are devoid
of good cards you cannot make tricks; but should your
partner hold one good suit out of the three, you will

very likely bring it in for him by leading from strength
in trumps. For, even if you have a poor hand out of
trumps, you will discover in the course of play (*i.e.*, by
the suits led or discarded by the other players) what
your partner's suit is, and will be able to lead it to
him each time you get the lead with your long trumps.
Besides, if your hand is weak out of trumps, you are
placed in the disadvantageous position of leading from
a weak suit unless you lead trumps.

You should not be deterred from leading trumps
because an honour is turned up to your right, nor
necessarily lead them because the same happens to
your left; either is proper if the circumstances of the
hand require it, but neither otherwise. To illustrate
this proposition, take this hand: ace, queen, and three
small spades (trumps), three small hearts, three small
clubs, and two small diamonds. The king of spades
is turned up fourth hand. The best lead is disputed;
but the author has no hesitation in advising the lead
of the smallest trump, notwithstanding that there is a
certain finesse over the king. A little consideration
will render this apparent. By leading the trump suit
originally, you obtain the advantages just enumerated,
and make the dealer open a suit up to your partner.
Your partner, as soon as he gets the lead, will return
the trump, and you thus obtain the command of
trumps whether the king was forced out in the first
round or not.

Bearing in mind the severe consequences of leaving
the adversary with the long trump, you must be
cautious in leading trumps from less than five; four

trumps and a moderate hand not justifying an original trump **lead**. You should, instead, lead your strong plain suit, and if you establish it, and the adversaries do not meantime show any great strength, as by leading or calling for trumps (pp. 106, 107), you may then, with four trumps, mostly venture a trump lead. With strength in trumps you may generally finesse more freely in the second and third rounds of trumps than you would in plain suits. In plain suits an unsuccessful finesse may result in the best being afterwards **trumped, which** cannot happen in trumps. Moreover, by finessing, you keep the winning trump, and so obtain the lead after the third round. This is especially important when you have a suit established and but four trumps. Here you should, generally, not merely finesse in the second round, but hold up the winning trump, and sometimes at this juncture refuse to part with it even if the trump lead comes from the adversary.

An **example** will render this more clear. The leader (A) has **ace**, and three small trumps, a strong suit, headed by ace, king, queen, and a probable trick, say king and another, in a third suit. A should, in the writer's judgment, lead a trump. If B (A's partner) wins the first trick in trumps, and returns it, A, as a rule, should not part with his ace. When A or B obtain the lead again they play a third round of trumps, which, being won by the ace, enables A, by leading his **tierce** major, **to** get a force (*i.e.* to compel one of his adversaries to trump in order to win the trick), in which case nothing short of five trumps in one hand against him can prevent A's bringing in his suit.

You must be prepared for similar tactics on the part
of the adversaries, and not conclude that they have
not the best trump because they suffer you to win the
first or second round.

With a well protected hand containing four trumps,
two being honours, a trump may be led originally.
For here the chance of gaining by the trump lead may
be taken as greater than the chance of losing. Thus
with queen, knave, and two small trumps, a four suit
with an honour, say for example, knave, ten, nine, and
a small one, king guarded in the third suit, and queen
guarded in the fourth, a small trump if it finds partner
with an honour is by no means unlikely to win the
game. If partner turns out very weak in trumps the
leader must alter his plan, and, instead of continuing
the trump lead, play to make three, five or seven tricks
according to the fall of the cards in plain suits.

Trump leads, without strength in trumps, can only
be right in consequence of some special circumstance
in the state of the game, or of the score. For instance,
great commanding strength in all the plain suits may
call for a trump lead; or it may be necessitated to stop
a *cross ruff* (*i.e.*, the alternate trumping by partners of
different suits, each leading the suit in which the other
renounces), in which case it is generally advisable to
take out two rounds if possible; so with the winning
trump you play it out, whatever your others are.
Again, if you have a wretched hand and you are love
to three or four, you assume that the game is lost,
unless your partner is very strong; and if he *is* very
strong, the trump is the best lead for him. This

doctrine is frequently carried to excess, as, by concealing your weakness, you often stand a better chance
of saving a point, if not the game, than by at once
exposing it. If, therefore, you have one four suit,
headed by an honour, you would generally do better
to choose that.

The trump lead is so much more important than
any other that you should almost always return your
partner's lead of trumps *immediately*, except he has led
from weakness, when you are not bound to return it
unless it suits your hand.

If you find one of the adversaries without a trump,
you should mostly proceed to establish your long suit,
and abstain from drawing two trumps for one; to say
nothing of the probability that the adversary who has
not renounced is unusually strong in trumps. Besides,
when he has the lead, he will very likely lead trumps
in order to draw two for one; and it is more advantageous to you that the lead should come from him.
On the other hand, if your partner has no trump, it is
often right to endeavour to weaken the adversaries by
continuing even their trump lead.

It is a common artifice, if you wish a trump to be
led, to drop a high card to the adversary's lead, to
induce him to believe that you will trump it next
round, whereupon the leader will very likely change
the suit, and perhaps lead trumps. Thus, if he leads
king (from ace, king, and others), and you hold queen
and one other, it is evident that you cannot make the
queen. If you throw the queen to his king, he may
lead a trump to prevent your trumping his ace; but if

he goes on with the suit, and you drop your small
card, it may fairly be inferred that you have been en-
deavouring to get him to lead a trump. Your partner
should now take the hint, and, if he gets the lead,
lead trumps; for, if you want them led, it is of little
consequence from whom the lead comes. By an extension of this system to lower cards it is understood
that, whenever you throw away an *unnecessarily* high
card, it is a sign (after the smaller card drops) that
you want trumps led. This is a recognised signal,
and is called *asking for trumps*.

It is not always requisite to wait the completion of
the signal. Thus, if your partner does not trump,
but discards (say) an honour in another suit, it is clear
that his hand must consist mainly of trumps and of
the fourth suit, with considerable strength in each.
The higher his discard, the more certainly is this so.
In such cases, your best game is to lead trumps to
him, to clear them, that he may bring in his strong
suit. If, then, he wants trumps led, he would naturally
discard the highest card he could spare, and when he
afterwards plays a lower, it is clear that he has been
asking you for trumps.

When your partner asks for trumps, and you have
four or more, lead the smallest, unless you have three
honours, or queen, knave, ten; if you have only two
or three trumps, lead from the highest downwards,
whatever they are (and *see* Appendix B, p. 267).

Before answering the signal, be sure that the higher
card, previously dropped, is *unnecessarily* high. For
instance, a higher card is often played before a lower,

to show that you command the suit, or that you hold the intermediate cards, or to get out of your partner's way. It is very important to distinguish between covering second hand and discarding an unnecessarily high card. For example, with knave, **ten, and one** other (say the three), it is usual to play the ten second hand on a small card. When your three comes down in the next round, it is not a signal for trumps, unless your partner can infer that you **do not hold the knave.** Moderate players, who know of the signal, never consider this; so with them the choice of the least evil **is** generally not to cover, for you otherwise run the terrible risk of having a strengthening trump led to you with a weak hand. **To** ask for trumps, second hand, with knave, ten, and one other, you must play the knave.

The use of strength in trumps being **to** disarm the opponents, it follows that you should as much as possible husband your strength for that purpose. Therefore when second player,

14. DO NOT TRUMP A DOUBTFUL CARD IF STRONG IN TRUMPS.

By a doubtful card is meant a card of a suit of which your partner *may* have the best.

Whether you should trump or refuse to **trump a** doubtful card depends almost entirely on your strength in trumps. It has already been mentioned that it is an advantage to trump when you are weak, for you thus make a little trump, which is not available for the other uses of trumps, and which, if not used for trumping, will presently be drawn by the strong hand. It is conversely a disadvantage to trump a doubtful card when you are strong in trumps, for by trumping you weaken your numerical power, and diminish the probability of your bringing in a suit. If, instead of trumping, you throw away a losing card, you inform your partner that you have strength in trumps (either four, at least, or one or two honours guarded), and also, by your discard, what your strong suit is; and if your partner has any strength in the suit led, you put him in a favourable position.

If you refuse to overtrump, or to trump a certain winning card, your partner should conclude either that you have no trump, or more probably four trumps and a powerful hand besides. He should presume you are reserving your trumps to bring in a suit, and should assist you by leading trumps as soon as he can. A refusal to be thus forced is seldom requisite if you have more than four trumps; with six you are mostly strong enough to trump and to lead trumps; with five you may do the same, if your suit is established; but if not, it is generally best to take the force, and to lead your suit.

The situations in which it is most necessary to refuse to overtrump your right-hand adversary, or to refuse to trump a winning card, occur when you have four trumps and a very strong suit, or a suit established early in a hand. For then, by trumping, you prejudice your chance of bringing in the suit in order to secure one trick. By refusing to part with a trump in these cases, you obtain the advantages just enumerated, at the time when they are most likely to become of service; and, where you refuse to over-trump, your adversary is left with one trump less, by which your hand is strengthened.

Many players run into the extreme of always refusing to be forced by a winning card when they are strong in trumps. The situations, however, just indicated, are almost the only ones in which it answers to hold up; and these even are liable to several exceptions. For instance :—1. You should not persist in refusing to be forced if you find that the adversary has the entire command of his suit. 2. You should not refuse if your partner evidently intends to force you; and, 3. You should not refuse to overtrump if you have reason to conclude that your left-hand adversary is strong in trumps.

With an untaught partner it is useless to refuse to trump; he will not understand it, but will continue to force you. With such, the best course is rather to make tricks when you can than to play for a great game.

From what has just been said, it is evidently an advantage to

15. FORCE A STRONG TRUMP HAND OF THE ADVERSARY.

For you thereby take the best chance of preventing his making use of his trumps for bringing in a suit. If he refuses to take a force, keep on giving it to him.

For instance, if he passes your king (led from king, queen, &c.), and the king wins, continue the suit, and so on. Some players can never be brought to understand this; they do not like to see their winning cards trumped, and therefore frequently change their suit or even lead trumps when an adversary refuses to be forced.

It now hardly requires to be stated that it is bad play intentionally to force a weak adversary, and still worse to lead a suit to which both adversaries renounce, as the weak will trump and the strong get rid of a losing card.

If you have numerical strength in trumps, you are justified in forcing your partner, relying on your own strength to disarm the opponents. But

16. DO NOT FORCE YOUR PARTNER IF YOU ARE WEAK IN TRUMPS.

For you thus weaken him; and so leave it in the power of the antagonists to draw all the trumps, and bring in their suit. If, then, a good partner refrains from forcing you, you may be sure he is weak; on the other hand, if he evidently *intends* to force you (as by leading a losing card of a suit he knows you must trump), you may assume that he is strong in trumps, and you should take the force willingly, even though you do not want to be forced, depending on his strength to exhaust the adversaries' trumps.

You may, however, though weak, force your partner

under these circumstances. **1.** When he has already shown a desire to be **forced, or** weakness in trumps, as by trumping a doubtful card, or by refraining from **forcing you. 2.** When you have a cross-ruff, which secures several tricks at once, and is therefore often more advantageous than trying to establish a **suit. 3.** Sometimes when you are playing a close game, as for the odd trick, and often when one trick saves or wins the game or **a** point. And 4. Sometimes when great strength in **trumps** has been declared against you.

If your partner leads a thirteenth card, **or a** card of a suit in which he knows that both you and the fourth player renounce, **your play** must depend on your partner's strength in **trumps.** If he is strong, he wants you to **put** on your best trump, either to make the trumps separately, **or** to force out one or two high ones, to leave himself with the command. If he is weak in trumps, he wants you to pass the card, that the fourth player may obtain the lead, and lead up to your hand. No general rule can be given as to the course to be pursued with regard to **thirteenth** cards. You must judge of the **leader's intention** by the score and the previous fall of the cards.

PLAYING TO THE BOARD.

17. PLAY TO THE SCORE;
AND
18. WATCH THE FALL OF THE CARDS, AND DRAW YOUR INFERENCES AT THE TIME.

These two all-important principles have already been mentioned as causing differences in the play. The commonest form in which the former is presented to us is this: at the score of Love-all five tricks save the game against two by honours. It is often right, therefore, when two by honours have been declared against you, to go for the fifth trick by leading off a winning card, or by putting one on second or third hand.

To explain further what is meant by playing to the score, put yourself in this situation. Four trumps remain in, the adversaries have the two best trumps, it being uncertain whether they are in one hand or divided; you have the two losing trumps, two forcing cards, and the lead; you can only play correctly by referring to the score. Thus, if the adversary is at four, and you have won five, or even six tricks, your game would be to secure two tricks by forcing; for if you play a trump and the two against you are in the same hand, you lose the game. But suppose you are at the point of two, and the adversaries are not at four, and you have won six tricks, your game would be to risk the trump; for if you bring down the other

I

trumps you win the game; but by playing to force you make certain of scoring only four. By applying this mode of reasoning you will often be directed as to a finesse late in a hand.

For simple examples of drawing inferences at the time of the fall of the cards take the following:—
1. You lead a small card from ace, knave, &c.; your partner wins with the queen; you should *immediately* (*i.e.*, before another card is led) infer that the king cannot be with your right-hand adversary. Hence, on the return of the suit, you would not finesse the knave.
2. You are second player, and a suit is led in which you have king, ten, and one small one. You play the small one. The third hand plays the queen, which is won with the ace. You should *at once* infer that the third hand cannot have the knave, and that you may safely finesse the ten next round.

You will greatly assist your memory by systematically recording inferences in the above manner. In addition to this you should apply your knowledge of the principles to noting important points, not attempting too much at first. Begin by counting the trumps as they fall, and notice, at all events, the honours, and remember the turn-up card. By degrees you will find yourself able to recollect the ten and nine, and then the smaller trumps. Next attend to the suit led originally by each player, and watch in the second round whether the lead was from strength or weakness. Try also to remember the fall of the cards in your own strong suit, that you may know when it is established. Beyond this, experience will enable you to judge what to retain and what to reject in each hand; so that, with practice, you will acquire what may be termed a *whist memory*, which will enable you, without any great effort, to recollect the principal features of every hand.

The following Examples are inserted to give an idea of the cases that occur in practice in which playing to the board is involved.

CASE I.

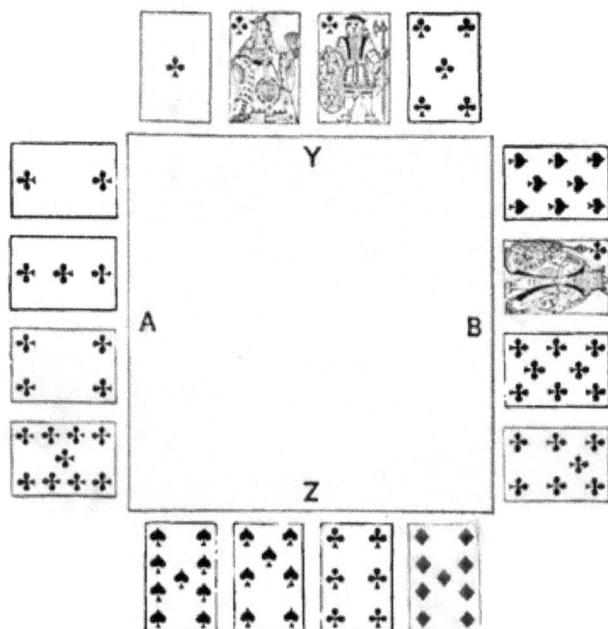

Score: AB, three; YZ, four. Spades trumps.

AB have six tricks and have played two by honours. It is known from the fall of the cards that A has no trump; also that Z has the long diamond.

I 2

THE PLAY AND REMARKS.—A leads a small club.
Y puts on the ace second hand. In order to save
(and win) the game, Y and his partner must win every
trick (*see* statement of score and of fall of the cards).
Y sees that to do this Z must have two of the three
remaining trumps. This being so, Z can have but
one club, and Y therefore puts on the ace of clubs
second hand.

For other illustrations *see* Hands VII and XIII.

CASE II.

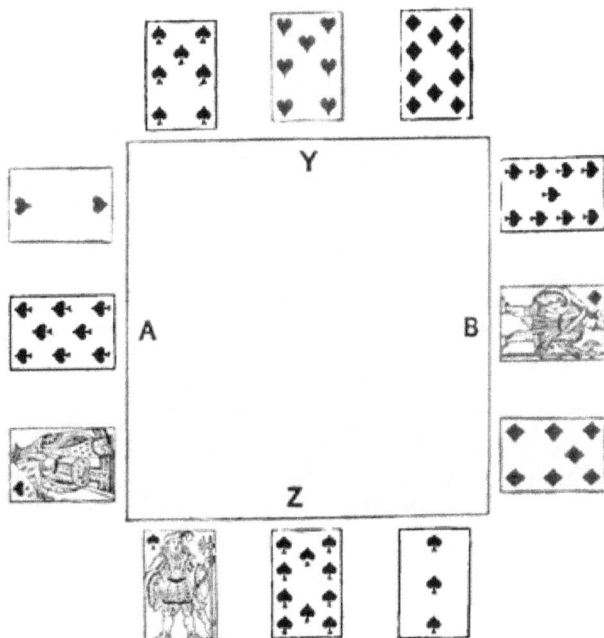

Score: AB want two tricks to save the game.
Hearts trumps.

A knows Y to have the best heart; also B to have the best diamond and weak spades.

THE PLAY AND REMARKS.—A leads the queen of spades, and then the losing trump. A takes the only chance of winning two tricks. To accomplish this Y must hold one spade and one diamond, as will appear by placing the unknown cards in any other way. A therefore plays on the assumption that Y holds a spade and a diamond in addition to the trump which is declared in his hand.

For another illustration of leading a losing trump to place the lead *see* Hand XXXV.

CASE III.

It is the duty of a player to make the game as easy to his partner as he can. The play often depends on the sort of partner. For example : you lead the ten from king, queen, knave, ten, &c., or from king, knave, ten, &c. Your ten forces the ace from the fourth hand. You obtain the lead again. The proper lead now is the queen, as your partner knows you have king, knave, whereas he is uncertain about the queen. But, with an indifferent partner, the better lead is the king, as he may not have drawn the correct inference from the first lead, and knowing the queen is not the best, he may trump it.

However good your partner may be, you should not put him into unnecessary difficulties. For example :—

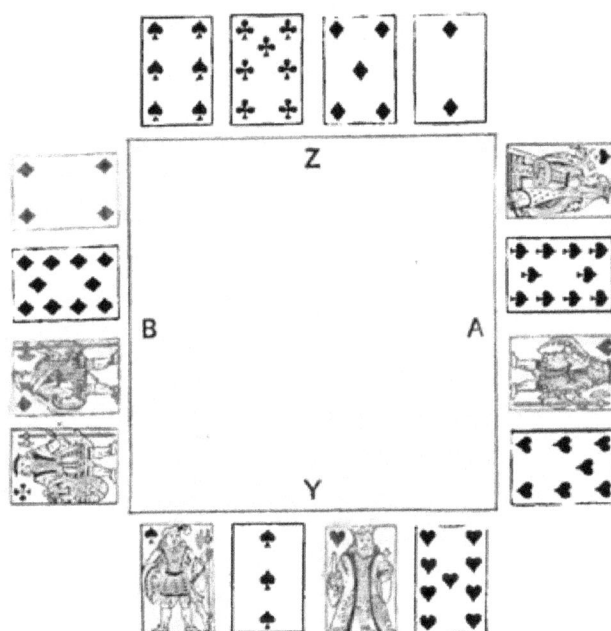

Spades trumps. Y can count two hearts, and queen, ten of spades in A's hand, and a small spade in Z's hand.

THE PLAY AND REMARKS.—A leads the seven of hearts. Y should put on the king, though certain of being able to win with the nine. For, if Y wins with the nine, he compels Z to play a coup, viz., to trump the best heart, in order to get the lead through the queen, ten of spades; but, if Y wins with the king and leads the losing heart, it requires no ingenuity on Z's part to trump it.

COUPS.

There is no Whist principle which should not be occasionally violated, owing to the knowledge of the hands derived from inference during the play. Some of the more frequent of the cases, *where a general rule can be given for departing from rule*, may advantageously close this Section.

LEADING FROM WEAKEST SUIT.

It is advisable in most cases where the game is desperate, and where it is clear that your partner must be strong in your weak suit, to save the game to lead your weakest suit, notwithstanding Principle 1 (p. 55). Your partner should finesse deeply in the suit you lead him, and should not return it, but, actuated by motives similar to yours, should lead his weakest suit, in which you should finesse deeply, and continue your weak suit, and so on.

For example: AB (partners) lead trumps. They win the first three tricks, and show four by honours, and three more trumps remain in A's hand. Consequently, if AB win another trick, they win the game. Y or Z now has the lead for the first time. *His lead should be from his weakest suit*, on this principle: if his partner has not the command of it, or a successful finesse in it, the game is lost. Say Y leads, and Z wins the trick. Z should not return Y's lead, but should similarly lead his weakest suit.

For an illustration of this coup, *see* Hand XXV.

TREATING LONG SUITS LIKE SHORT ONES, AND VICE VERSA.

It often happens towards the end of a hand, that an unplayed suit, of which the leader holds (say) four cards, can only go round twice, *e.g.*, there may be two trumps left in in one of the opponents' hands. In such a case, if your suit is headed by queen or knave, you should treat it as a suit of two cards only, and lead your highest, as this gives the best chance of making two tricks in the suit.

The following case illustrates this point with reference to the play of the second hand :—

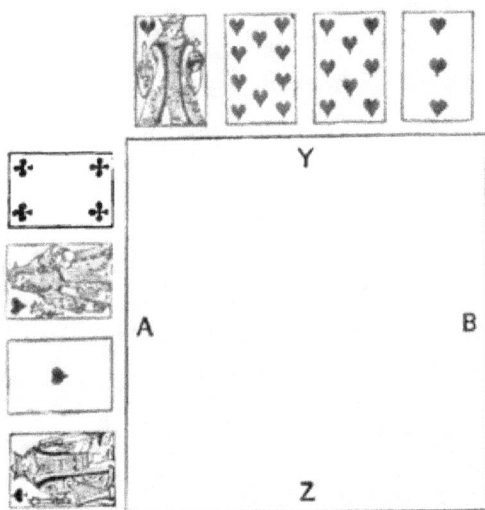

A (leader) has the last trump (clubs), the best spade, both declared in his hand, and the ace, queen of hearts (a suit which has never been led). A leads the queen of hearts the second hand ought to cover with the king.

This case happened in actual play. Y was a very good player. Z remonstrated with him for not covering; Y defended his play by saying, that it is not the game to cover with four of the suit (*see* Analysis of Play of Second Hand, p. 81). But here Y should have reflected that the suit could only be played twice, and therefore he should have played as though he only had king and one small heart, and have covered the queen.

In the reverse case, where a suit can only go round once, it is obvious that a small card should be led, so as not to tempt partner to finesse. Thus, holding queen and one small card of an unplayed suit, which you are about to lead, all the opponents' cards but one being winning cards, the proper lead is the small card.

For an illustration *see* Hand XX. ·

There is another case, known as *Deschapelles' coup*, where the proper card to lead is not determined by the leader's numerical power in the suit. It is this: all the adversaries' and partner's trumps are exhausted, and the leader's partner remains with an established suit. If the leader (not having any of his partner's suit left) is obliged to open a fresh suit headed by king, queen, or knave, he should lead the highest card, irrespective of the number of cards he holds in the suit, that being the best chance of subsequently procuring the lead for his partner.

For an illustration of this coup, *see* Hand XXVI.

Deschapelles' coup often succeeds in practice, but it may generally be defeated by an attentive player. When the above-described position of the cards occurs, the adversary, if he has the ace of the fresh suit led, should not put it on first round. The suit will, in all probability, be continued with a low card, when the third player will most likely be compelled to play his highest, which will be taken by the ace; and, having lost the card of re-entry, he never brings in his suit, unless he gets the lead in some other way.

REFUSING TO WIN THE SECOND ROUND OF A SUIT.

This is a case of by no means infrequent occurrence. For example : one of the adversaries has a long suit declared in his favour, which is led a second time. Only one trump remains in, which is in the hand of the second or fourth player. As a rule, the second round of the suit should not be trumped. The third round will probably exhaust the adverse hand, which is numerically weak in the suit. If it so happens that the player who is numerically strong in it has no card of re-entry in any other suit, he will then never bring in his long suit, as his partner, whose hand is exhausted, cannot lead it again, should he get the lead after the third round. If there is a card of re-entry in the hand of the player who has numerical strength, he must bring in the suit, whether the second round is trumped or not.

See Hand XXVII for an illustration of this position.

A similar rule applies, but less frequently, when one adversary has the long trumps, and his partner a long suit nearly established.

For an illustration of this position, *see* Hand XXVIII.

DECLINING TO DRAW THE LOSING TRUMP.

When all the trumps are out but two, and the leader remains with the best trump, the losing trump being in the hand of his adversary, the natural and obvious play is to draw the last trump.

But there is a class of cases in which the trump should not be drawn as a matter of course, viz., if one adversary has a long suit established, and his partner has a card of that suit to lead.

The case usually happens in this way: YZ (partners) lead a suit, and after two rounds establish it. They then lead trumps from a suit of four trumps (*see* p. 104). Eleven trumps come out, and A (YZ's adversary) has the lead and the best trump, one of the opponents having the losing trump. The question then arises, Should A draw the trump?

A should draw the trump if he has also an established suit; or, if B (A's partner) has an established suit, and A can put the lead into B's hand. For, in these two cases, A or B cannot do better than bring in

their suit. Again, A should draw the trump, if the
adversary who has a suit established (say Z) has also
the losing trump, for then, if either Y or Z has a card
of re-entry in either of the other two suits, Z cannot
be prevented from bringing in his established suit.
Lastly, A should draw the trump if Y (Z's partner) has
the losing trump, and Z has declared in his hand two
cards of re-entry. This last case may be dismissed as
of but little practical use, as, at the time when A has
to decide whether he will draw the trump, he will
seldom know enough about the remaining cards to be
positive that Z has two cards of re-entry.

In the above cases, A, by not drawing the trump,
makes his adversaries a present of a trick.

On the other hand, A should not draw the trump if
one opponent (Z) has an established suit, which Y (Z's
partner) can lead, the losing trump being in Y's hand.
And, it is especially incumbent on A not to draw the
trump, if either he or his partner has a suit which will
probably be established by leading it, and if A can
infer from the fall of the cards that Y has *only one card*
of his partner's established suit in his hand, subject,
of course, to the qualifications already noted.

The point aimed at in not drawing the trump, is to
force the card of re-entry in A's or B's long suit out
of the adverse hand. Y or Z thus obtains the lead,
and continues the established suit, which A trumps
with the winning trump. If, now, Z has no card of
re-entry in the fourth—or unopened—suit, he never
brings in his established suit, Y not having another
card of it to lead.

The case is difficult to carry when stated thus generally; for an illustration, *see* Hand XXIX.

REFUSING TO OVERTRUMP.

Cases often happen where it is not advisable to overtrump. Most of these depend on the fall of the cards and on inferences from the play (*see* Hands XXI, XXII, XXIII), and cannot be generalised. But there is one case in which it is *never right* to overtrump, viz., when three cards remain in each hand, and one player holds the second and third best trumps, with one of which he trumps the card led. If the player to his left has the best and fourth best trumps, he can never gain anything by overtrumping, and may lose a trick, as the following example shows :—

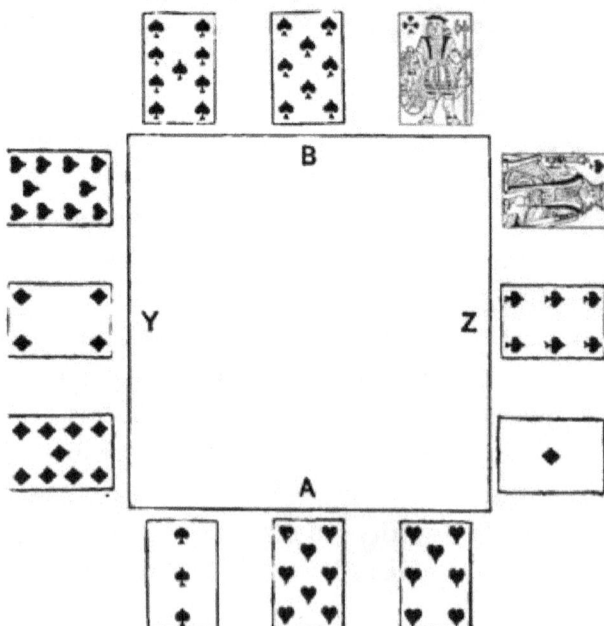

The position of the trumps (spades) is known. A leads a heart, B trumps it. If Z overtrumps he loses the other two tricks, but if he throws the ace of diamonds he wins the other two tricks.

This rule for not overtrumping cannot be laid down absolutely when there are more than three cards in hand; but when only four trumps remain in, second and third best against best and fourth, it is so frequently advisable not to overtrump, that the player should consider well the position of the remaining cards before overtrumping.

For an illustration of this case, *see* Hand XXX.

It follows, from the fact that it is often right not to overtrump under these circumstances, that when the case arises the player who holds second and third best should, as a rule, attempt to defeat the coup by playing a false card—*i. e.*, he should trump with the higher card in hopes of deceiving his left hand opponent as to the position of the third best trump.

THROWING HIGH CARDS TO PLACE THE LEAD.

This coup presents itself in a variety of forms; the following are selected as likely to be of use.

Whenever you are left at the end of a hand with the tenace in trumps (either best and third best, or second best guarded) over the player to your right, and two

other cards, both being cards of the suit led by him,
you, second hand, should *always* throw the highest
card of his lead to that trick. You can never lose
by so doing, and may win. For example: you
have nine and five of the suit led. Throw the
nine. For, in the second round of the suit, it
may so happen that you get the lead with the nine.
If the cards lie thus, for instance :—

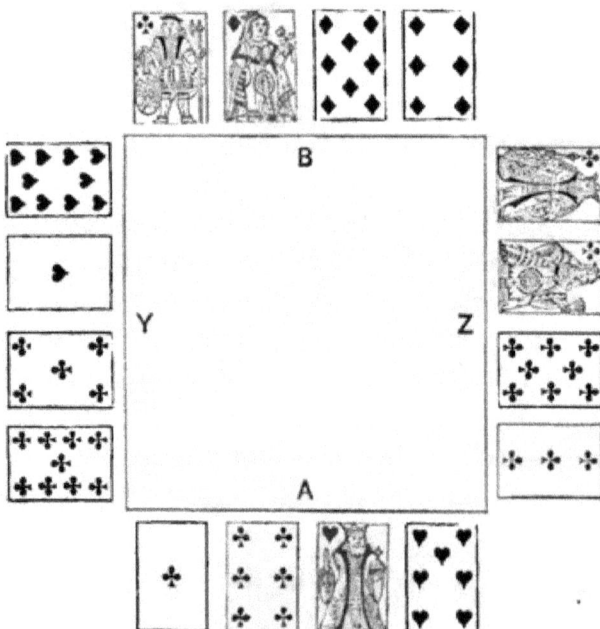

Y has the tenace in hearts (trumps) over A. A
leads ace of clubs. If Y does not throw the nine, and
Z plays carelessly and fails to win Y's nine in the next
round, YZ lose a trick. Of course, Z ought to win
the second round, but it is Y's duty to render it

impossible for Z not to do so (*see* Remarks on Making it Easy to Partner, p. 117).

The typical example of this coup is the case where the leader plays the ace, and the second player has king guarded, as in the following example :—

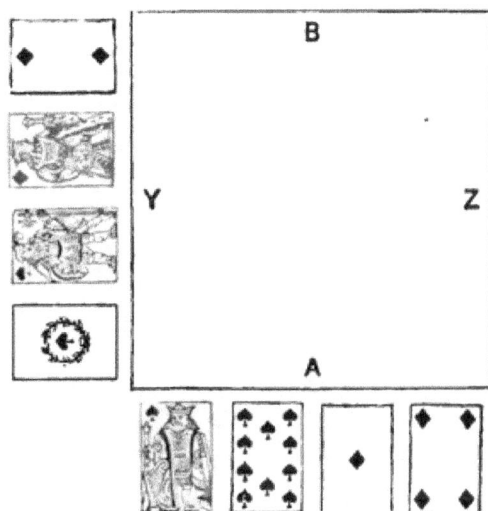

Spades trumps. There are only four spades in, and Y knows that A has the king, ten. B's and Z's cards are immaterial.

A leads the ace of diamonds. If Y plays the two of diamonds he can only make two tricks; but, if he throws the king to the ace, he still makes two tricks, and, if his partner has the queen of diamonds, he makes three tricks.

This coup may be similarly played in plain suits. For an illustration, *see* Hand XXXI.

The following fine coup (which occurred in actual play) exemplifies a similar, but more complicated, case :—

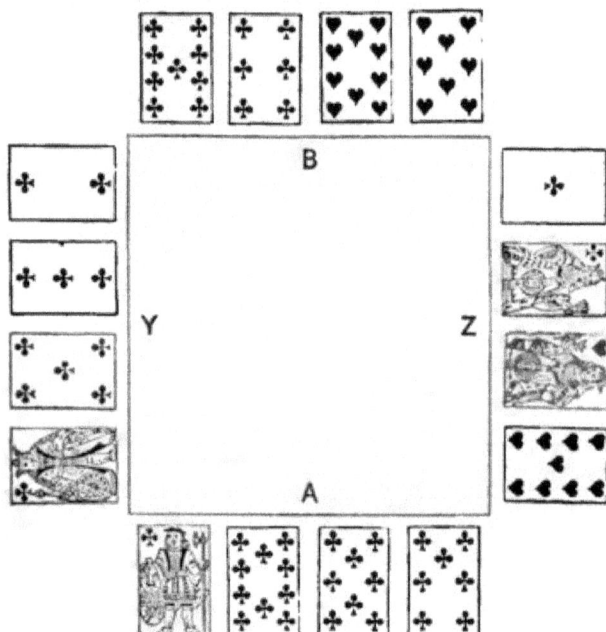

Score: YZ require every trick. Hearts trumps. It is known that the trumps lie between B and Z.

A leads a club; Y and B play small clubs. Z, knowing that B holds the second best trump guarded, takes the only chance of saving the game, by winning the first trick in clubs with the ace, and returning the queen. Y, seeing his partner's anxiety to get rid of the lead, rightly conjectures him to hold the major tenace in trumps. He, therefore, wins his partner's queen of clubs with the king, and saves the game.

It being known that the remaining trumps lie between B and Z, Y would be right to win the second round of clubs under all circumstances of the score.

For another illustration of this coup, *see* Hand XXXII.

On a similar principle, the leader not infrequently leads a losing plain card, or a losing trump, at the end of a hand, in order to place the lead. For illustrations, *see* Case II, p. 116, and Hands XIV, XV, and XXXV.

THE GRAND COUP.

The *Grand Coup* consists in throwing away a superfluous trump. At the first glance it appears impossible to have a superabundance of trumps; but cases sometimes happen where a player has *a trump too many*. To get rid of this trump—as by undertrumping a trick already trumped by your partner, or by trumping a trick which he has won, or which you know he may win—is to play the *grand coup*.

The opportunity for playing the *grand coup* generally happens in this way. Two rounds of trumps come out, leaving five trumps in, two in the hand of (say) A, and three in the hand of Y (the player to his left). If A has the best and third best trumps, or the second best guarded, and trumps are not led again, nor used for trumping, it is clear that at the eleventh trick Y must obtain the lead, and must lead up to the tenace in trumps. If, before the eleventh trick, Y trumps a trick of his partner's (or, in the case of only seven trumps coming out in two rounds, undertrumps a

trick already trumped by his partner), and the lead at
the eleventh trick can thus be kept in—or put into—
Y's partner's hand, the *grand coup* comes off, as in the
following example :—

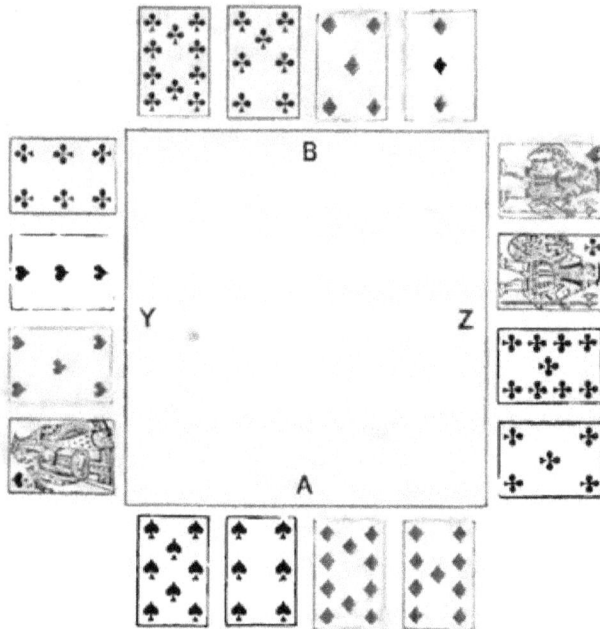

Clubs trumps. Z knows that B has ten and
another trump. A leads the ten of diamonds; Y
trumps with the six of clubs; Z undertrumps with
the five. If he retains his three trumps, and B refuses
to trump the queen of spades next led by Y, Z loses a
trick in clubs.

The opportunity for playing the *grand coup* is often
missed. A player should always be on the look-out
for it when he has five trumps, especially if a trump is

led to his right. It should be added also, that if
the player who attempts it retains a high card in
his hand, he may be just as badly off as though he
remained with three trumps. Thus, holding three
trumps against two, and ace and another card of
another suit, it is not sufficient that he disposes of
one of his trumps; he should also get rid of his
ace (*see* Remarks on Throwing High Cards to place
the Lead, pp. 126-130). The following example will
render this more clear :—

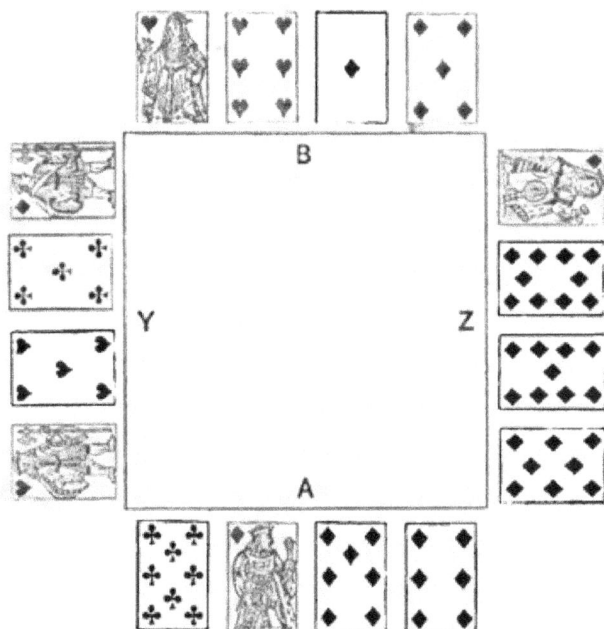

Hearts trumps. B has already got rid of his superfluous trump. A leads the eight of clubs. B should
throw the ace of diamonds to it. For, if B has the
lead after the next trick, he might just as well have

kept his third trump. If A has the king of diamonds, B wins a trick by discarding the ace; and, if A has not the king, B loses nothing by throwing the ace.

An exception to this rule is when A has winning cards to go on with. Thus, if A had another club, B should not discard the ace of diamonds. This is too obvious to require working out.

The following is another aspect under which the *grand coup* may present itself :—

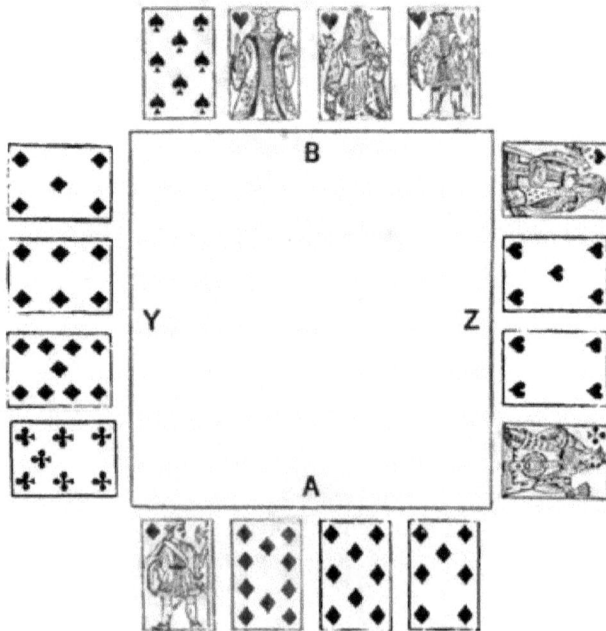

Hearts trumps. It is known that B has king, queen, knave of trumps, and a losing spade or club—but uncertain which.

A leads the knave of diamonds. B trumps it. Z

should throw away a small trump, undertrumping B
in order to keep two winning queens.   If he discards
a queen, he must do so at random, and perhaps throw
away the suit of which B has the small one.   By discarding his useless trump (which B would proceed to
draw) he defers parting with either queen till after the
next round, when the fall of the cards may assist him.
B now leads a trump, and Y discards the losing club.
B then leads another trump, and Z now knows that he
ought to keep the spade.   This case actually occurred
in the presence of the writer, but Z, instead of undertrumping, discarded the wrong queen at random, and
eventually lost the rubber in consequence.

For further illustrations of the *Grand Coup, see*
Hands XXXVII and XXXVIII.

If the foregoing principles are reflectively perused, it
will be seen that they mould the Theory of Whist into
a harmonious whole.   The Theory of Whist tells you
how to play your own hand to the greatest advantage,
how to assist your partner, and how to weaken and to
obstruct your opponents; in short, it teaches how to
take the best chance of making the greatest number
of tricks.   This knowledge constitutes a *sound* player.
If to theoretical perfection you add the power of accu-
rate observation, and of acute perception, together with
a thorough comprehension of the whist capacities of
partners and of opponents, you have all the elements
necessary to form a Master of the Science.

PART II.
HANDS.

THE following hands are given in illustration of the general principles discussed in Part I. The plan adopted in the arrangement of the hands is to imitate closely the circumstances of actual play. Thus, at starting, one player's hand is known, together with the score and the turn-up card. Each player is then caused to play a card in his turn, and at the end of the trick, the one player whose hand is known makes observations, and draws inferences from the play, as though he were at the whist table.

A, Y, B, and Z, are the four players throughout. They are placed at the table in the above order, A and B being partners against Y and Z. A is the first leader, and Z the dealer. In "the play," the cards of each trick are placed in the order in which the players sit round the table, the card played by the person whose hand is under consideration being the one nearest to the reader. The capital letter by each card shows to which player it belongs.

All the players are supposed to follow the ordinary rules of play, as laid down in Part I, and in the Appendices. Thus, each player is credited with leading originally from his strongest suit, and with leading the card of it indicated in the Analysis of Leads (pp. 63-66) and in Appendix A; with playing the lowest of a sequence when not leading; with returning the highest of two remaining cards, the lowest of more than two, and so on.

HAND I.

A's HAND.

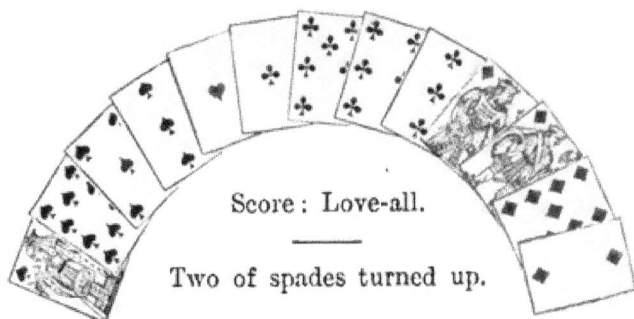

Score : Love-all.

———

Two of spades turned up.

THE PLAY.

TRICK 1.

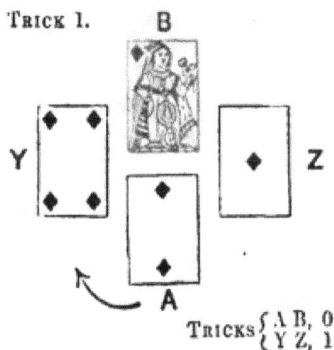

TRICKS $\begin{cases} \text{A B, 0} \\ \text{Y Z, 1} \end{cases}$

REMARK.—A leads from his strongest suit (*see* p. 55). Having no sequence, he leads the lowest card of the suit (*see* p. 59).

The fall of the queen and ace in this round, leaves A

TRICK 2.

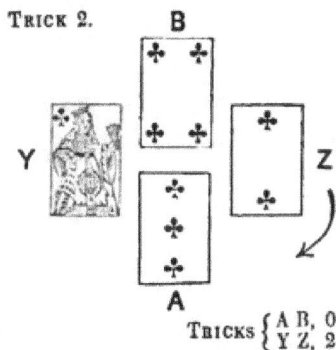

TRICKS $\begin{cases} \text{A B, 0} \\ \text{Y Z, 2} \end{cases}$

REMARK.—A plays his lowest card second hand (*see* p. 77).

B allowing the queen to win, may be presumed not to have the king.

with the winning diamonds and a small one. His suit may be said to be established (*see* p. 56).

TRICK 3.

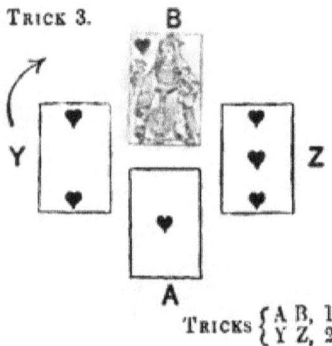

TRICKS { A B, 1
        { Y Z, 2

REMARK.—It is unlucky that A is obliged to win his partner's queen. The probability is that B has the king, as queen is scarcely ever put on when a small card is led, unless the second hand has king also (*see* p. 81).

TRICK 4.

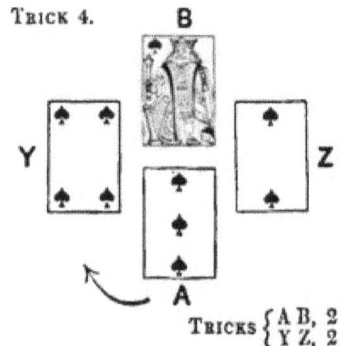

TRICKS { A B, 2
        { Y Z, 2

REMARK.—This is an instructive trump lead. A, at the first start, with but four trumps, would not have been justified in leading a trump. But, his strong suit being established, and his partner having in all probability the best heart, his game is now to lead trumps. Consider carefully the management of trumps (pp. 102-105), and apply the arguments there made use of to the present situation.

TRICK 5.

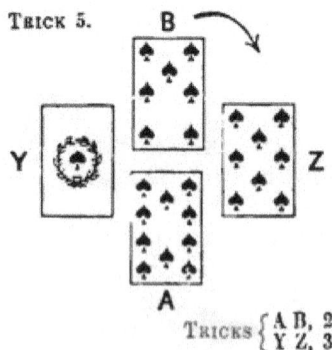

TRICKS { A B, 2
        { Y Z, 3

TRICK 6.

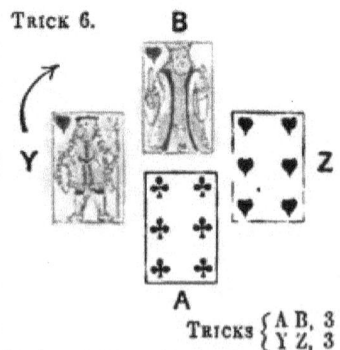

TRICKS { A B, 3
        { Y Z, 3

REMARK (Trick 5).—A finesses the ten (*see* p. 85).

TRICK 7.

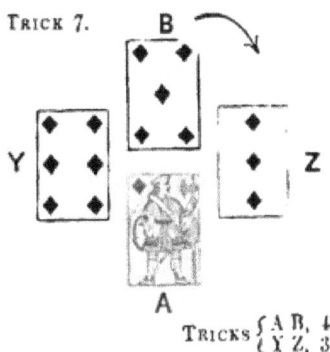

TRICKS $\begin{cases} A \ B, \ 4 \\ Y \ Z, \ 3 \end{cases}$

TRICK 8.

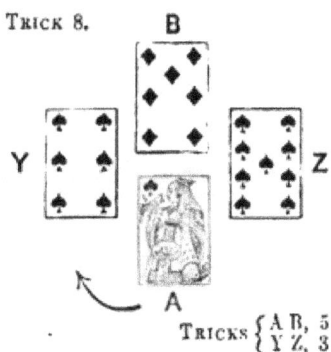

TRICKS $\begin{cases} A \ B, \ 5 \\ Y \ Z, \ 3 \end{cases}$

TRICK 9.

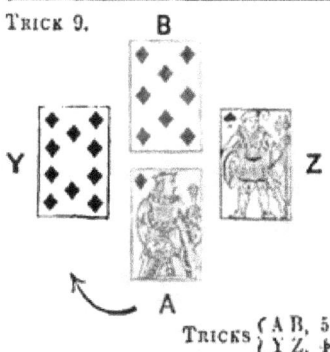

TRICKS $\begin{cases} A \ B, \ 5 \\ Y \ Z, \ 4 \end{cases}$

TRICK 10.

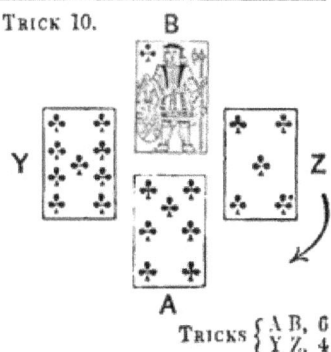

TRICKS $\begin{cases} A \ B, \ 6 \\ Y \ Z, \ 4 \end{cases}$

REMARK.—A forces the best trump. and remains with the thirteenth to bring in his long diamond.

REMARK.—Well played by A. The general rule is to put on the winning card in the second round of a suit. In this case, if A follows the rule he will, after making his trump and diamond. be left with a losing club, the king being against him (*see* Remark, Trick 2). But if the king of clubs is in Z's hand (and there is nothing to show that it is not), A, by passing this trick, gives his partner a chance of making the knave, and still retains the ace to capture the king.

TRICKS 11 to 13.—Whatever B leads, A makes the remaining tricks, and

A B win three by cards.

THE HANDS.

(A's hand is given above.)

Y's HAND.	B's HAND.	Z's HAND.
Ace, 6, 4 . . ♠	Kg, 7 . . . . ♠	Knv, 9, 8, 2 . ♠
Knv, 10, 8, 2 . ♥	Kg, Qn, 9, 5, 4 ♥	7, 6, 3 . . . . ♥
Qn. 10, 9 . . ♣	Knv, 4 . . . ♣	Kg, 8, 5, 2 . ♣
10, 6, 4 . . . ♦	Qn, 8, 7, 5 . . ♦	Ace, 3 . . . ♦

HAND II.

Trump lead from four moderate trumps.

B's HAND.

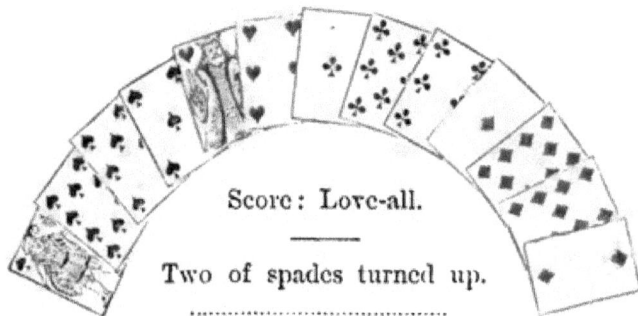

Score: Love-all.

———

Two of spades turned up.

THE PLAY.

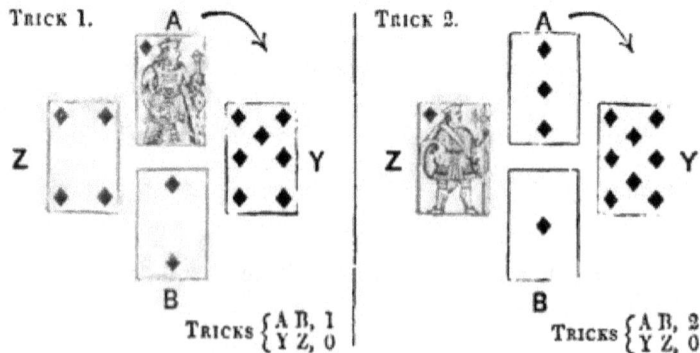

TRICK 1.

A

Z   Y

B

TRICKS { A B, 1
        { Y Z, 0

TRICK 2.

A

Z   Y

B

TRICKS { A B, 2
        { Y Z, 0

TRICK 3.

A

Z

Y

B

TRICKS $\left\{\begin{array}{l}A B, 2 \\ Y Z, 1\end{array}\right.$

TRICK 4.

A

Z

Y

B

TRICKS $\left\{\begin{array}{l}A B, 3 \\ Y Z, 1\end{array}\right.$

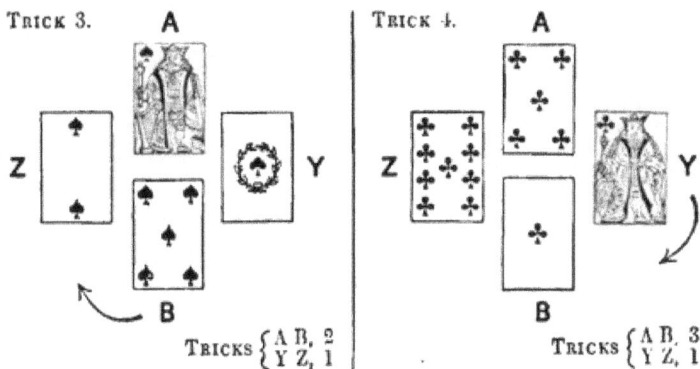

REMARK (Trick 3).—B has four trumps, and defence in hearts and clubs, his partner's suit is established, and no adverse strength in trumps has been exhibited. B therefore leads trumps. (Consider carefully the arguments at pp. 104, 105, respecting leads from four trumps, and apply them to this case.) To judge when to lead from four moderate trumps is an important point in the game, which hands such as this are given to illustrate and explain.

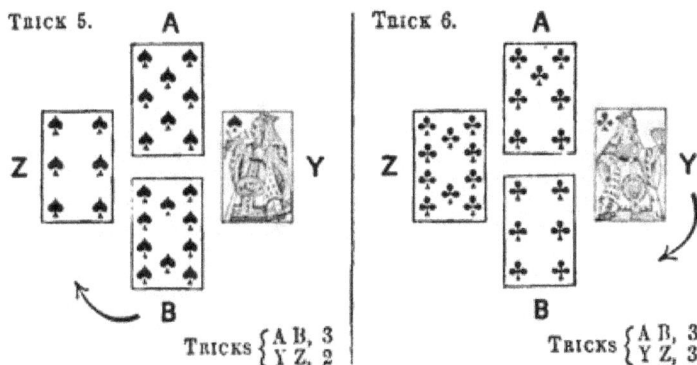

TRICK 5.

A

Z

Y

B

TRICKS $\left\{\begin{array}{l}A B, 3 \\ Y Z, 2\end{array}\right.$

TRICK 6.

A

Z

Y

B

TRICKS $\left\{\begin{array}{l}A B, 3 \\ Y Z, 3\end{array}\right.$

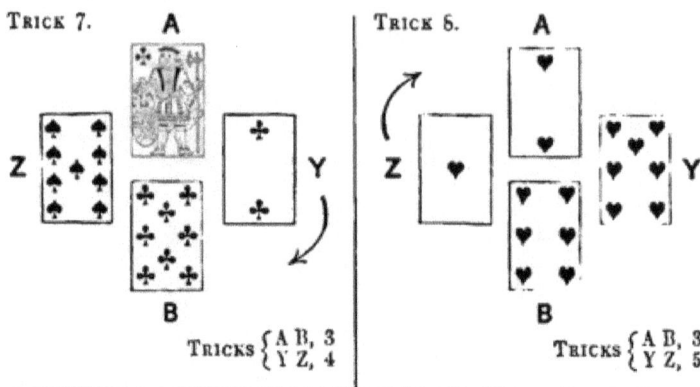

TRICK 7.

TRICKS { A B, 3
       { Y Z, 4

TRICK 8.

TRICKS { A B, 3
       { Y Z, 5

TRICKS 9 to 13.—Z leads queen of hearts which B wins. B draws the two trumps (if he remembers that the seven is the best) and brings in the diamonds, and

A B win two by cards.

THE HANDS.

(B's hand is given above.)

A'S HAND.	Y'S HAND.	Z'S HAND.
Kg, 8 . . . ♠	Ace, Qn, 4, 3 . ♠	9, 6, 2 . . . ♠
5, 3, 2 . . . ♥	10, 7 . . . . ♥	Ace, Q, Kv, 9, 8, 4 ♥
Knv, 7, 5 . . ♣	Kg, Qn, 4, 3, 2 ♣	10, 9 . . . . ♣
Kg, Qn, 6, 5, 3 ♦	8, 7 . . . . ♦	Knv, 4 . . . ♦

HAND III.

A simple elementary hand, save in one point which demands strict attention to the rule respecting returned leads (*see* pp. 74-76).

A's HAND.

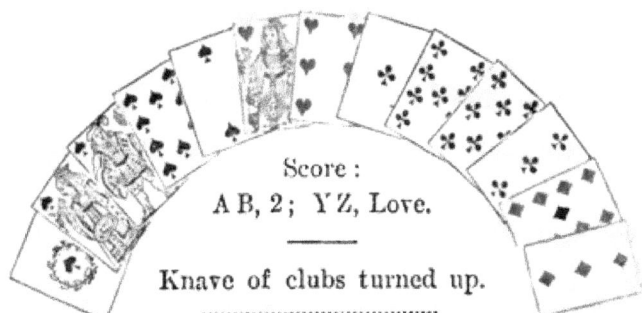

Score :
A B, 2; Y Z, Love.

———

Knave of clubs turned up.

THE PLAY.

TRICK 1.

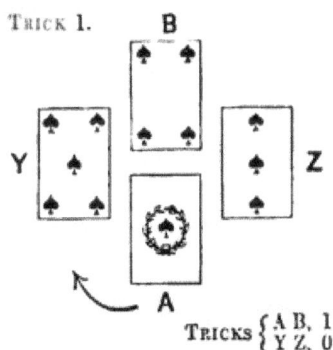

TRICKS $\begin{cases} \text{A B, 1} \\ \text{Y Z, 0} \end{cases}$

REMARK.—A leads from his strongest suit (*see* p. 55). Holding ace, queen, knave, he leads out ace and queen (*see* Analysis of Leads, p. 64).

TRICK 2.

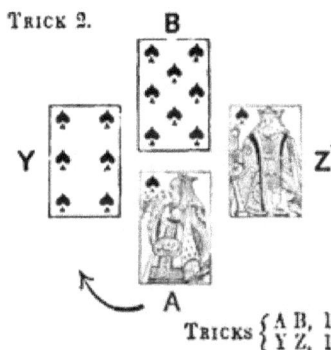

TRICKS $\begin{cases} \text{A B, 1} \\ \text{Y Z, 1} \end{cases}$

REMARK.—A continues his suit (*see* p. 69).

As the cards happen to lie A would have been able to make a successful finesse against the king of spades.

But A, not having seen Z's hand, can only play on general principles.

TRICK 3. B

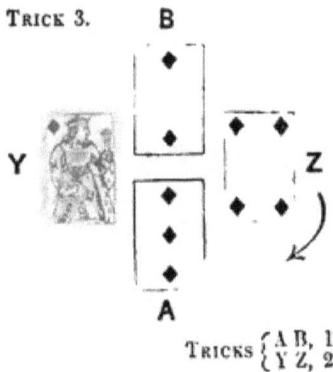

TRICKS $\begin{cases} A\,B,\ 1 \\ Y\,Z,\ 2 \end{cases}$

TRICK 4. B

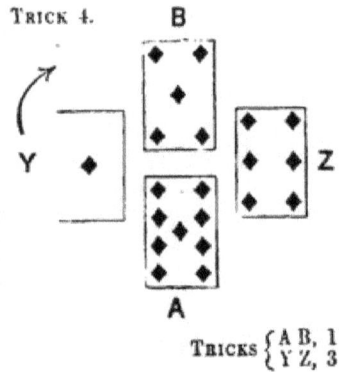

TRICKS $\begin{cases} A\,B,\ 1 \\ Y\,Z,\ 3 \end{cases}$

TRICK 5. B

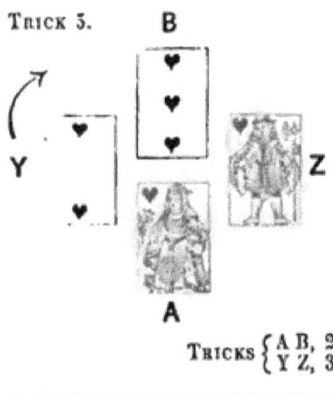

TRICKS $\begin{cases} A\,B,\ 2 \\ Y\,Z,\ 3 \end{cases}$

TRICK 6. B

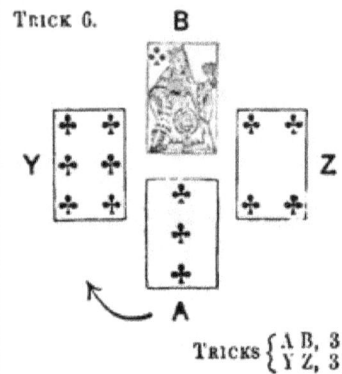

TRICKS $\begin{cases} A\,B,\ 3 \\ Y\,Z,\ 3 \end{cases}$

REMARK (Trick 6).—A has now the command of his suit, and four trumps. The adversaries have not shown any particular strength in trumps, either by leading them or by calling for them, though they have had the opportunity of doing both, and A therefore assumes that the trumps are pretty evenly divided, and leads a trump (*see* p. 104). A is not deterred from opening the trump suit because an honour was turned up (*see* p. 103).

B's winning the trick with the queen shows that Z has not got the king.

TRICK 7.   B

Y   Z

A

TRICKS $\begin{cases} \text{A B, 4} \\ \text{Y Z, 3} \end{cases}$

TRICK 8.   B

Y   Z

A

TRICKS $\begin{cases} \text{A B, 4} \\ \text{Y Z, 4} \end{cases}$

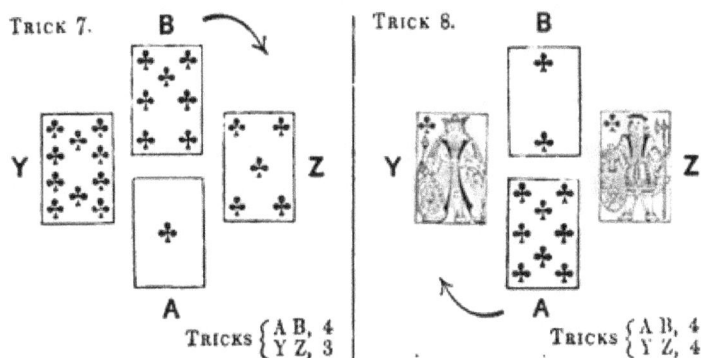

REMARK (Trick 7).—B returns his partner's lead of trumps (*see* p. 106).

This is the important trick of the hand. Note the card returned by B, the seven, and if in doubt as to the fall of the trumps, look at the previous trick (*see* Law 91, p. 18). In that trick, the small clubs that fall are the three, six, and four, and in the present one, the seven, five, and ten. Nobody having played the two, A may place it by inference in B's hand, for the adversaries not winning the trick may be supposed to play their lowest cards. Assuming B to hold the two, it may be inferred that he has that card and no other left in the suit. For he returns the seven, a higher card than the two; and the rule is to return the highest of two remaining cards, the lowest if holding more than two (*see* p. 75. Consider carefully the example given there, and apply it to the present situation).

The king and knave are therefore in the opponents' hands, and divided. Z has the knave (which he turned up), and he has not the king, as he could not win the queen in the previous trick. Y must consequently hold it.

It may be objected that this train of reasoning is too close and elaborate to serve the purpose of inexperienced players. It is, perhaps, a little difficult for an elementary hand; but the careful observance of the rule of play respecting returned leads is so important, that it has been deemed advisable to insist strongly upon it. Of course, when playing with those who do not attend to the conversation of the game, all pains bestowed on working out the position of the cards from such data as the preceding is so much trouble thrown away.

Assuming, then, that A's partner can be depended on to play according to rule, it is morally certain that the trumps are evenly divided, and that a third round will leave A with a long trump to bring in his spades. Accordingly, A leads the eight of clubs (*see* Trick 8, above).

TRICK 9.

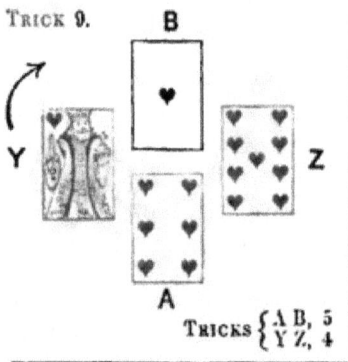

TRICKS 10 to 13.—B (Trick 10) leads a small diamond, though, as the cards happen to lie, his lead is immaterial. A trumps the diamond, and brings in the spades; and

A B win three by cards.

THE HANDS.

(A's hand is given above.)

Y's HAND.	B's HAND.	Z's HAND.
9, 6, 5 . . . ♠	8, 4 . . . . ♠	Kg, 7, 3 . . ♠
Kg. 10, 8, 4, 2 ♥	Ace, 7, 5, 3 . ♥	Knv, 9 . . . ♥
Kg. 10. 6 . . ♣	Qn, 7, 2 . . ♣	Knv, 5, 4 . . ♣
Ace. Kg. . . ♦	Knv, 8, 5, 2 . ♦	Qn, 10, 7, 6, 4 ♦

L

HAND IV.

An instructive hand, illustrative of playing to the score.

A'S HAND.

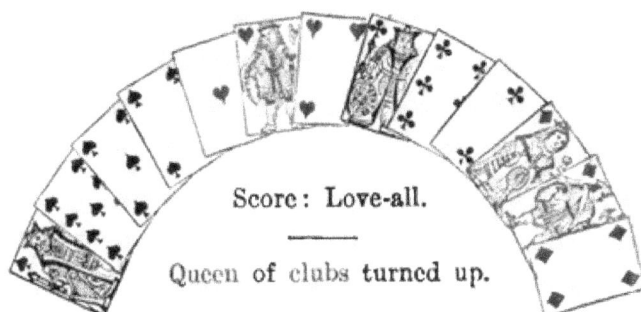

Score: Love-all.

———

Queen of clubs turned up.

....

THE PLAY.

TRICK 1.

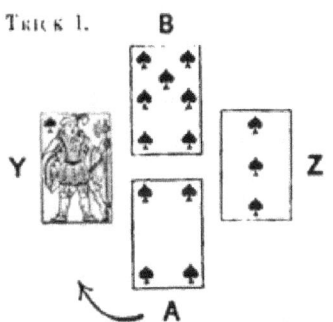

TRICKS {A B, 0
       {Y Z, 1

REMARK.—A leads from his strongest suit (*see* p. 55.)

TRICK 2.

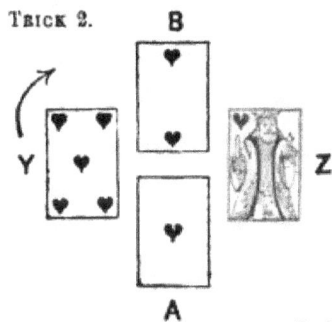

TRICKS {A B, 1
       {Y Z, 1

REMARK.—It may be inferred that hearts are Y's strongest suit.

TRICK 3.

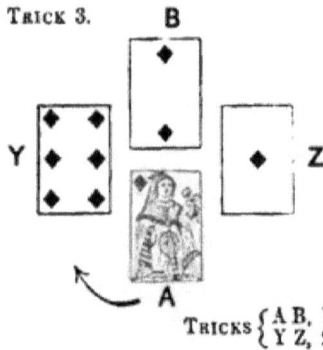

REMARK (Trick 3).—A having found his partner weak in
spades (*see* Trick 1), does not continue his suit (*see* p. 70).

TRICK 4.

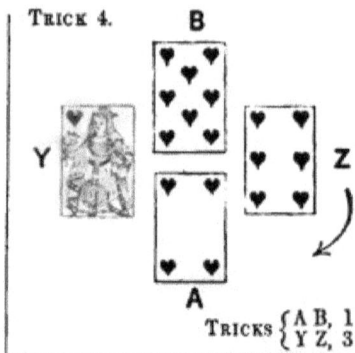

TRICK 5.

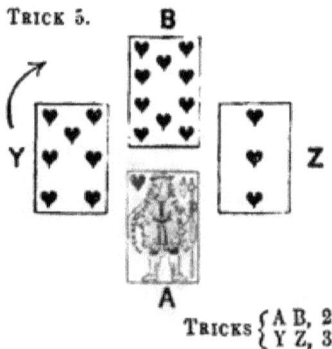

REMARK.—Presuming the
players are to be depended
on for following the ele-
mentary rules of the game,
it is clear from the fall of
the cards that Y holds the
remaining heart, the nine.
B drops the ten, so he ought
not to have the nine, the

TRICK 6.

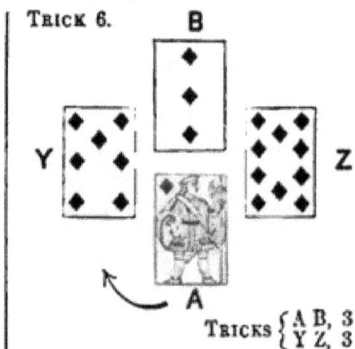

REMARK.—It is evident
that Z, dropping the ten,
will trump the next round
of diamonds. Nevertheless,
A's game is to continue the
diamond (Trick 7), to give
Z the lead, and to make B
last player.

rule being to play the lowest card when not able to win the
trick. Z ought not to have another heart, for he returned
the six (*see* Trick 4), and now plays the three. Having
returned the higher card he can hold no more (*see* p. 74).

L 2

TRICK 7.

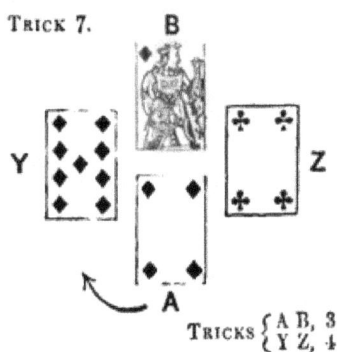

TRICK 8.

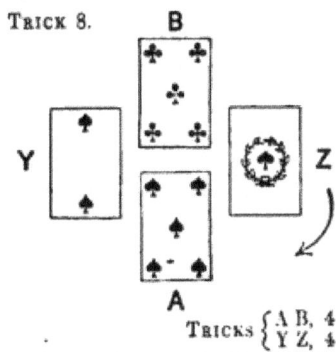

TRICKS { A B, 3 / Y Z, 4

TRICKS { A B, 4 / Y Z, 4

REMARK (Trick 7).—Y, dropping the nine of diamonds, may be taken to have no more, as, not being able to win the trick, he is assumed to play his smallest. The remaining diamonds are therefore with B.

TRICK 9.

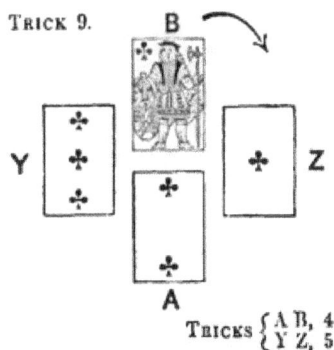

TRICK 10.

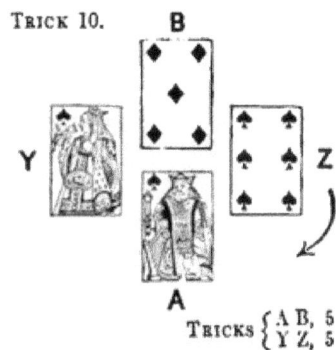

TRICKS { A B, 4 / Y Z, 5

TRICKS { A B, 5 / Y Z, 5

REMARK.—Z, with ace, queen, second hand (*see* his hand below), follows the usual rule (*see* p. 80). It is open to argument whether Z should depart from rule in this case. But Z's hand is not the one under examination.

REMARK.—The fall of the queen of spades from Y shows A that the two remaining spades are in Z's hand. Z's third card is the queen of clubs, which he turned up.

TRICK 11.

TRICKS $\begin{cases} A B, 6 \\ Y Z, 5 \end{cases}$

TRICK 12.

TRICKS $\begin{cases} A B, 7 \\ Y Z, 5 \end{cases}$

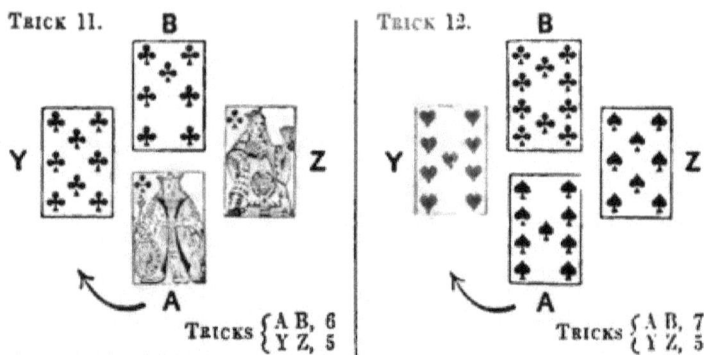

REMARK (Trick 12).—A's lead here is instructive. He knows his partner (B) has one diamond and no spade and no heart (*see* Tricks 5, 7, and 10). B's other card must therefore be a club (trump). If it is the best trump, A wins two by cards by leading a trump. But if it is not the winning trump, a trump lead loses the odd trick. It is better to make certain of the odd trick than to risk losing it for the chance of winning two by cards; for the odd trick makes a difference of two to the score. A, therefore, properly ensures the odd trick by forcing his partner (*see* p. 113).

Suppose the score to be A B three, and Y Z one. Then A would be justified in leading the trump at Trick 12. For, if B has the ten, AB win two by cards and the game; and, if B has not the ten, AB lose the odd trick; the score remaining AB three, YZ two. It is better to run the risk of this score for the sake of the game, than to make certain of scoring only four and of leaving the adversaries at one.

A B win the odd trick.

THE HANDS.

(A's hand is given above.)

Y's HAND.	B's HAND.	Z's HAND.
Qn, Knv, 2 . ♠	7 . . . . . ♠	Ace, 10, 8, 6, 3 ♠
Qn, 9, 7, 5. . ♥	10, 8, 2 . . . ♥	Kg, 6, 3 . . ♥
9, 8, 3 . . . ♣	Knv, 10, 7, 5 . ♣	Ace, Qn, 4. . ♣
9, 7, 6 . . . ♦	Kg, 8, 5, 3, 2 . ♦	Ace, 10 . . . ♦

In the following hands the comments will be fewer,
it being assumed that explanations of ordinary play
are unnecessary.

HAND V.

Illustrative of the advantage of returning the highest
of a short suit.

A's HAND.

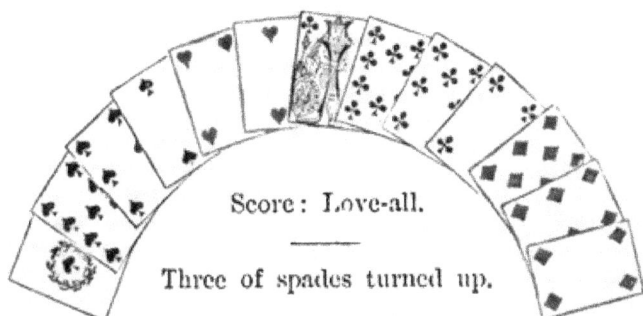

Score: Love-all.

———

Three of spades turned up.

THE PLAY.

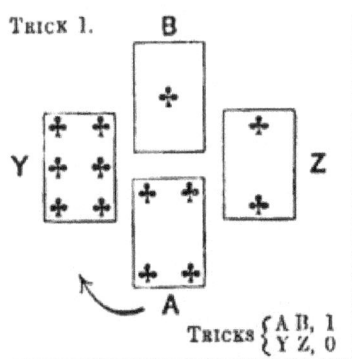

TRICK 1.

TRICKS { A B, 1
        { Y Z, 0

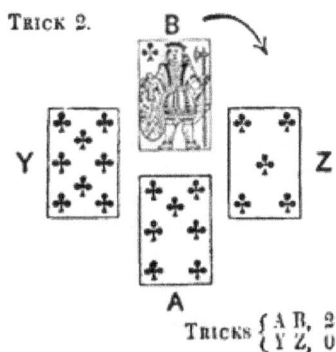

TRICK 2.

TRICKS { A B, 2
        { Y Z, 0

REMARK (Trick 2).—A's finesse here is justifiable, because
he has strength in trumps (*see* A's hand). With only three
trumps, A's better play would be to secure the trick at once.

TRICK 3.

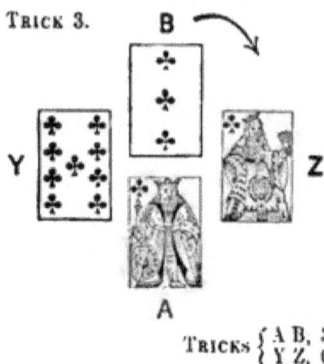

TRICKS $\begin{cases} \text{A B, 3} \\ \text{Y Z, 0} \end{cases}$

REMARK.—Note the advantage of the return of the strengthening card at Trick 2, in accordance with General Principle 5 (p. 74). The command is left with the presumably strong hand; and the queen is completely hemmed in. It is true the queen might have been in Y's hand. In that case the queen must make whatever card is returned. A similar position occurs at Trick 9.

TRICK 4.

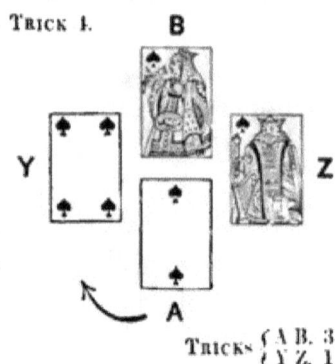

TRICKS $\begin{cases} \text{A B, 3} \\ \text{Y Z, 1} \end{cases}$

REMARK.—A did not lead the trump at first: but now he does so for these reasons: he has the long card of his suit; trumps are his strongest suit (p. 101); and the adversaries have had the opportunity of calling for trumps (see pp. 106-108), and have not made use of it, which is negative evidence that there is no very great strength of trumps in one hand.

TRICK 5.

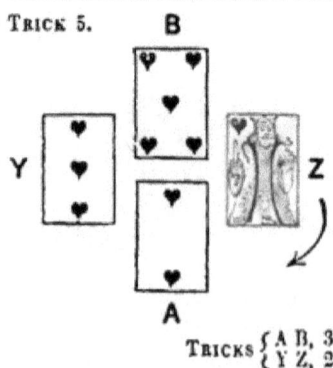

TRICKS $\begin{cases} \text{A B, 3} \\ \text{Y Z, 2} \end{cases}$

TRICK 6.

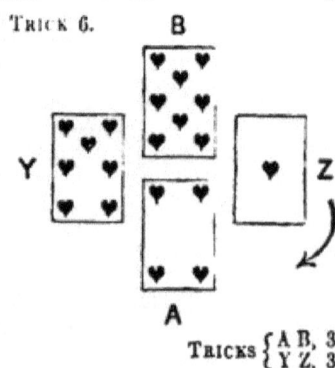

TRICKS $\begin{cases} \text{A B, 3} \\ \text{Y Z, 3} \end{cases}$

TRICK 7.

TRICK 8.

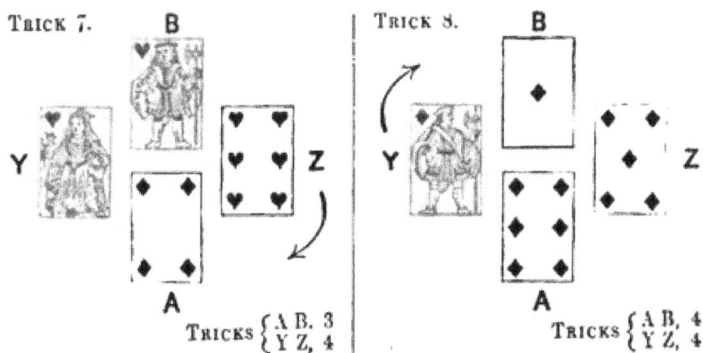

REMARK (Trick 7).—A being strong in trumps passes the doubtful card (*see* p. 108).

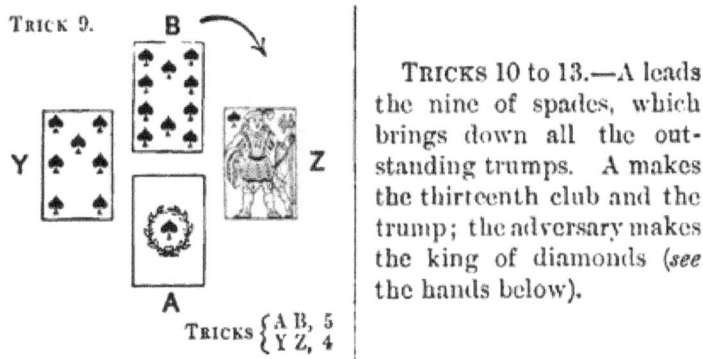

TRICK 9.

TRICKS 10 to 13.—A leads the nine of spades, which brings down all the outstanding trumps. A makes the thirteenth club and the trump; the adversary makes the king of diamonds (*see* the hands below).

A B win two by cards.

THE HANDS.

(A's hand is given above.)

Y's HAND.	B's HAND.	Z's HAND.
8, 7, 4 . . . ♠	Qn, 10, 5 . . ♠	Kg, Knv, 3 . ♠
Qn, 10, 7, 3 . ♥	Knv, 8, 5 . . ♥	Ace, Kg, 9, 6 . ♥
9, 8, 6 . . . ♣	Ace, Knv, 3 . ♣	Qn, 5, 2 . . ♣
Knv, 10, 9 . ♦	Ace, Qn, 3, 2 . ♦	Kg, 7, 5 . . ♦

HAND VI.

Playing to the score.

Y's HAND.

Score: Love-all.

———

Two of diamonds turned up.

THE PLAY.

TRICK 1.

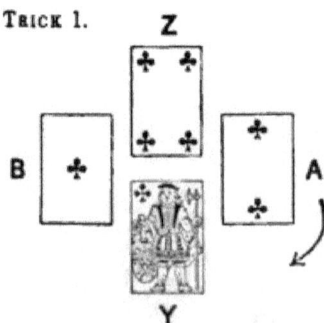

TRICKS $\begin{cases} A B, 1 \\ Y Z, 0 \end{cases}$

TRICK 2.

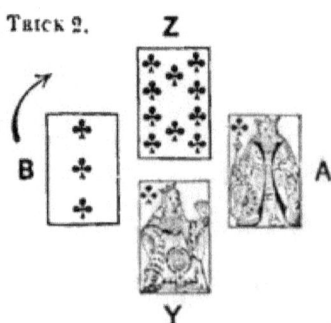

TRICKS $\begin{cases} A B, 2 \\ Y Z, 0 \end{cases}$

TRICK 3.

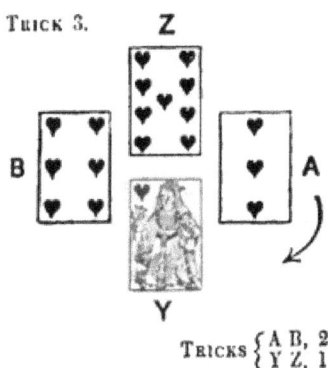

TRICKS $\left\{ \begin{array}{l} \text{A B, 2} \\ \text{Y Z, 1} \end{array} \right.$

TRICK 4.

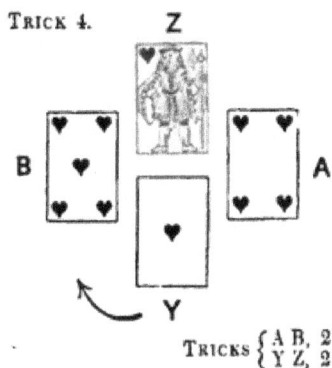

TRICKS $\left\{ \begin{array}{l} \text{A B, 2} \\ \text{Y Z, 2} \end{array} \right.$

TRICK 5.

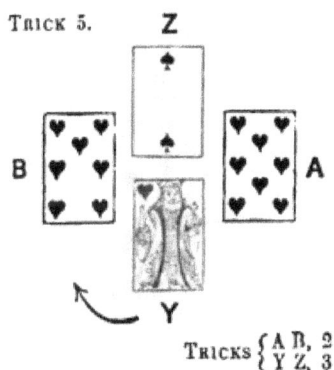

TRICKS $\left\{ \begin{array}{l} \text{A B, 2} \\ \text{Y Z, 3} \end{array} \right.$

TRICK 6.

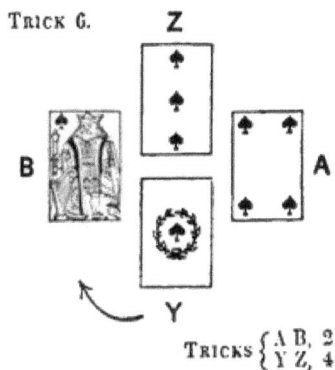

TRICKS $\left\{ \begin{array}{l} \text{A B, 2} \\ \text{Y Z, 4} \end{array} \right.$

REMARK (Trick 6).—The lead here is the point in the hand. Y has three tricks up; there is a whole suit (clubs) against him, and his adversary B has called for trumps (*see* Tricks 3 and 4). It is, consequently, Y's duty to make five tricks (which save the game if Z has an honour) as quickly as possible. He, therefore, leads the ace of spades to make the fourth trick, and (Trick 7) forces his partner (though without any strength of trumps in his own hand, *see* pp. 111, 112.) to make the fifth.

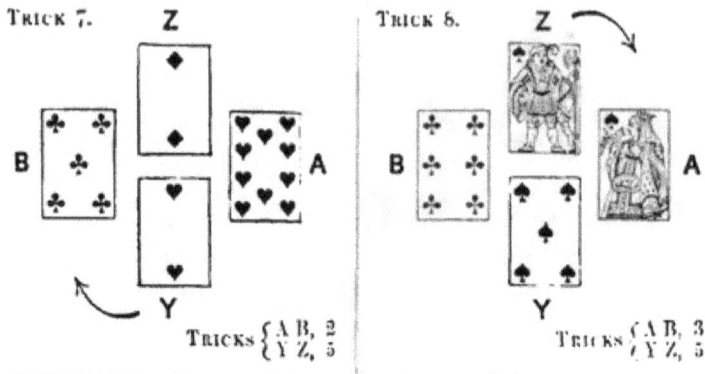

TRICK 7.

Z

B   A

Y

TRICKS { A B, 2
         { Y Z, 5

TRICK 8.

Z

B   A

Y

TRICKS { A B, 3
         { Y Z, 5

TRICKS 9 to 13.—A leads a trump (the knave, *see* his hand below), in obedience to the call. If B finesses (*see* his hand below), as he ought to do, he loses one more trick, and

A B score the odd trick and two by honours.

THE HANDS.

(Y's hand is given above.)

A's HAND.	B's HAND.	Z's HAND.
Qn, 4 . . . ♠	Kg . . . . ♠	Knv,10,9,7,3,2 ♠
10, 8, 4, 3 . . ♥	7, 6, 5 . . . ♥	Knv, 9 . . . ♥
Kg, 9, 7, 2 . . ♣	Ace, 8, 6, 5, 3 . ♣	10, 4 . . . . ♣
Knv, 5, 3 . . ♦	Ace, Kg, 10, 7 ♦	Qn, 9, 2 . . . ♦

At Trick 2, B, with the club suit well-nigh established (assuming his partner to have led from strength), and four trumps, two honours, should risk a trump lead. He cannot lose the game; and if his partner has an average hand, a trump lead will, in all probability, give A B a good score. As a matter of fact it would win the game, but that proves nothing.

HAND VII.

Playing to the score and to the fall of the cards.

Z's HAND.

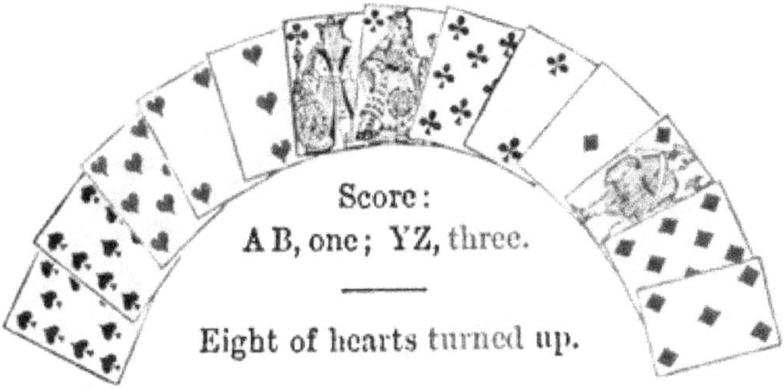

Score:
A B, one; YZ, three.

———

Eight of hearts turned up.

THE PLAY.

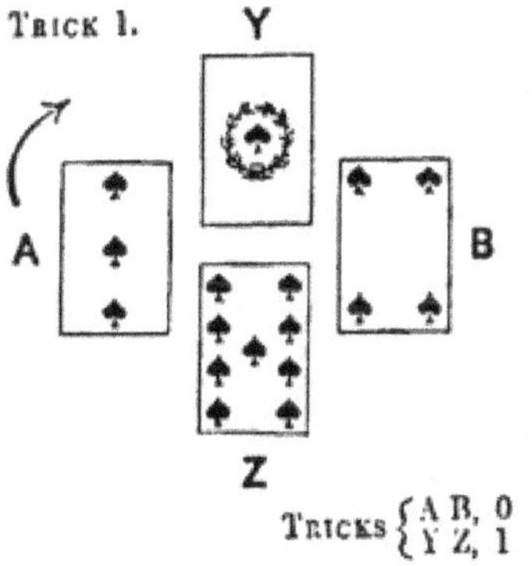

TRICK 1.   Y

A   B

Z

TRICKS { A B, 0
         Y Z, 1

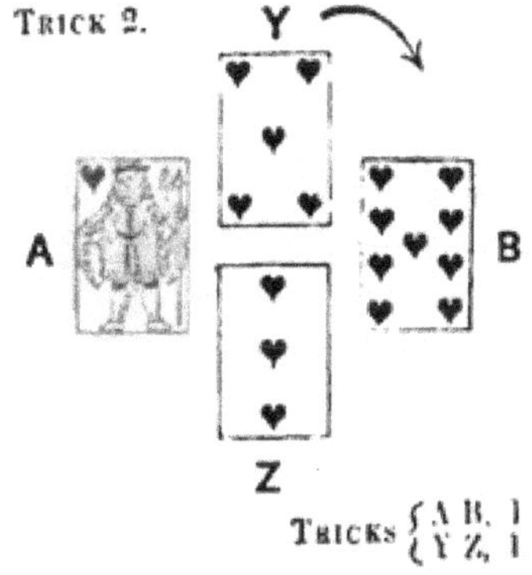

TRICK 2.   Y

A   B

Z

TRICKS { A B, 1
         Y Z, 1

TRICK 3.

TRICKS $\begin{cases} A B, & 1 \\ Y Z, & 2 \end{cases}$

TRICK 4.

TRICKS $\begin{cases} A B, & 2 \\ Y Z, & 2 \end{cases}$

TRICK 5.

TRICKS $\begin{cases} A B, & 3 \\ Y Z, & 2 \end{cases}$

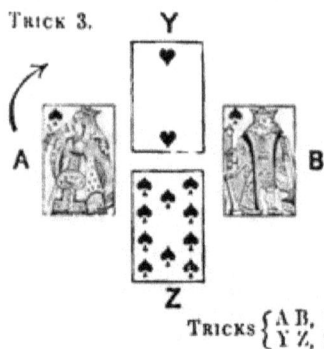

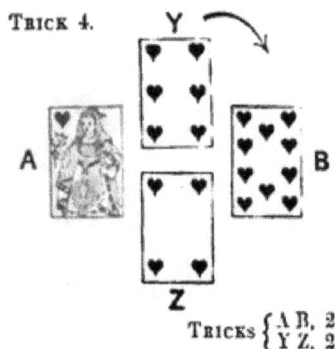

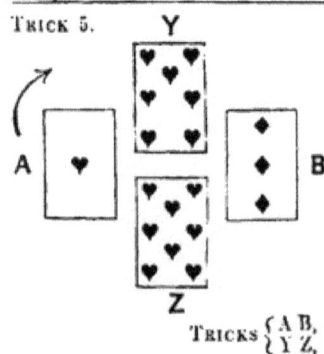

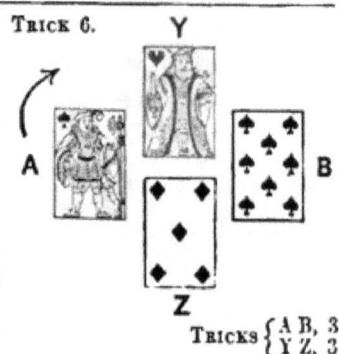

REMARK.—Drawing two for one.

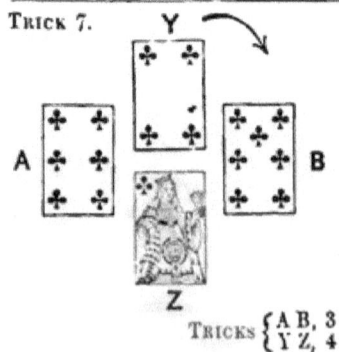

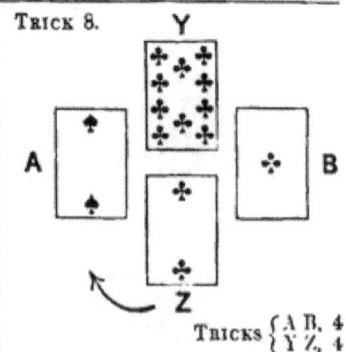

TRICK 6.

TRICKS $\begin{cases} A B, & 3 \\ Y Z, & 3 \end{cases}$

TRICK 7.

TRICKS $\begin{cases} A B, & 3 \\ Y Z, & 4 \end{cases}$

TRICK 8.

TRICKS $\begin{cases} A B, & 4 \\ Y Z, & 4 \end{cases}$

REMARK.—Y must have knave.

TRICK 9.

TRICKS { A B, 4
{ Y Z, 5

TRICK 10.

TRICKS { A B, 4
{ Y Z, 6

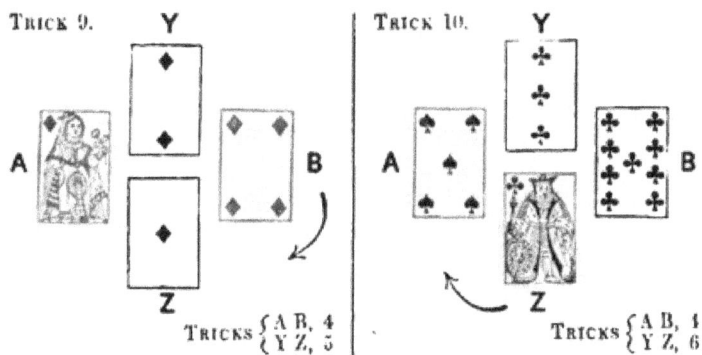

REMARK (Trick 9).—Z plays well to put on ace second hand, as he can then bring in the clubs. If A gets the lead he brings in the spades, and wins the game.

TRICKS 11 to 13.—Z (Trick 11) leads a club; Y makes two more tricks in clubs, and

Y Z win two by cards.

THE HANDS.

(Z's hand is given above.)

A'S HAND.	Y'S HAND.	B'S HAND.
Q. Kv.7,6,5,3,2 ♠	Ace . . . . ♠	Kg, 8, 4 . . ♠
Ace, Qu. Knv ♥	Kg, 7, 6, 5, 2 . ♥	10, 9 . . . . ♥
6 . . . . . ♣	Knv, 10, 5, 4, 3 ♣	Ace, 9, 7 . . ♣
Kg, Qu . . . ♦	7, 2 . . . . . ♦	10, 9, 6, 4, 3 . ♦

At Trick 3, Y plays badly to trump the doubtful spade (*see* p. 108). At same trick, B plays well to get rid of the command of his partner's suit (*see* p. 88), as A, from the lead, must have knave of spades, and Z, from the previous fall of the cards, must have the ten single.

At Trick 4, Y's continuing the trump is bad, after ruining his numerical strength. For he has no particular strength out of trumps (*see* his hand), and his partner is evidently very weak in trumps.

As the cards happen to lie, if Z does not put on ace of diamonds second hand at Trick 9, A brings in the spades, and Y Z lose the game instead of winning it.

HAND VIII.

Counting the cards.

Z'S HAND.

Score:
A B, three; YZ, love.

Two of clubs turned up.

THE PLAY.

TRICK 1.

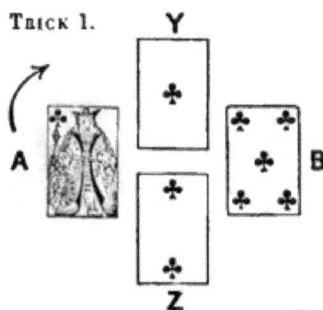

TRICKS { A B, 0 / Y Z, 1

REMARK.—A's lead is either from king, queen, ten, &c., or from four trumps only, headed by tierce to the king (see Analysis of Leads, p. 65).

TRICK 2.

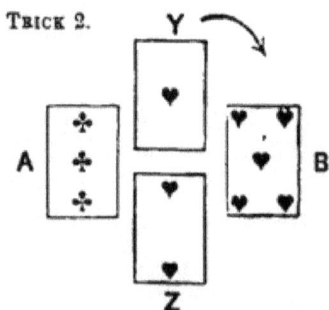

TRICKS { A B, 1 / Y Z, 1

REMARK.—Y's lead is from ace, queen, knave, &c., or from five at least (see Analysis of Leads, pp. 63, 64). It must be the latter, as Z holds the knave.

TRICK 3.

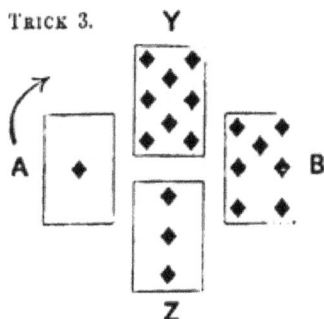

TRICKS { A B, 2
         Y Z, 1

REMARK.—The lead is from five diamonds at least.

TRICK 4.

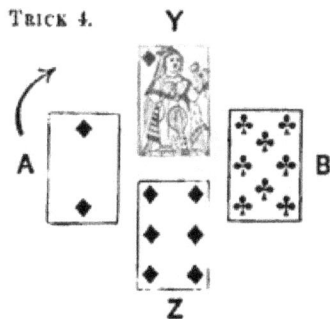

TRICKS { A B, 3
         Y Z, 1

REMARK.—Y putting on queen can have no more diamonds.

TRICK 5.

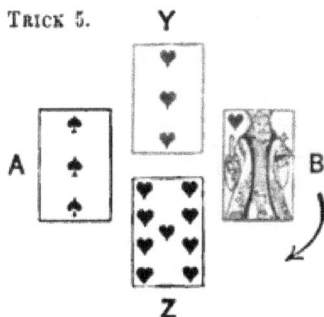

TRICKS { A B, 4
         Y Z, 1

REMARK.—From B's not returning his partner's trump lead, it is probable that he has no more trumps.

TRICK 6.

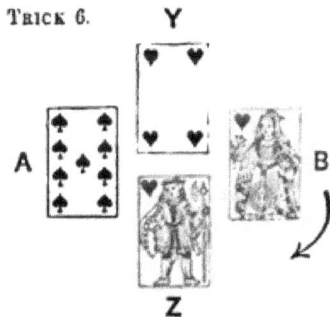

TRICKS { A B, 5
         Y Z, 1

REMARK.—The inference (Trick 5) is strengthened from the fact that B leads winning cards.

TRICK 7.

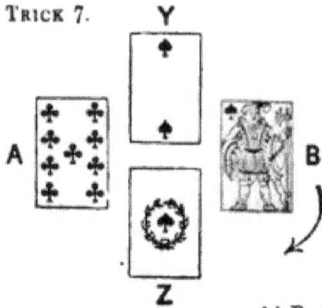

REMARK.—Y has king of spades.

TRICK 8.

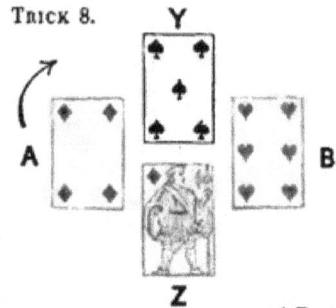

TRICKS 9 to 13.—Z can now count all the hands. A has the three remaining diamonds, and queen, ten of clubs (*see* Remark, Trick 1); Y has two hearts, the best and another (for if B had the best heart he would have led it at Trick 7), king of spades, and knave and another trump. Z's correct lead, therefore, is the trump, notwithstanding that the adversary has led trumps, and that the lead will draw two for one. By leading the trump, Z makes certain of all the remaining tricks but one. If Z leads the diamond, and then the trump, he may equally make every trick but one; but, by playing in this way, he puts Y into difficulties. Z accordingly (Trick 9) leads six of clubs. A wins, and (Trick 10) leads five of diamonds. Z wins, and (Trick 11) leads seven of clubs; Y Z make the remaining tricks, and

A B win the odd trick.

THE HANDS.

(Z's hand is given above.)

A's HAND.	Y's HAND.	B's HAND.
9, 3 . . . . ♠	Kg, 5, 2 . . ♠	Knv, 10, 8, 7, 6 ♠
Kg, Qn, 10, 9, 3 ♣	Ace, 10, 8, 4, 3 ♥	Kg, Qn, 7, 6, 5 ♥
Ace, 10, 9, 5, 4, 2 ♦	Ace, Knv, 4 . ♣	8, 5 . . . . . ♣
	Qn, 8 . . . ♦	7 . . . . . . ♦

M

HAND IX.

Counting the hands; success of irregular play.

B's HAND.

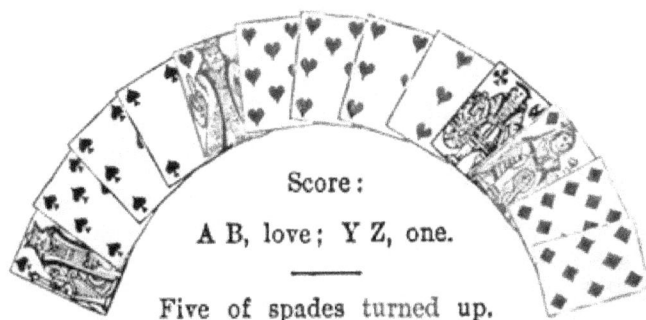

Score:

A B, love; Y Z, one.

———

Five of spades turned up.

THE PLAY.

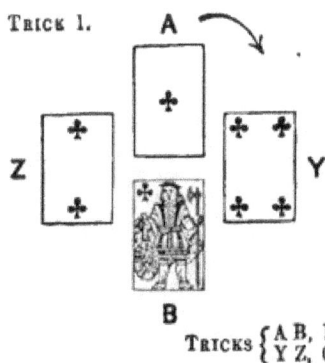

TRICK 1.

TRICKS { A B, 1
Y Z, 0

REMARK.—A's lead, ace and a small one (*see* Trick 2), shows five clubs at least.

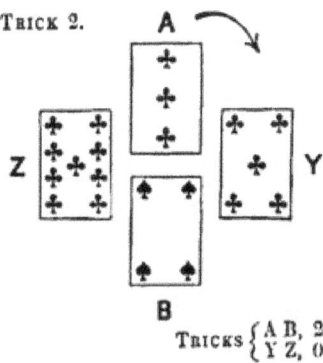

TRICK 2.

TRICKS { A B, 2
Y Z, 0

REMARK.—The king of clubs is most probably in Z's hand.

TRICK 3.

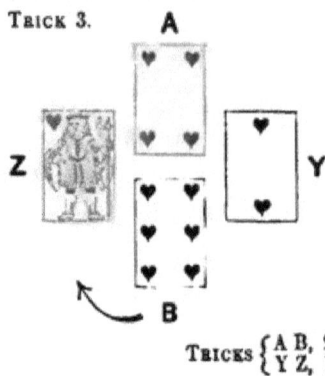

TRICKS $\begin{cases} A\,B, & 2 \\ Y\,Z, & 1 \end{cases}$

TRICK 4.

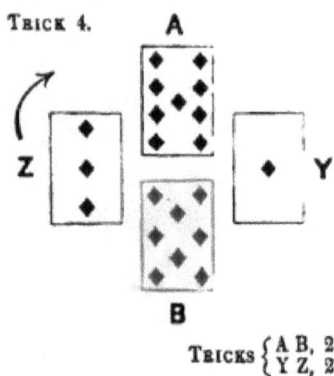

TRICKS $\begin{cases} A\,B, & 2 \\ Y\,Z, & 2 \end{cases}$

TRICK 5.

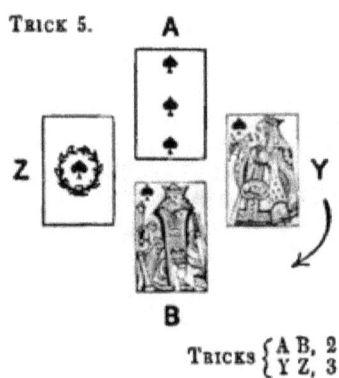

TRICKS $\begin{cases} A\,B, & 2 \\ Y\,Z, & 3 \end{cases}$

TRICK 6.

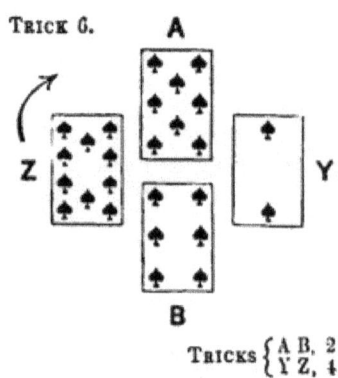

TRICKS $\begin{cases} A\,B, & 2 \\ Y\,Z, & 4 \end{cases}$

TRICK 7.

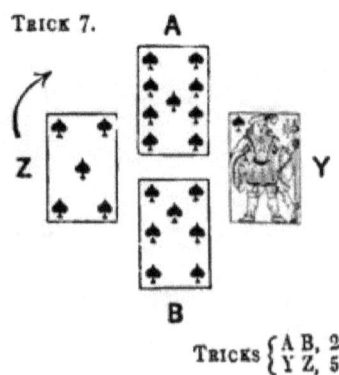

TRICKS $\begin{cases} A\,B, & 2 \\ Y\,Z, & 5 \end{cases}$

TRICK 8.

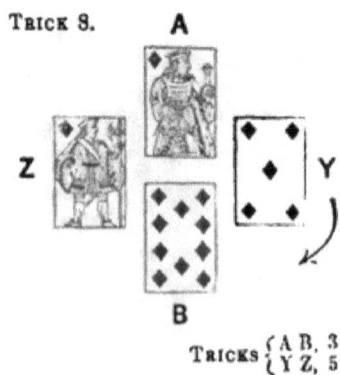

TRICKS $\begin{cases} A\,B, & 3 \\ Y\,Z, & 5 \end{cases}$

M 2

TRICK 9.   A

Z   Y

                  B

TRICKS { A B, 4
        { Y Z, 5

TRICK 10.   A

Z   Y

                  B

TRICKS { A B, 4
        { Y Z, 6

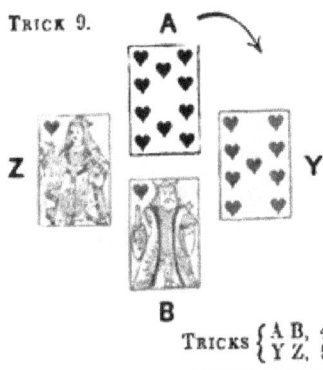

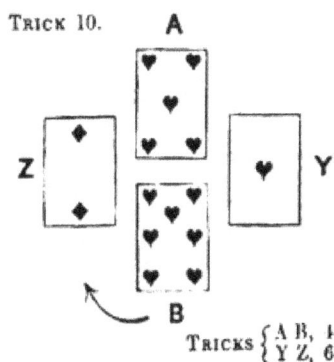

REMARK (Trick 10).—B is in a position of difficulty. Acting on his inference (Trick 2), he places the remaining cards thus before he leads: Y, ace of hearts, two of diamonds (Y returned the five at Trick 8, and so may very well hold the two), and two losing clubs; Z, king of clubs (*see* Remark, Trick 2), and the remainder of his hand diamonds. B, therefore, concludes, that if he clears the heart suit he will get the lead with the queen of diamonds, and make two more tricks, only losing the odd.

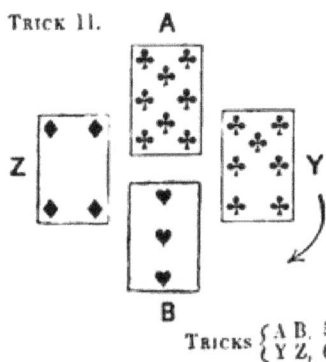

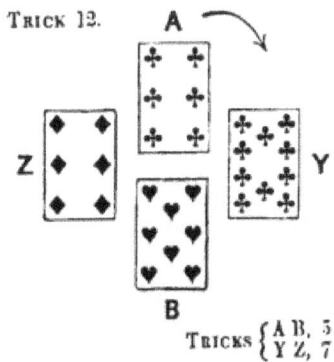

TRICK 11.   A

Z   Y

                  B

TRICKS { A B, 5
        { Y Z, 6

TRICK 12.   A

Z   Y

                  B

TRICKS { A B, 5
        { Y Z, 7

TRICK 13.—The king of clubs turns out after all to be in Y's hand.   Y makes the last trick, and

Y Z score two by cards and two by honours.

THE HANDS.

(B's hand is given above.)

A's Hand.	Y's Hand.	Z's Hand.
9. 8, 3 . . . ♠	Qn, Knv, 2 . ♠	Ace, 10, 5 . . ♠
10, 5, 4 . . . ♥	Ace, 9, 2 . . ♥	Qn, Knv . . ♥
Ace, Qn, 8, 6, 3 ♣	Kg, 10, 7, 5, 4 ♣	9, 2 . . . . ♣
Kg, 9 . . . ♦	Ace, 5 . . . ♦	Knv, 7, 6, 4, 3, 2 ♦

At Trick 2, Y's play in passing the club, with only three trumps in hand, is not good. Y knows that either B or Z will be obliged to trump; and Y, being numerically weak in trumps, should not run the risk of allowing his partner to be forced. Y's play turns out very luckily. It causes B to place the king of clubs probably in Z's hand, because the chances are against any given player (in this case Y) being strong in trumps, and only strength in trumps would justify Y in risking a force on his partner. Consequently, B miscounts the hands, and loses the game. *The result, however, is no criterion.*

At Trick 10, if B could place either the remainder of the club or diamond suit with certainty, he could save the game by leading queen of diamonds. The hand is unusual, partly owing to the fact that the hands cannot be counted even at this late period. It is also instructive, as warning *not to judge by results:* for B's good play loses him the game, and Y's bad play wins it.

Y plays very well at Trick 9 in not putting on ace of hearts; it being demonstrable that if he does so he cannot win two by cards (for he can count the hands, but the inferences being long, and not bearing on B's play, are omitted). Y also plays well at Trick 11, in leading the under club, so as to secure the tenace.

HAND X.

Discarding, and playing to the score.

Z's HAND.

Score: Love-all.

———

Six of hearts turned up.

THE PLAY.

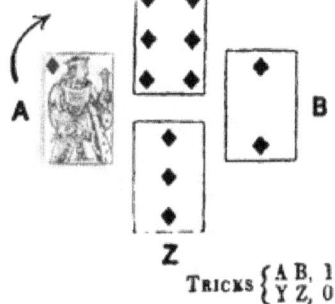

TRICK 1.

TRICKS $\left\{\begin{array}{l} \text{A B, 1} \\ \text{Y Z, 0} \end{array}\right.$

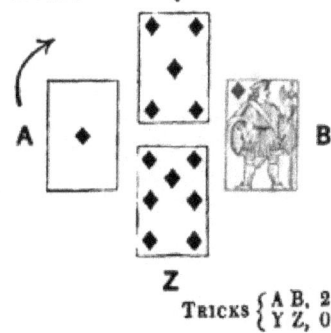

TRICK 2.

TRICKS $\left\{\begin{array}{l} \text{A B, 2} \\ \text{Y Z, 0} \end{array}\right.$

REMARK.—Y has called for trumps.

TRICK 3.

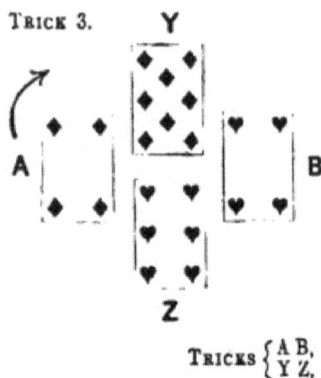

A   B

TRICKS { A B, 2
        { Y Z, 1

TRICK 4.

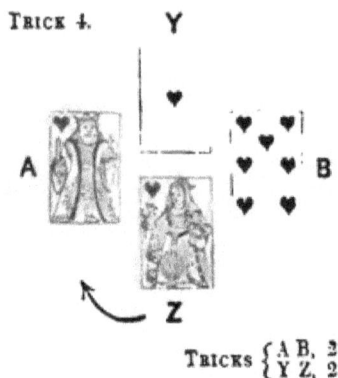

A   B

TRICKS { A B, 2
        { Y Z, 2

TRICK 5.

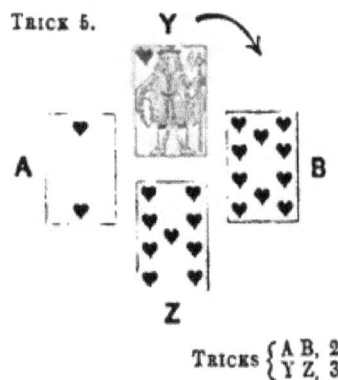

A   B

TRICKS { A B, 2
        { Y Z, 3

TRICK 6.

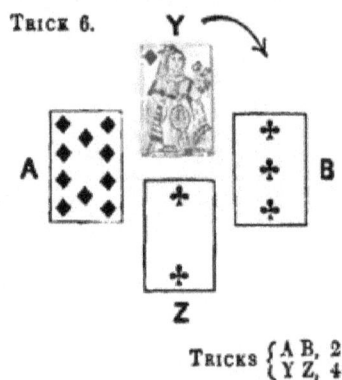

A   B

TRICKS { A B, 2
        { Y Z, 4

TRICK 7.

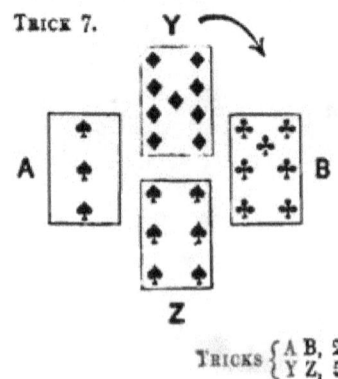

A   B

TRICKS { A B, 2
        { Y Z, 5

TRICK 8.

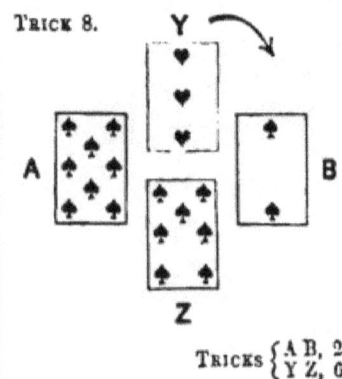

A   B

TRICKS { A B, 2
        { Y Z, 6

TRICKS 9 to 13.—Y (Trick 9) leads a spade. Z puts on the ace, as that card and the two trumps in Y's hand make the game. If Z finesses he only scores four, as will be seen by referring to the hands below.

The hand is instructive on these grounds. Y is directed to the spade suit by Z's *original discard* of a club at Trick 6 (*see* p. 93), notwithstanding that Z has since discarded two spades. Z plays properly to keep his queen of clubs guarded after his first discard, as he only wants at most two tricks besides the two trumps which he knows to be in Y's hand. Y, at Trick 8, leads a heart to show that he has all the other hearts, as it is possible that the best heart may be held up by the adversary. Y thus tells Z not to finesse if he has one trick certain (*see* score).

Z's play would not be good if he had only five tricks up, as he would then want one more trick to win the game. In that case he should finesse. This is a good illustration of playing to the score.

Y Z score three by cards and two by honours.

THE HANDS.

(Z's hand is given above.)

A's HAND.	Y's HAND.	B's HAND.
Kg, 9, 8, 3 . . ♠	5 . . . . . ♠	Knv, 10, 4, 2 . ♠
Kg, 2 . . . ♥	Ace, Knv, 8, 5, 3 ♥	10, 7, 4 . . . ♥
Kg, 9, 5 . . ♣	Knv, 6 . . . ♣	Ace, 10, 7, 3 . ♣
Ace, Kg, 10, 4 ♦	Qn, 9, 8, 6, 5 . ♦	Knv, 2 . . . ♦

HAND XI.

Getting rid of command of partner's suit, and
conveying information.

Z's Hand.

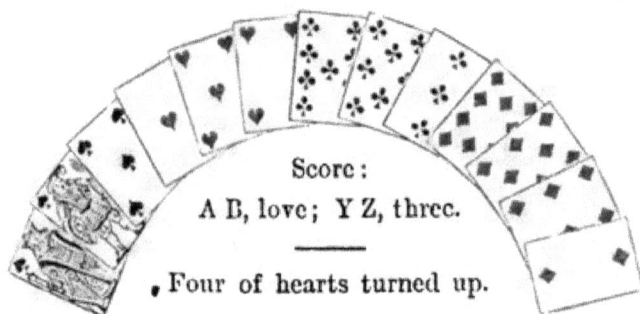

Score:

A B, love; Y Z, three.

———

Four of hearts turned up.

THE PLAY.

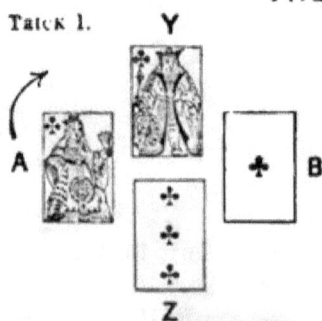

Trick 1.

Y

A

B

Z

Tricks { A B, 1
Y Z, 0

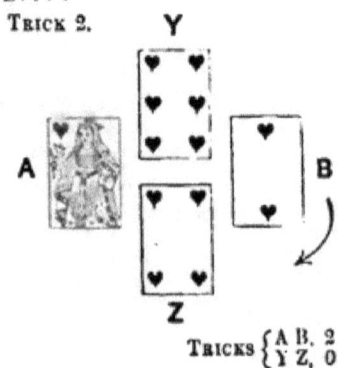

Trick 2.

Y

A

B

Z

Tricks { A B, 2
Y Z, 0

TRICK 3. Y

A B

Z

TRICKS { A B, 2
Y Z, 1

TRICK 4. Y

A B

Z

TRICKS { A B, 3
Y Z, 1

TRICK 5. Y

A B

Z

TRICKS { A B, 3
Y Z, 2

TRICK 6. Y

A B

Z

TRICKS { A B, 3
Y Z, 3

TRICK 7. Y

A B

Z

TRICKS { A B, 3
Y Z, 4

TRICK 8. Y

A B

Z

TRICKS { A B, 3
Y Z, 5

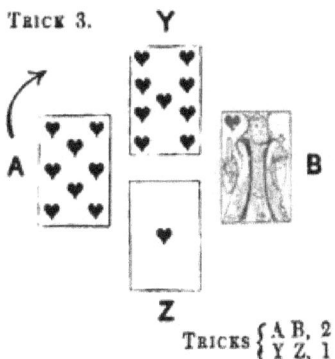

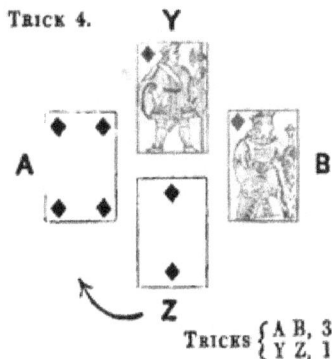

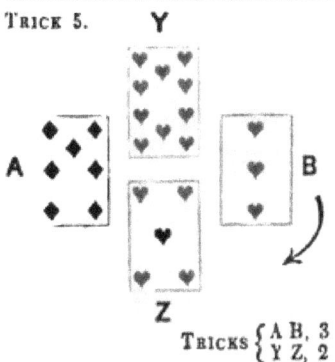

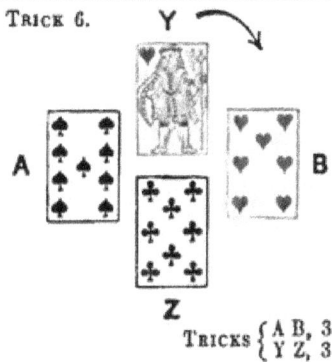

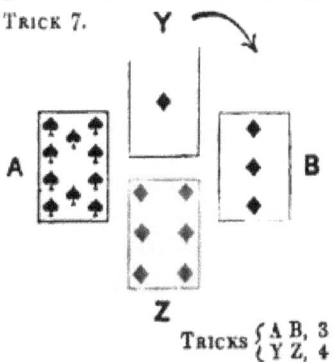

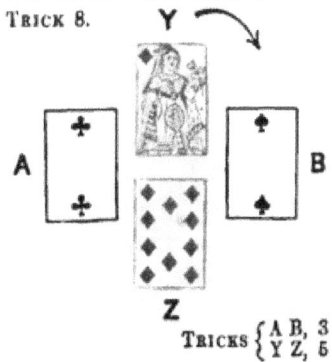

REMARK (Trick 8).—Z, finding that all the remaining diamonds (viz., the 9 and 5) are in Y's hand, throws the ten on the queen that he may leave the command in the hand which has the greatest numerical strength (*see* p. 88). If he does not play thus he loses the odd trick, as will appear by referring to the hands below.

Y plays badly in leading the queen. He should feel certain that Z's lead was from four diamonds, and should therefore have led the small diamond in order to keep the command in his own hand.

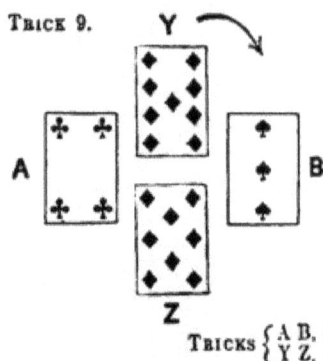

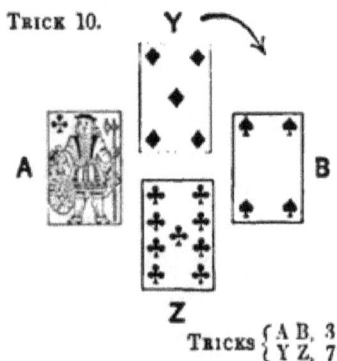

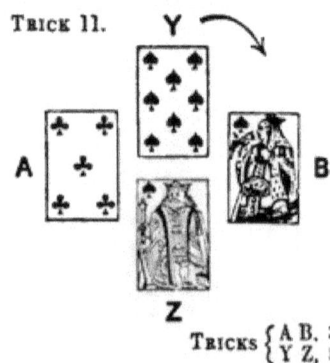

TRICK 9.

Y

A ♣♣ ♣♣ B ♠ ♠ ♠

Z

TRICKS { A B, 3 / Y Z, 6 }

TRICK 10.

Y

A ♣(King) B ♠ ♠ ♠

Z (clubs)

TRICKS { A B, 3 / Y Z, 7 }

TRICK 11.

Y (spades)

A ♣ ♣ ♣ ♣ B (diamond court card)

Z (court card)

TRICKS { A B, 3 / Y Z, 8 }

REMARK (Trick 11). — B (who has ace of spades and a club) plays disgracefully here. He should save the game by putting on the ace of spades, and leading the club, of which it is evident A has the command, for he led the queen originally (and king and ace being out), the lead is almost certainly from queen, knave, ten, &c. (*see* Analysis of Leads, p. 66). Besides, to make assurance doubly sure, A (Trick 10) discards the best club, showing that he has the entire command of the suit (*see* p. 100).

YZ win two by cards.

THE HANDS.

(Z's hand is given above.)

A's Hand.	Y's Hand.	B's Hand.
10, 9 . . . ♠	8, 7, 6 . . . ♠	Ace, Qn, 4, 3, 2 ♠
Qn, 8 . . . ♥	Knv, 10, 9, 6 . ♥	Kg, 7, 3, 2 . ♥
Q, Kv, 10, 6, 5, 4, 2 ♣	Kg . . . . ♣	Ace, 7 . . . ♣
7, 4 . . . . ♦	Ace, Q, Knv, 9, 5 ♦	Kg, 3 . . . ♦

HAND XII.

Finessing.

A's Hand.

Score: Four-all.

Ten of clubs turned up.

THE PLAY.

Trick 1.

Tricks { A B, 1
        { Y Z, 0

Trick 2.

Tricks { A B, 1
        { Y Z, 1

TRICK 3.

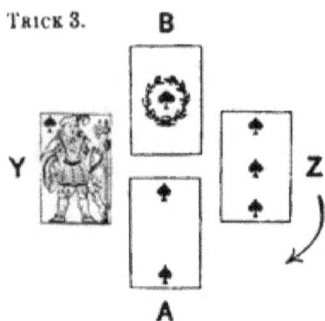

TRICKS { A B, 2
{ Y Z, 1

TRICK 4.

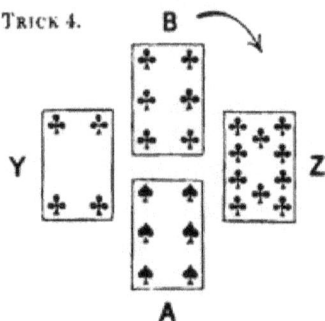

TRICKS { A B, 2
{ Y Z, 2

TRICK 5.

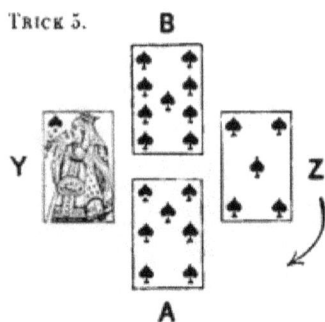

TRICKS { A B, 2
{ Y Z, 3

TRICK 6.

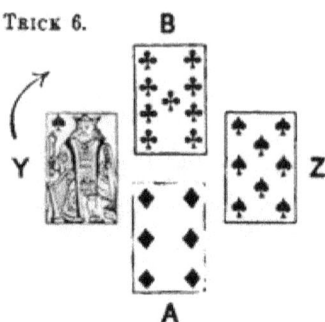

TRICKS { A B, 3
{ Y Z, 3

TRICK 7.

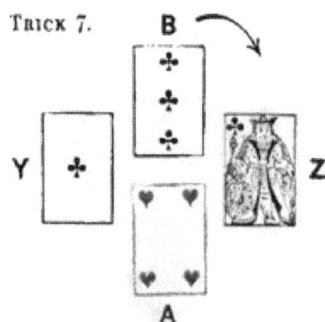

TRICKS { A B, 3
{ Y Z, 4

TRICK 8.

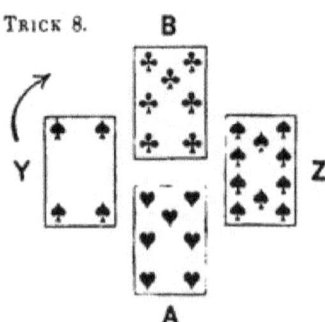

TRICKS { A B, 4
{ Y Z, 4

TRICK 9.

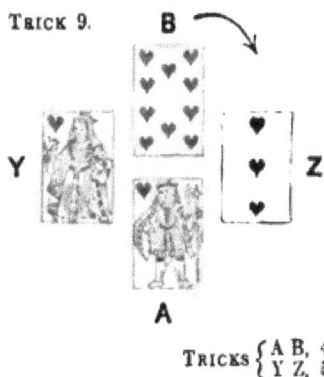

REMARK (Trick 9).—A's finesse is unlucky. He has no indication as to the position of the queen. *The finesse must not be judged by the result.* It is generally right against one card if the success of the finesse wins the game.

TRICKS $\begin{cases} \text{A B, } 4 \\ \text{Y Z, } 5 \end{cases}$

TRICKS 10 to 13.—YZ make two tricks in diamonds (*see* their hands below); and

YZ win the odd trick.

THE HANDS.

(A's hand is given above.)

Y's HAND.	B's HAND.	Z's HAND.
Kg. Qn, Knv, 4 ♠	Ace, 9 . . . ♠	10, 8, 5, 3 . . ♠
Qn, 5 . . . ♥	Ace, 10 . . . ♥	8, 3, 2 . . . ♥
Ace, 4, 2 . . ♣	9, 8, 7, 6, 5, 3 . ♣	Kg, Qn, 10 . ♣
Kg, Knv, 8, 5 ♦	Qn, 9, 3 . . ♦	Ace, 4, 2 . . ♦

HAND XIII.

Counting the hands, and refusing a finesse.

Z's HAND.

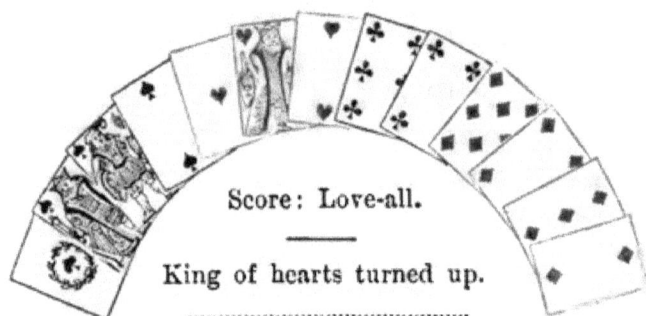

Score: Love-all.

———

King of hearts turned up.

THE PLAY.

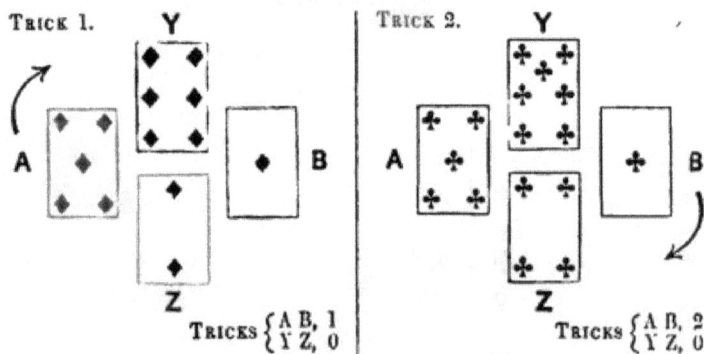

TRICK 1. Y

A   B

Z

TRICKS { A B, 1
          { Y Z, 0

TRICK 2. Y

A   B

Z

TRICKS { A B, 2
          { Y Z, 0

REMARK (Trick 1).—A has not both king and queen of diamonds, or he would have led one. B has not either king or queen of diamonds, or he would have played one of them instead of the ace. Therefore, Y must have one of those cards. Z draws this inference *at the time*. It will not be of any use to him until near the end of the hand.

TRICK 3.

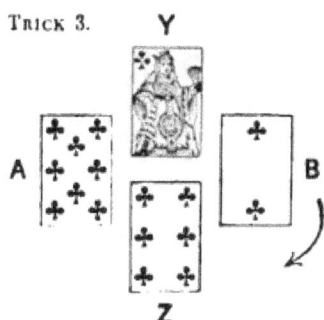

TRICKS $\begin{cases} A B, & 2 \\ Y Z, & 1 \end{cases}$

REMARK.—B has led from at least five clubs.

TRICK 4.

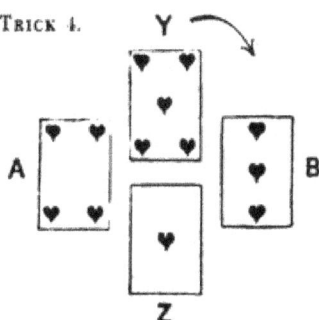

TRICKS $\begin{cases} A B, & 2 \\ Y Z, & 2 \end{cases}$

TRICK 5.

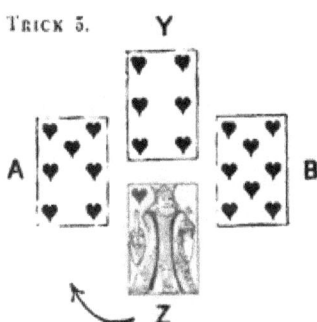

TRICKS $\begin{cases} A B, & 2 \\ Y Z, & 3 \end{cases}$

TRICK 6.

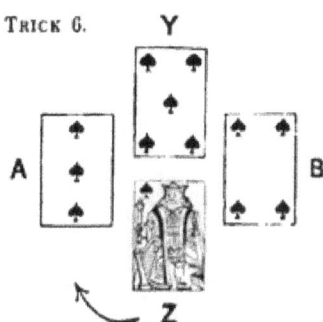

TRICKS $\begin{cases} A B & 2 \\ Y Z, & 4 \end{cases}$

REMARK (Trick 6).—The policy of this lead is doubtful. Players are apt to show their suits in this manner. But it is clear, the opponents having led diamonds and clubs, that if Z has strength in any suit it is in spades. The objections to showing a suit in this way are: 1, that it may be trumped the first round; 2, that partner may have only one card of it. In the latter case he cannot return the lead, and must open or continue another suit to a disadvantage.

TRICK 7.

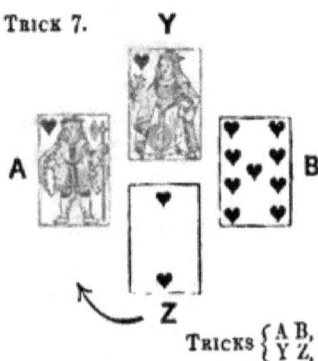

TRICKS $\begin{cases} A\,B, & 2 \\ Y\,Z, & 5 \end{cases}$

REMARK.—Y has the long trump.

TRICK 8.

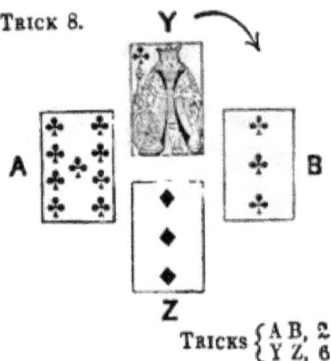

TRICKS $\begin{cases} A\,B, & 2 \\ Y\,Z, & 6 \end{cases}$

TRICK 9.

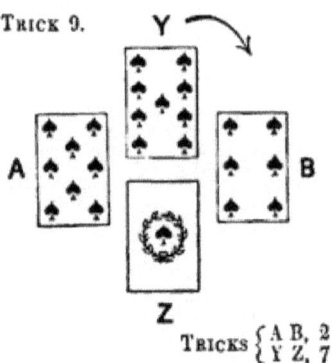

TRICKS $\begin{cases} A\,B, & 2 \\ Y\,Z, & 7 \end{cases}$

TRICK 10.

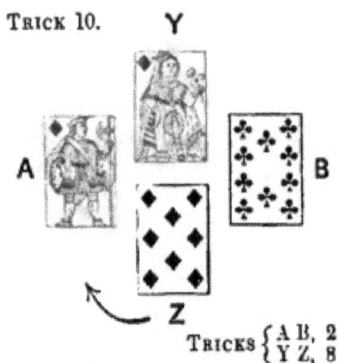

TRICKS $\begin{cases} A\,B, & 2 \\ Y\,Z, & 8 \end{cases}$

REMARK (Trick 9).—Z's play in not finessing is very good. He can count Y's hand, thus: Y has no more clubs (*see* Remark, Trick 3), he has the last trump, and three other cards. These cards must either be queen, ten of spades, and a diamond, in which case Z's play does not matter; or the nine returned by Y must be his best spade, in which case he can only have one more, as he would return the highest of two remaining cards (*see* p. 75), and his other cards must then be two diamonds. Therefore, assuming the case in which Z's play does matter (*i.e.*, of Y's nine being his best spade), Y's diamond must be guarded.

N

Consequently, Z, by not finessing, makes sure of the game. He requires one more trick besides the ace of spades and his partner's trump, and this trick Y is certain to make in diamonds if Z leads through A's hand (*see* Remark, Trick 1).

TRICKS 10 to 13.—Z (Trick 10) leads a diamond, and, however A plays,

YZ score three by cards and two by honours.

THE HANDS.

(Z's hand is given above.)

A's HAND.	Y's HAND.	B's HAND.
Qn, 8, 3 . . ♠	9, 5 . . . . ♠	10, 7, 6, 4 . . ♠
Knv, 7, 4 . . ♥	Qn, 10, 6, 5 . ♥	9, 8, 3 . . . ♥
9, 8, 5 . . . ♣	Kg, Qn, 7 . . ♣	Ace, Kv,10,3,2 ♣
Kg, Knv, 7, 5 ♦	Qn, 10, 9, 6 . ♦	Ace . . . . ♦

As the cards happen to lie, YZ only score four if Z finesses at Trick 9, and A plays properly. A, on winning this trick with the queen of spades, should see that his only chance of making two more tricks is to be led up to in diamonds. He should therefore (Trick 10) lead the seven of diamonds, which Y is compelled to take, and AB save the game.

HAND XIV.

Leading losing card to place the lead
(*see* pp. 126-130).

B's HAND.

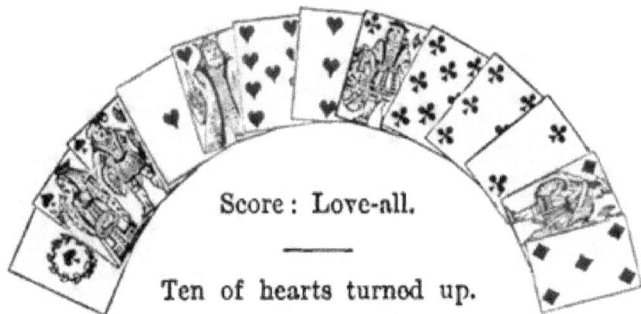

Score : Love-all.

———

Ten of hearts turned up.

THE PLAY.

TRICK 1.

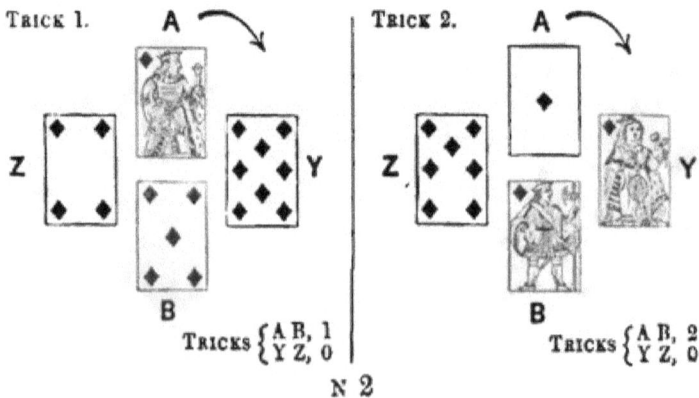

TRICKS $\left\{ \begin{array}{l} A\ B,\ 1 \\ Y\ Z,\ 0 \end{array} \right.$

TRICK 2.

TRICKS $\left\{ \begin{array}{l} A\ B,\ 2 \\ Y\ Z,\ 0 \end{array} \right.$

N 2

TRICK 3. A

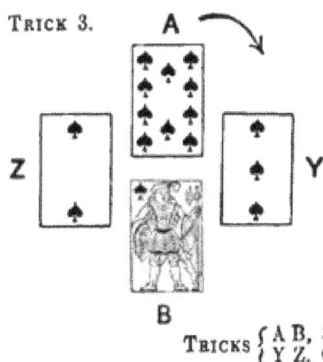

Z

Y

B

TRICKS $\begin{cases} \text{A B, } 3 \\ \text{Y Z, } 0 \end{cases}$

REMARK.—Y has the king of spades.

TRICK 4. A

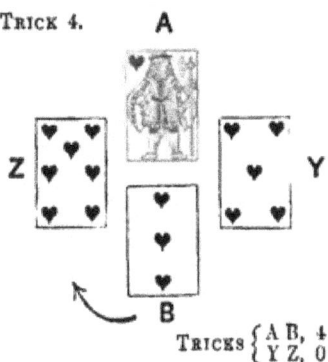

Z

Y

B

TRICKS $\begin{cases} \text{A B, } 4 \\ \text{Y Z, } 0 \end{cases}$

REMARK.—It is probable that A is weak in trumps, as he refused to force his partner in diamonds. Nevertheless, B leads a trump, as he is well provided in spades, and has some defence in the club suit.

TRICK 5. A

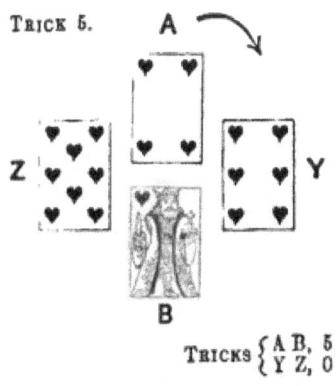

Z

Y

B

TRICKS $\begin{cases} \text{A B, } 5 \\ \text{Y Z, } 0 \end{cases}$

TRICK 6. A

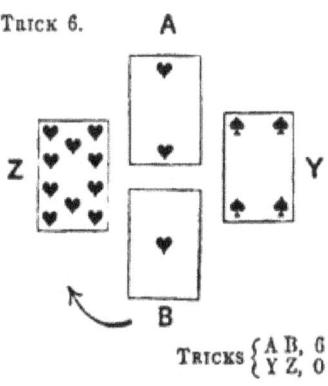

Z

Y

B

TRICKS $\begin{cases} \text{A B, } 6 \\ \text{Y Z, } 0 \end{cases}$

REMARK (Trick 6).—The queen of hearts must be in Z's hand, as A returned the four and now plays the two, and Y renounces.

TRICK 7.

TRICK 8.

TRICK 9.

TRICK 10.

TRICKS { A B, 6 — Y Z, 1

TRICKS { A B, 6 — Y Z, 2

TRICKS { A B, 7 — Y Z, 2

TRICKS { A B, 7 — Y Z, 3

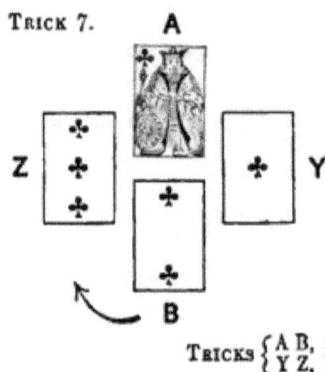

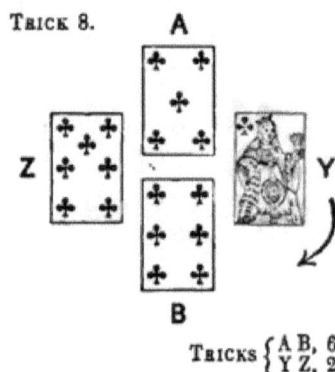

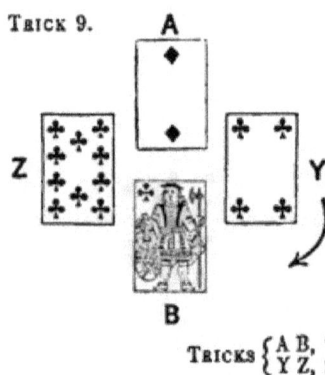

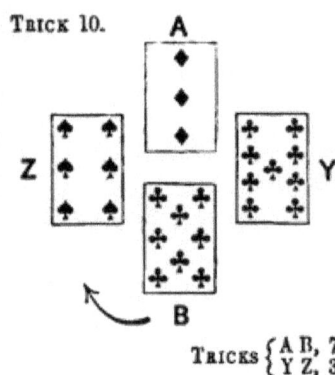

REMARK (Trick 10).—B leads the losing club to throw the lead into Y's hand. Y will then be obliged to lead a spade, as he has no other suit. Z will have to follow suit, or will be forced with the queen of trumps, and B will make the ace of spades and the last trump.

....

TRICKS 11 to 13.—Y (Trick 11) leads a spade, B puts on the queen, and

A B score three by cards and two by honours.

THE HANDS.

(B's hand is given above.)

A's Hand.	Y's Hand.	Z's Hand.
10, 9, 7 . . . ♠	Kg, 8, 5, 3, 4 . ♠	6, 2 . . . . ♠
Knv, 4, 2 . . ♥	6, 5 . . . . ♥	Qn, 10, 8, 7 . ♥
Kg, 5 . . . ♣	Ace, Qn, 9, 4 . ♣	10, 7, 3 . . . ♣
Ace, Kg, 6, 3, 2 ♦	Qn, 8 . . . ♦	10, 9, 7, 4 . . ♦

HAND XV.

Leading losing card to place the lead (*see* pp. 126-130).

Y's Hand.

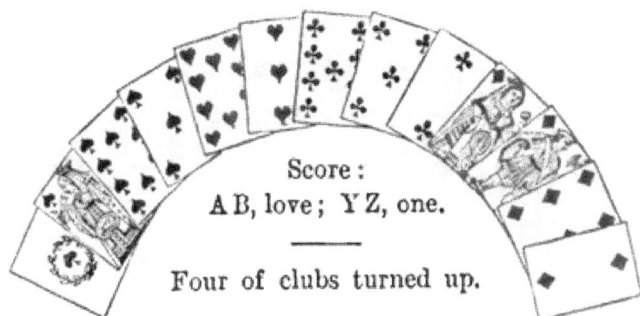

Score :
A B, love ; Y Z, one.

———

Four of clubs turned up.

THE PLAY.

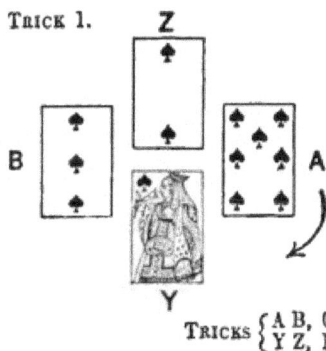

TRICK 1.

TRICKS { A B, 0 / Y Z, 1

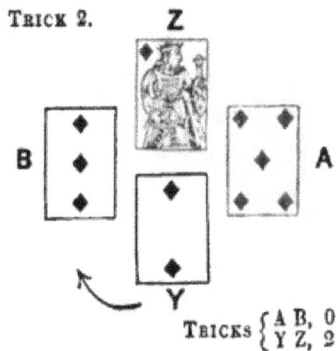

TRICK 2.

TRICKS { A B, 0 / Y Z, 2

TRICK 3.

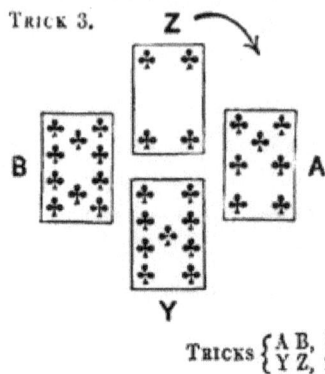

TRICKS $\begin{cases} \text{A B, 1} \\ \text{Y Z, 2} \end{cases}$

TRICK 4.

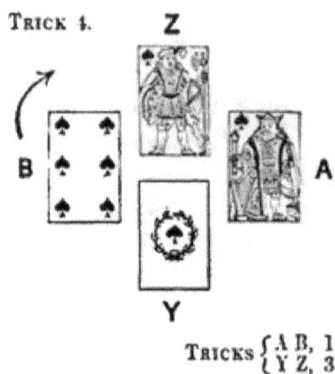

TRICKS $\begin{cases} \text{A B, 1} \\ \text{Y Z, 3} \end{cases}$

TRICK 5.

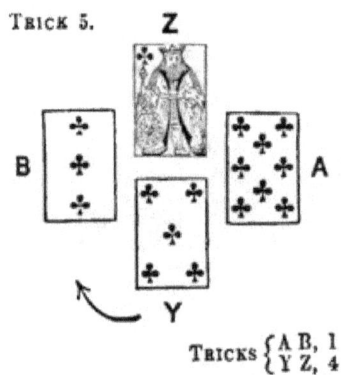

TRICKS $\begin{cases} \text{A B, 1} \\ \text{Y Z, 4} \end{cases}$

TRICK 6.

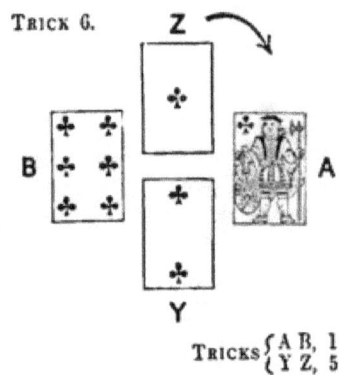

TRICKS $\begin{cases} \text{A B, 1} \\ \text{Y Z, 5} \end{cases}$

TRICK 7.

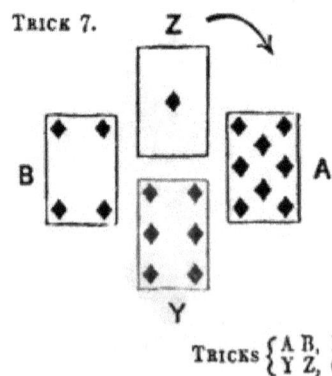

TRICKS $\begin{cases} \text{A B, 1} \\ \text{Y Z, 6} \end{cases}$

TRICK 8.

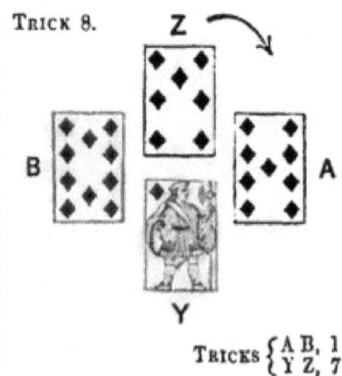

TRICKS $\begin{cases} \text{A B, 1} \\ \text{Y Z, 7} \end{cases}$

TRICK 9.   **Z**

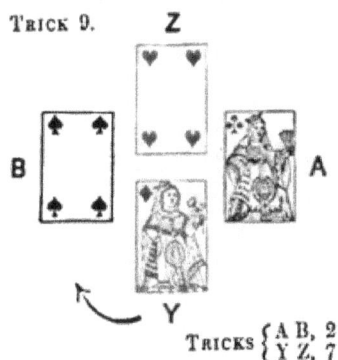

TRICKS $\begin{cases} \text{A B, 2} \\ \text{Y Z, 7} \end{cases}$

TRICK 10.   **Z**

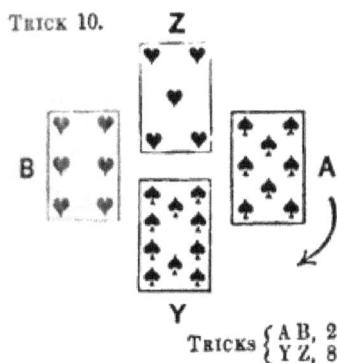

TRICKS $\begin{cases} \text{A B, 2} \\ \text{Y Z, 8} \end{cases}$

TRICK 11.   **Z**

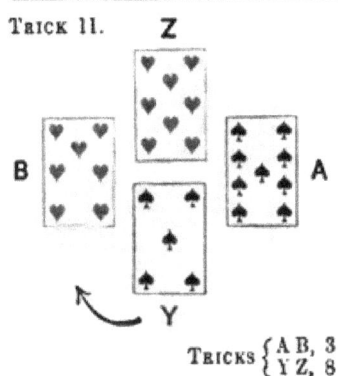

TRICKS $\begin{cases} \text{A B, 3} \\ \text{Y Z, 8} \end{cases}$

REMARK (Trick 11).—Y leads the losing spade to put the lead into A's hand (*see* fall of the spades, Tricks 1, 4, and 10), and so compel A to lead hearts up to Z. At this score (YZ, one) this is the best chance of four by cards. If the score were YZ, love, Y should lead a heart, as leading the spade gives up all chance of five by cards.

TRICKS 12 and 13.—Z has ace, queen of hearts; and YZ win four by cards.

THE HANDS.

(Y's hand is given above.)

A's HAND.	B's HAND.	Z's HAND.
Kg, 9, 8, 7 . ♠	6, 4, 3 . . . ♠	Knv, 2 . . . ♠
Kg, 2 . . . ♥	Knv, 9, 7, 6 . ♥	Ace, Qn, 8, 5, 4 ♥
Qn, Knv, 8, 7 . ♣	10, 6, 3 . . . ♣	Ace, Kg, 4 . . ♣
9, 8, 5 . . . ♦	10, 4, 3 . . . ♦	Ace, Kg, 7 . ♦

HAND XVI.

Underplay.

Z's HAND.

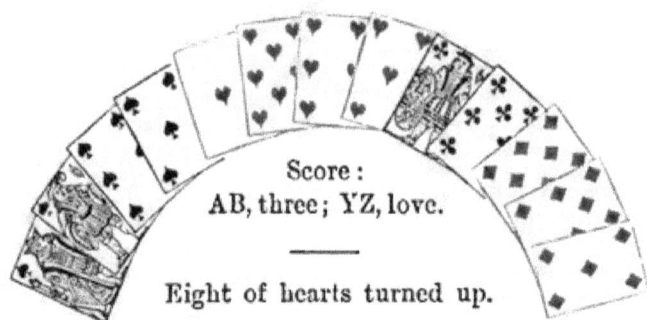

Score:
AB, three; YZ, love.

———

Eight of hearts turned up.

THE PLAY.

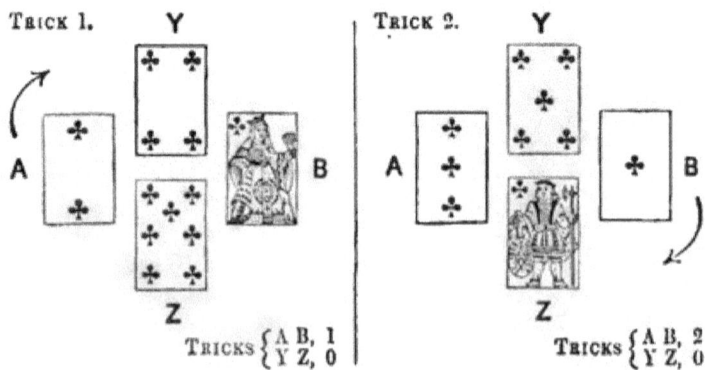

Trick 1.

Y

A   B

Z

TRICKS $\begin{cases} \text{A B, 1} \\ \text{Y Z, 0} \end{cases}$

Trick 2.

Y

A   B

Z

TRICKS $\begin{cases} \text{A B, 2} \\ \text{Y Z, 0} \end{cases}$

TRICK 3.

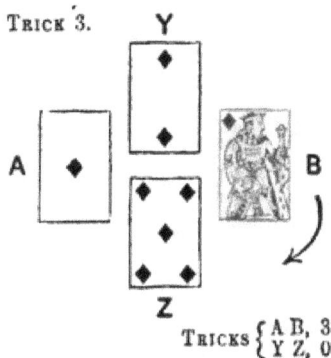

TRICKS $\begin{cases} \text{A B, 3} \\ \text{Y Z, 0} \end{cases}$

TRICK 4.

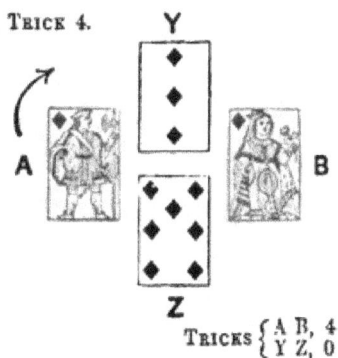

TRICKS $\begin{cases} \text{A B, 4} \\ \text{Y Z, 0} \end{cases}$

TRICK 5.

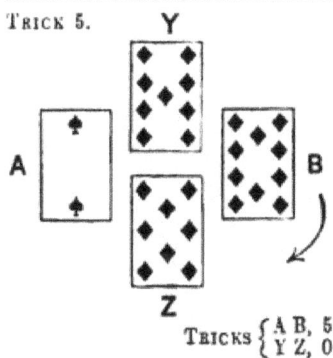

TRICKS $\begin{cases} \text{A B, 5} \\ \text{Y Z, 0} \end{cases}$

TRICK 6.

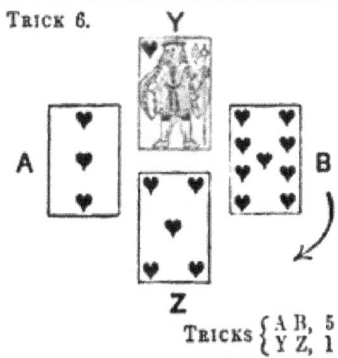

TRICKS $\begin{cases} \text{A B, 5} \\ \text{Y Z, 1} \end{cases}$

REMARK.—The nine of hearts looks like the best of a weak suit (*see* p. 67).

TRICK 7.

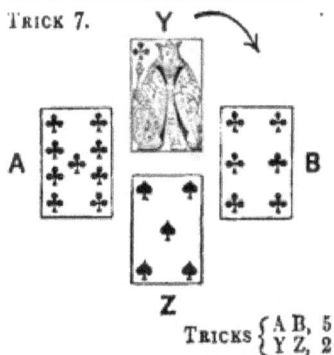

TRICKS $\begin{cases} \text{A B, 5} \\ \text{Y Z, 2} \end{cases}$

TRICK 8.

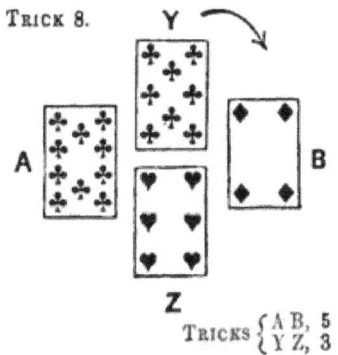

TRICKS $\begin{cases} \text{A B, 5} \\ \text{Y Z, 3} \end{cases}$

TRICK 9.

TRICKS {A B, 6
       {Y Z, 3

TRICK 10.

TRICKS {A B, 6
       {Y Z, 4

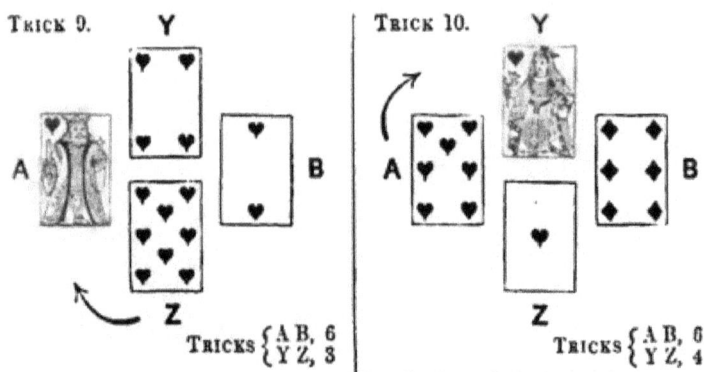

REMARK (Trick 9).—This is an example of underplay (*see* pp. 90-93). Z leads an under trump up to the weak hand (*see* Remark, Trick 6), in hopes that Y may win the trick, and be able to give some assistance in the spade suit, whereby the three tricks necessary to save the game may be made out of the remaining five.

A, suspecting underplay, puts on the king second hand.

TRICKS 11 to 13.—Z leads a spade, which Y wins with the ace, and returns. On the return Z does not finesse, as there is another trump in. Were all the trumps out the finesse would be safe; for then there would be only spades left in, and, consequently, no fear of losing the game by not making the king.

A B win the odd trick.

THE HANDS.

Z's hand is given above.

A's HAND.	Y's HAND.	B's HAND.
Qn, 4, 2 . . ♠	Ace, 9, 3 . . ♠	10, 8, 7 . . . ♠
Kg, 10, 7, 3 . ♥	Qn, Knv, 4 . ♥	9, 2 . . . . . ♥
10, 9, 3, 2 . . ♣	Kg, 8, 5, 4 . ♣	Ace, Qn, 6 . ♣
Ace, Knv . . ♦	9, 3, 2 . . . ♦	Kg, Qn, 10, 6, 4 ♦

HAND XVII.

Underplay, and playing to the score.

Y's HAND.

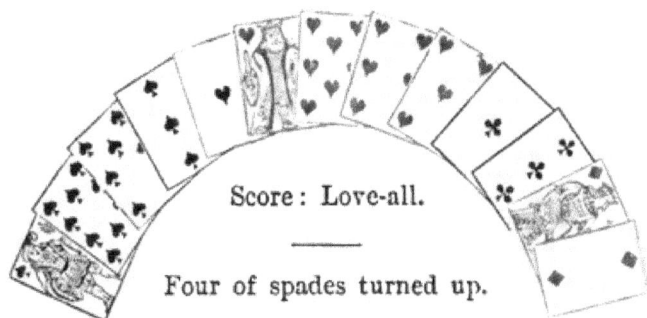

Score : Love-all.

––––––

Four of spades turned up.

THE PLAY.

TRICK 1.

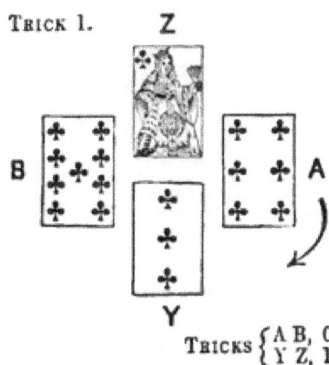

TRICKS $\begin{cases} \text{A B, 0} \\ \text{Y Z, 1} \end{cases}$

TRICK 2.

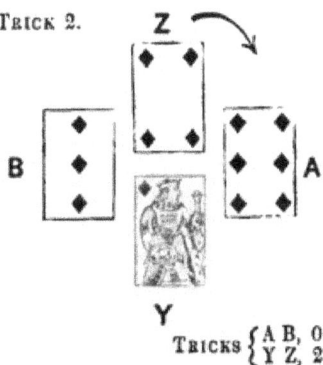

TRICKS $\begin{cases} \text{A B, 0} \\ \text{Y Z, 2} \end{cases}$

TRICK 3. Z	TRICK 4. Z
B ♠ A	B ♣ A
Y	Y
TRICKS { A B, 1 / Y Z, 2	TRICKS { A B, 1 / Y Z, 3

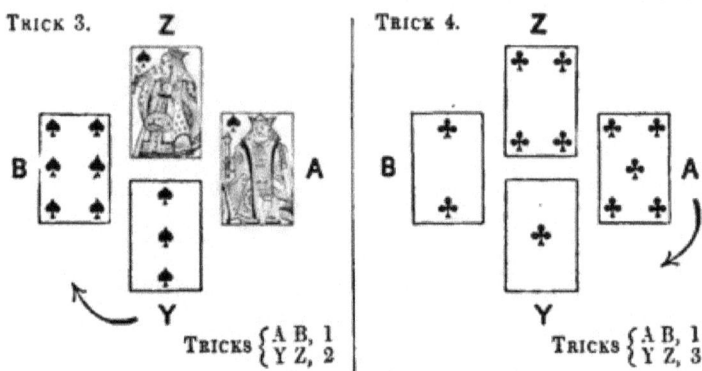

REMARK (Trick 3).—Y is justified in playing a forward game. He has four trumps (*see* pp. 104, 105), ace of the opponent's suit, and a fine heart suit : and his partner has declared strength in diamonds by choosing that suit for his original lead.

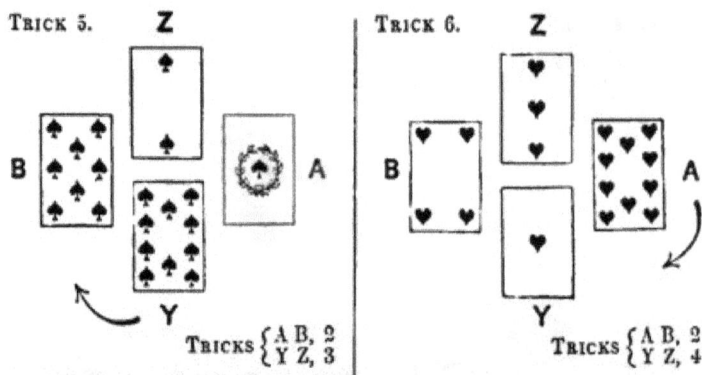

TRICK 5. Z	TRICK 6. Z
B ♠ A	B ♥ A
Y	Y
TRICKS { A B, 2 / Y Z, 3	TRICKS { A B, 2 / Y Z, 4

REMARK (Trick 6).—Y is justified in playing a false card here, notwithstanding General Principle 12 (p. 95). The heart is a forced lead, and the card led (the ten) is almost certainly A's best. Y's scheme is to take another round of trumps, and then to underplay in hearts (*see* p. 90); so he puts on the ace to deceive B as to the position of the king.

Trick 7.   Z

TRICKS { A B, 2
{ Y Z, 5

Trick 8.   Z

TRICKS { A B, 2
{ Y Z, 6

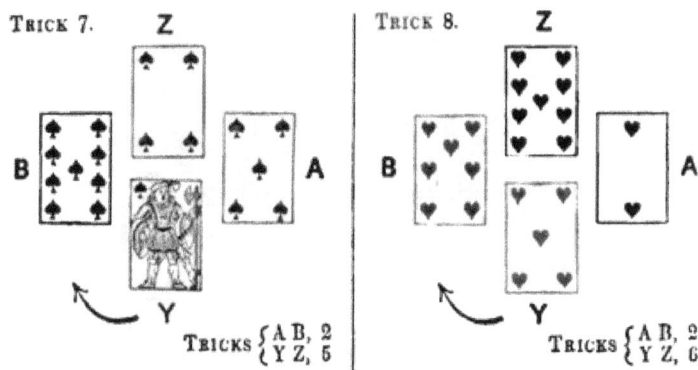

TRICKS 9 to 13.—Z leads the king of clubs, on which Y discards the two of diamonds.   Z then leads the knave of hearts. on which Y puts the king; the queen falls (*see* the hands below); Y brings in the hearts; and

Y Z win five by cards.

THE HANDS.

(Y's hand is given above.)

A's HAND.	B's HAND.	Z's HAND.
Ace, Kg, 5. . ♠	9, 8, 6 . . . ♠	Qn, 4, 2 . . ♠
10, 2. . . . ♥	Qn, 7, 4 . . ♥	Knv, 9, 3 . . ♥
Knv, 8, 7, 6, 5 ♣	10, 9, 2 . . . ♣	Kg, Qn, 4 . . ♣
Ace, 8, 6. . . ♦	10, 9, 7, 3 . . ♦	Qn, Knv, 5, 4 ♦

A and B both play the hand badly.   At Trick 6, A, in the face of an adverse trump lead and the command of his suit (clubs) against him, should lead the ace of diamonds to make the third trick and save the game.   At Trick 8 B should put on his queen of hearts.   He is fairly taken in by Y's dark play at Trick 6; but he ought not to have allowed himself to be so.   He should have argued that Y who has been playing a very strong game, would not be likely to put on ace second hand merely for the purpose of getting the lead or of making sure of a trick. Further, A having declared weakness in hearts by leading a strengthening ten, Z is sure to finesse if he has king, knave, or even king, nine. So B's best chance of making the queen is to put it on (*see* p. 91).

HAND XVIII.

Defensive trump lead, and playing to the score.

A's HAND.

Score : Love-all.

———

Nine of clubs turned up.

THE PLAY.

TRICK 1.

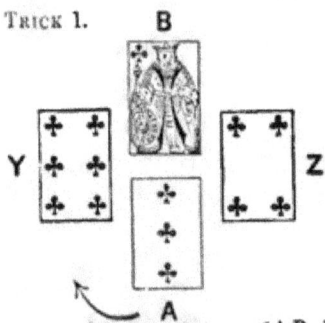

TRICKS $\begin{cases} \text{A B, 1} \\ \text{Y Z, 0} \end{cases}$

TRICK 2.

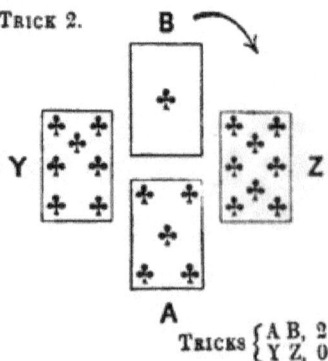

TRICKS $\begin{cases} \text{A B, 2} \\ \text{Y Z, 0} \end{cases}$

REMARK.— A defensive trump lead (*see* p. 101).

TRICK 3.   B

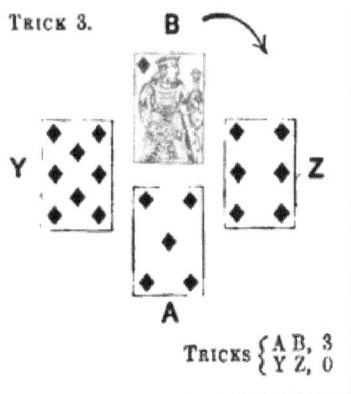

Y   Z

A

TRICKS $\begin{cases} \text{A B, 3} \\ \text{Y Z, 0} \end{cases}$

TRICK 4.   B

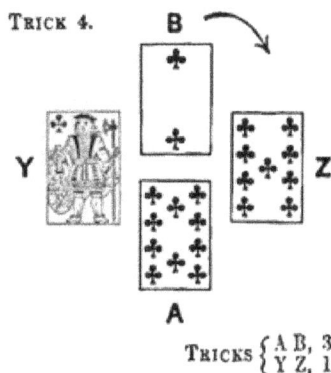

Y   Z

A

TRICKS $\begin{cases} \text{A B, 3} \\ \text{Y Z, 1} \end{cases}$

REMARK (Trick 4).—A's finesse is unlucky. He is, however, clearly justified in not parting with the command of trumps, as, even if the finesse does not succeed, he remains with the last trump, and will, in all probability, bring in his partner's diamonds.

TRICK 5.   B

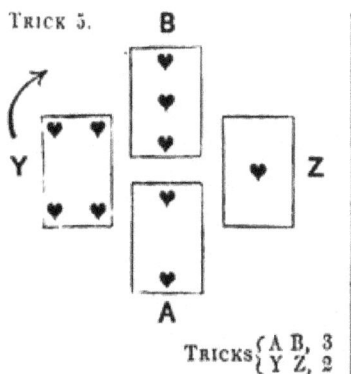

Y   Z

A

TRICKS $\begin{cases} \text{A B, 3} \\ \text{Y Z, 2} \end{cases}$

TRICK 6.   B

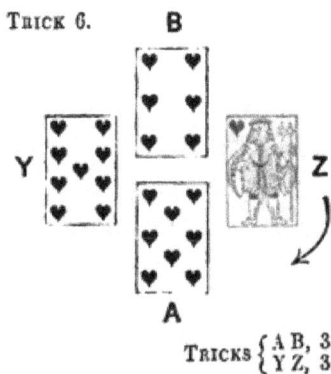

Y   Z

A

TRICKS $\begin{cases} \text{A B, 3} \\ \text{Y Z, 3} \end{cases}$

TRICK 7.	TRICK 8.

TRICKS { A B, 3 / Y Z, 4

TRICKS { A B, 4 / Y Z, 4

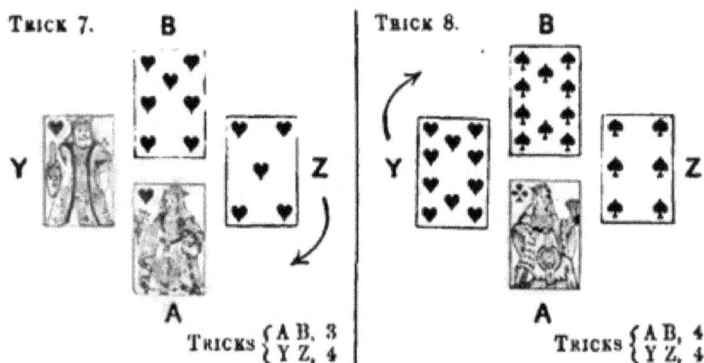

TRICKS 9 to 13.—A leads the queen of diamonds, and then the seven, finding his partner with the entire command of diamonds (*see* B's hand below); and

A B score three by cards and two by honours.

THE HANDS.

(A's hand is given above.)

Y's HAND.	B's HAND.	Z's HAND.
8, 7, 4, 3, 2 . ♠	10 . . . . ♠	Ace, Qn, 9, 6 . ♠
Kg, 10, 9, 4 . ♥	7, 6, 3 . . . ♥	Ace, Knv, 5 . ♥
Knv, 7, 6 . . ♣	Ace, Kg, 2 . ♣	9, 8, 4 . . . ♣
8 . . . . . ♦	A, Kg, Kv, 4, 3, 2 ♦	10, 9, 6 . . . ♦

It may be observed that Z loses the game by bad play at Trick 7. The fall of the cards in Tricks 5 and 6 shows that A has the queen of hearts, and Y the king. Z should therefore, at Trick 7, lead the ace of spades to make the fourth trick, and then the heart, making the fifth trick and saving the game.

At Trick 8, if Y leads a spade and Z does not finesse, the game may be saved. To finesse at that point would be very bad play, as the ace of spades makes the fifth trick. But Y's play at Trick 8, though unfortunate, is not wrong;

o

for Y cannot tell that Z has the ace of spades; indeed, the presumption is that he has not, or he would have led it. Y properly plays to force the long trump, and to make his partner fourth player.

HAND XIX.

A well judged trump lead, though the adversary has called for trumps.

B's HAND.

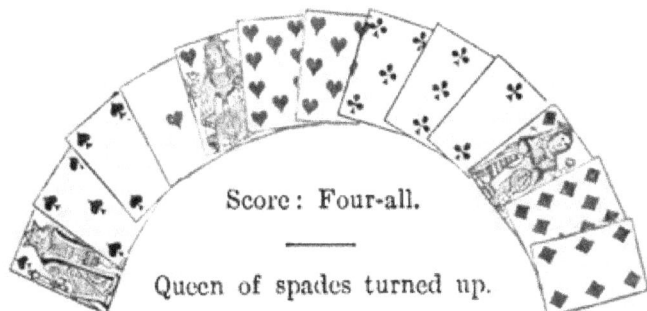

Score : Four-all.

———

Queen of spades turned up.

THE PLAY.

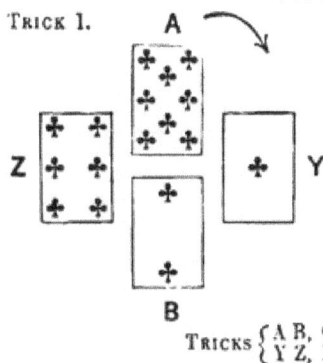

TRICK 1.

TRICKS { A B, 0
        { Y Z, 1

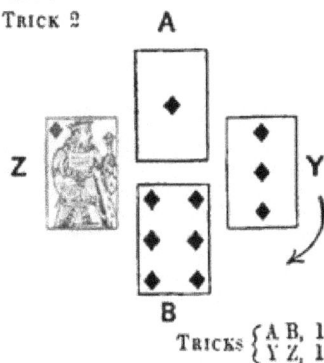

TRICK 2

TRICKS { A B, 1
        { Y Z, 1

TRICK 3. A

Z Y

B

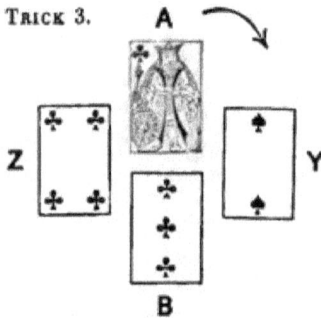

TRICKS $\begin{cases} A\,B, & 1 \\ Y\,Z, & 2 \end{cases}$

REMARK.—Z has called for trumps.

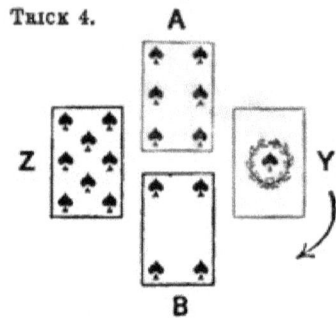

TRICK 4. A

Z Y

B

TRICKS $\begin{cases} A\,B, & 1 \\ Y\,Z, & 3 \end{cases}$

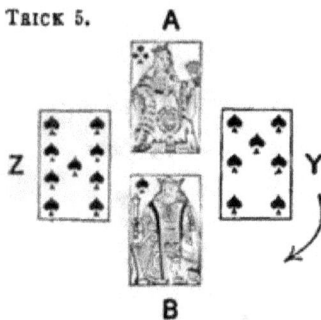

TRICK 5. A

Z Y

B

TRICKS $\begin{cases} A\,B, & 2 \\ Y\,Z, & 3 \end{cases}$

REMARK.—The fall of the spades (*see* Tricks 3, 4, and 5) shows that the three of the suit is in Y's hand.

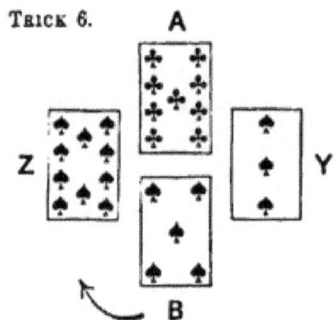

TRICK 6. A

Z Y

B

TRICKS $\begin{cases} A\,B, & 2 \\ Y\,Z, & 4 \end{cases}$

REMARK.—It is seldom right to continue trumps when led by the opponents; but this is an exceptional case. B plays very well in drawing two trumps for one, as it is evident that if Y and Z make their trumps separately they must win the odd trick.

o 2

TRICK 7.   A

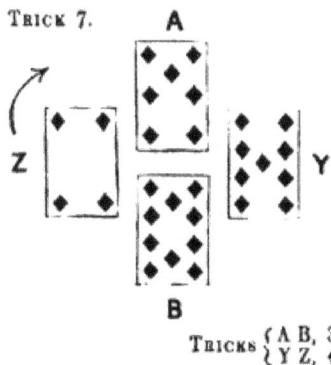

Z   Y

B

TRICKS { A B, 3
       { Y Z, 4

TRICK 8.   A

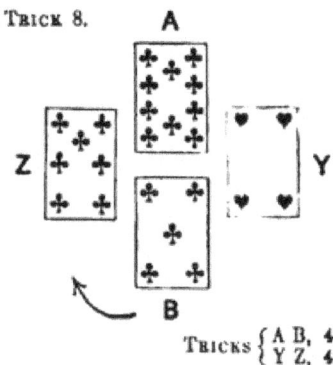

Z   Y

B

TRICKS { A B, 4
       { Y Z, 4

TRICK 9.   A

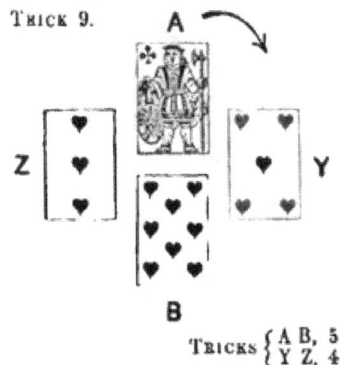

Z   Y

B

TRICKS { A B, 5
       { Y Z, 4

TRICK 10.   A

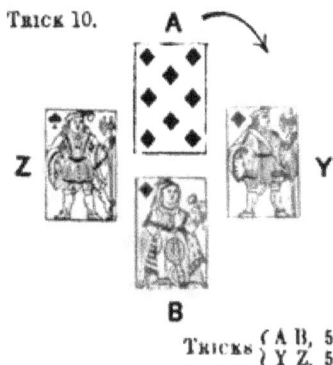

Z   Y

B

TRICKS { A B, 5
       { Y Z, 5

TRICKS 11 to 13.—Whatever Z leads, B makes ace, queen of hearts; and

AB win the odd trick.

THE HANDS.

(B's hand is given above.)

A's HAND.	Y's HAND.	Z's HAND.
6 . . . . . ♠	Ace, 7, 3, 2 . ♠	Qn,Knv,10,9,8 ♠
9, 6, 2 . . . ♥	7, 5, 4 . . . ♥	Kg, Knv, 3 . ♥
Kg,Q,Kv,10,9,8 ♣	Ace . . . . ♣	7, 6, 4 . . . ♣
Ace, 8, 7 . . ♦	Knv, 9, 5, 3, 2 ♦	Kg, 4 . . . ♦

HAND XX.

Returned lead, and refusing a force.

A's HAND.

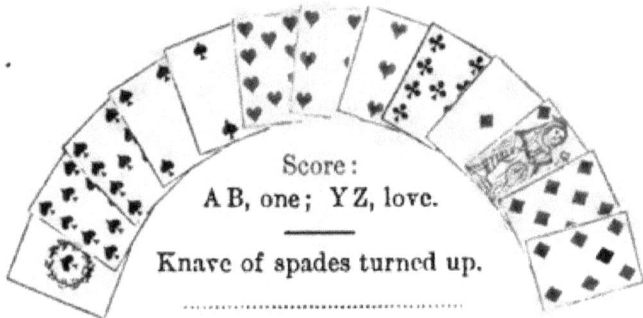

Score:
A B, one; Y Z, love.

Knave of spades turned up.

THE PLAY.

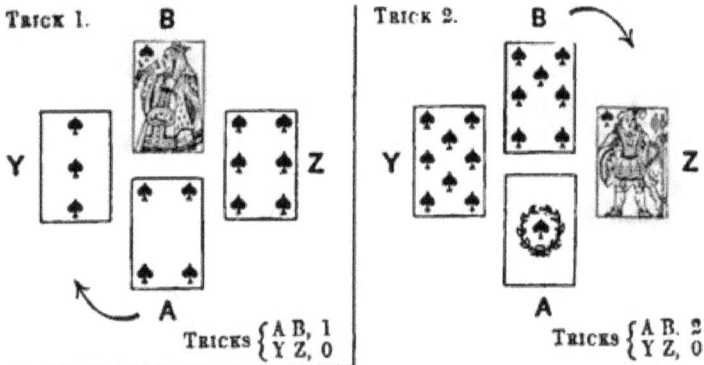

TRICK 1.

B

Y   Z

A

TRICKS {A B, 1
        {Y Z, 0

TRICK 2.

B

Y   Z

A

TRICKS {A B, 2
        {Y Z, 0

REMARK (Trick 2).—Note the card returned by B, the seven. From this card it may be inferred that B remains with the five and no more. For, had he both five and king (the only ones remaining in), he would have returned the five (*see* p. 74). If no false cards have been played (as is most probable), B has the five of spades, and Y the king. A, therefore, does not continue the trump, but leaves the small spade in his partner's hand.

TRICK 3.

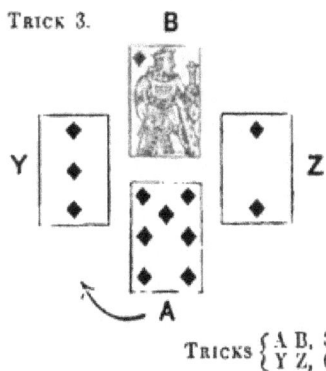

TRICKS { A B, 3
         { Y Z, 0

TRICK 4.

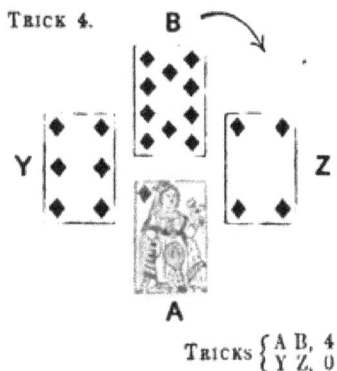

TRICKS { A B, 4
         { Y Z, 0

TRICK 5.

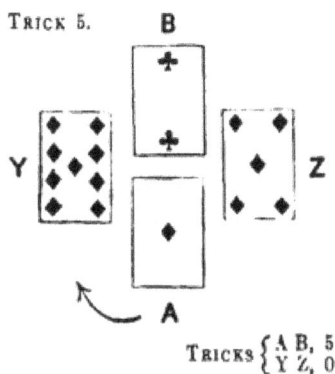

TRICKS { A B, 5
         { Y Z, 0

TRICK 6.

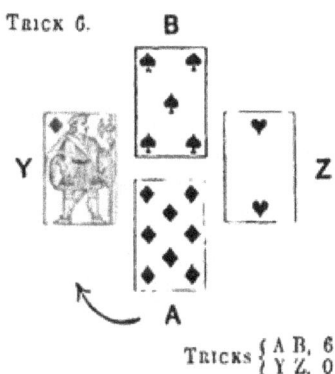

TRICKS { A B, 6
         { Y Z, 0

TRICK 7.

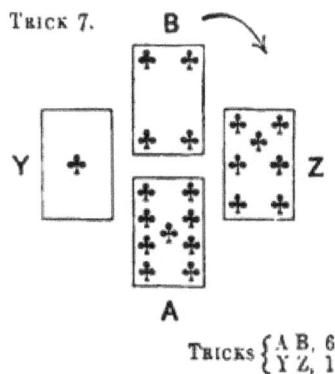

TRICKS { A B, 6
         { Y Z, 1

TRICK 8.

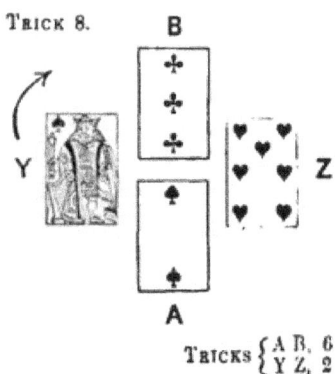

TRICKS { A B, 6
         { Y Z, 2

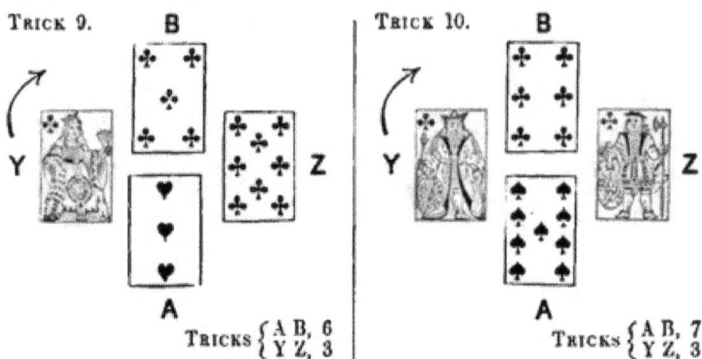

TRICK 9.   B   Y   Z   A   TRICKS { A B, 6 / Y Z, 3

TRICK 10.   B   Y   Z   A   TRICKS { A B, 7 / Y Z, 3

REMARK (Trick 9).—A knows B has at least two more clubs (*see* Tricks 7 and 8, and refer to Appendix A, p. 257). A, therefore, desires to leave the lead with Y, that he may go on with another club, and so clear B's suit.

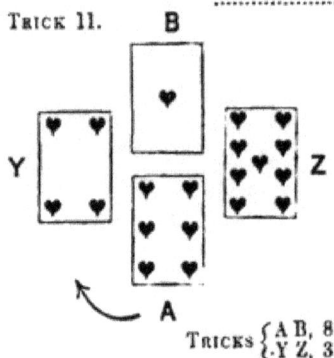

TRICK 11.   B   Y   Z   A   TRICKS { A B, 8 / Y Z, 3

REMARK (Trick 11).—A leads his smallest heart, as he does not want to tempt B to finesse (*see* p. 121). B has ace, queen of hearts (*see* his hand below), but he does not finesse, as the ace of hearts, last club, and A's trump make every trick.

A B win four by cards.

THE HANDS.

(A's hand is given above.)

Y's HAND.	B's HAND.	Z's HAND.
Kg, 8, 3 . . ♠	Qn, 7, 5 . . ♠	Knv, 6 . . . ♠
8, 5, 4 . . . ♥	Ace, Qn . . ♥	Kg, Knv, 9, 7, 2 ♥
Ace, Kg, Qn . ♣	10, 6, 5, 4, 3, 2 ♣	Knv, 8, 7 . . ♣
Knv, 9, 6, 3 . ♦	Kg, 10 . . . ♦	5, 4, 2 . . . ♦

HAND XXI.

Refusing to overtrump.

A's HAND.

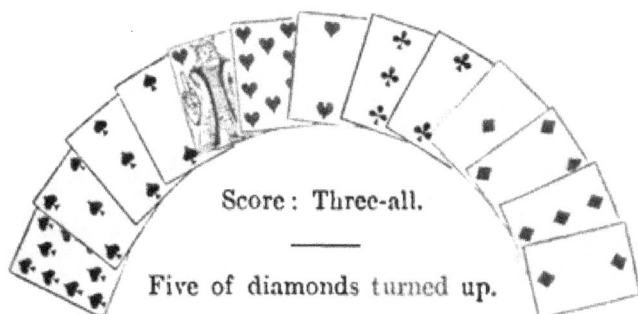

Score : Three-all.

———

Five of diamonds turned up.

THE PLAY.

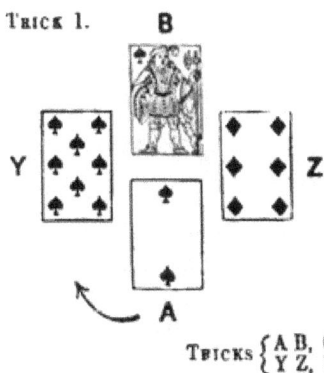	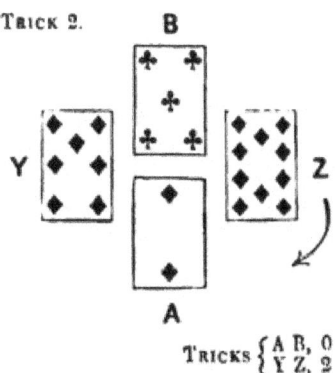

TRICK 1.   TRICK 2.

TRICKS { A B, 0 / Y Z, 1 }   TRICKS { A B, 0 / Y Z, 2 }

TRICK 3.

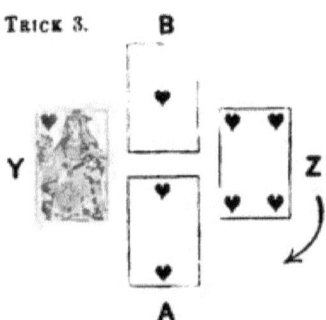

TRICKS $\begin{cases} A B, & 1 \\ Y Z, & 2 \end{cases}$

TRICK 4.

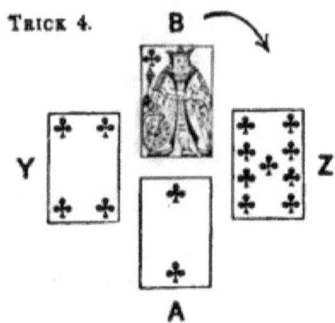

TRICKS $\begin{cases} A B, & 2 \\ Y Z, & 2 \end{cases}$

TRICK 5.

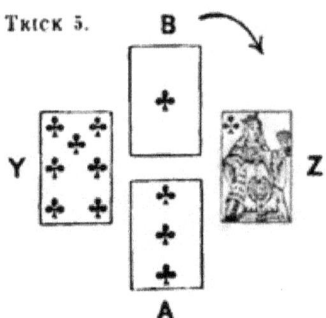

TRICKS $\begin{cases} A B, & 3 \\ Y Z, & 2 \end{cases}$

TRICK 6.

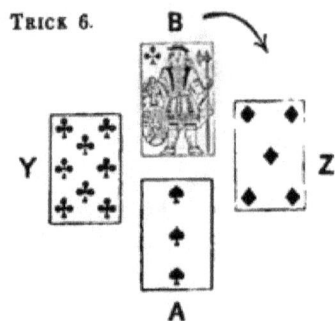

TRICKS $\begin{cases} A B & 3 \\ Y Z, & 3 \end{cases}$

REMARK (Trick 6).—A does not overtrump. This is the sort of *coup* for which no rule can be laid down in a book, as it depends entirely on the state of the game and the previous fall of the cards. A sees that his only chance of two by cards is for the remaining trumps to be divided, and for him to be able to get two rounds before he loses the command of hearts. If then his partner has ace, queen of spades, he may win the game even with his wretched hand.

TRICK 7.

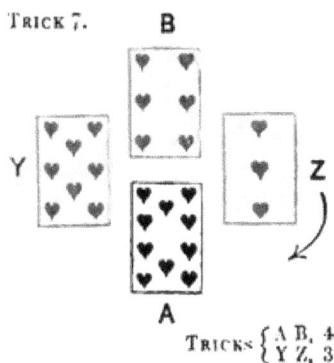

TRICKS { A B, 4 / Y Z, 3 }

TRICK 8.

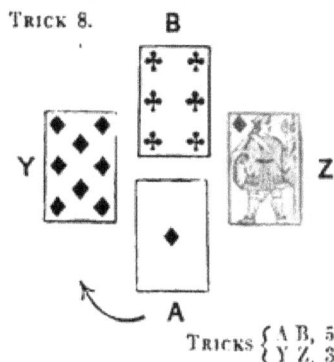

TRICKS { A B, 5 / Y Z, 3 }

TRICK 9.

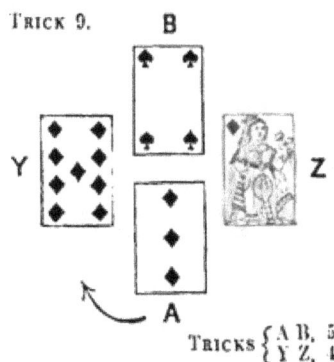

TRICKS { A B, 5 / Y Z, 4 }

TRICK 10.

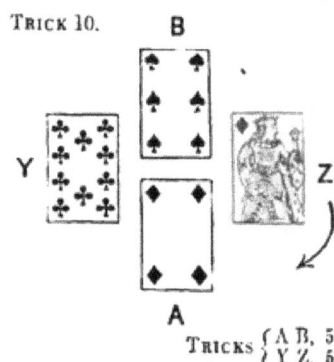

TRICKS { A B, 5 / Y Z, 5 }

TRICKS 11 to 13.—Z leads a heart, which A wins. A leads a spade, and finds his partner with ace, queen; and A B win two by cards (which score before honours).

THE HANDS.

(A's hand is given above.)

Y's HAND.	B's HAND.	Z's HAND.
Kg, 9, 8 . . ♠	Ace,Q,Kv,7,6,4 ♠	Knv, 7, 5, 4, 3 ♥
Qn, 9, 8 . . ♥	Ace, 6 . . . ♥	Qn, 9 . . . ♣
10, 8, 7, 4 . . ♣	Ace, Kg, Kv,6,5 ♣	Kg,Q,Kv,10,6,5 ♦
9, 8, 7 . . . ♦		

HAND XXII.

Refusing to overtrump.

Z's HAND.

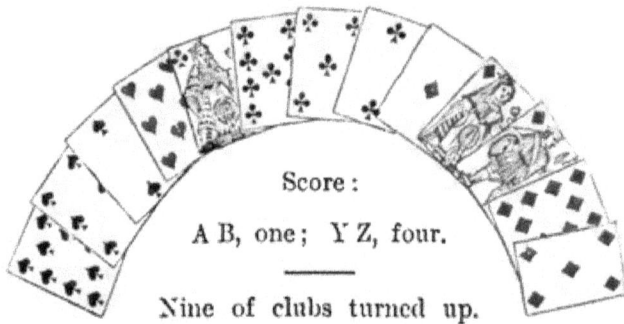

Score :

A B, one ; Y Z, four.

———

Nine of clubs turned up.

THE PLAY.

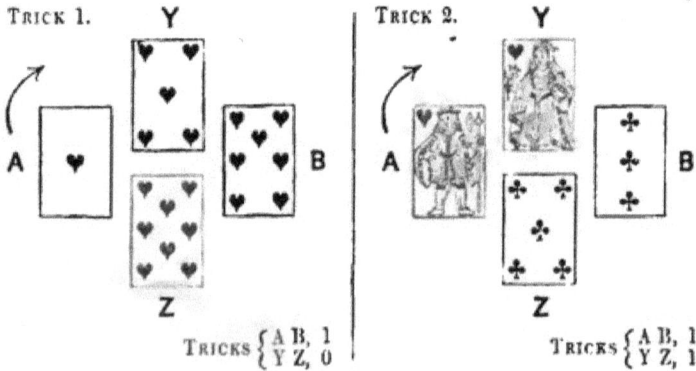

TRICK 1.

A   Y   B

Z

TRICKS { A B, 1
        { Y Z, 0

TRICK 2.

A   Y   B

Z

TRICKS { A B, 1
        { Y Z, 1

TRICK 3.

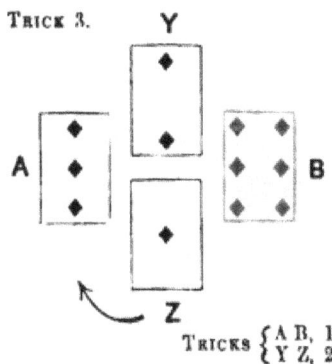

TRICKS $\begin{cases} A B, 1 \\ Y Z, 2 \end{cases}$

TRICK 4.

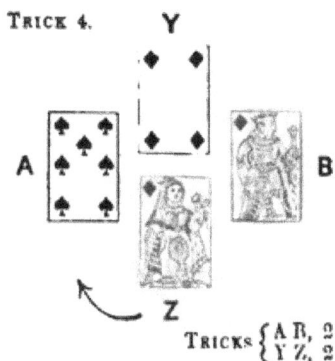

TRICKS $\begin{cases} A B, 2 \\ Y Z, 2 \end{cases}$

TRICK 5.

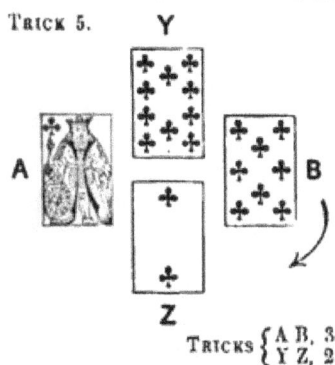

TRICKS $\begin{cases} A B, 3 \\ Y Z, 2 \end{cases}$

TRICK 6.

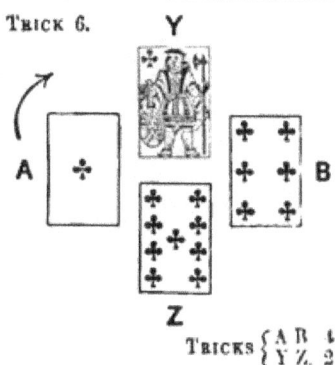

TRICKS $\begin{cases} A B, 4 \\ Y Z, 2 \end{cases}$

TRICK 7.

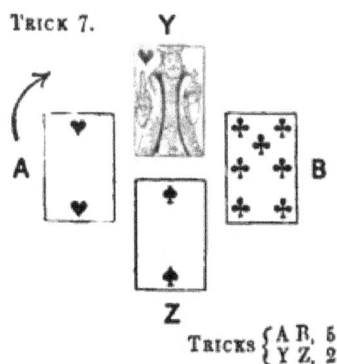

TRICKS $\begin{cases} A B, 5 \\ Y Z, 2 \end{cases}$

TRICK 8.

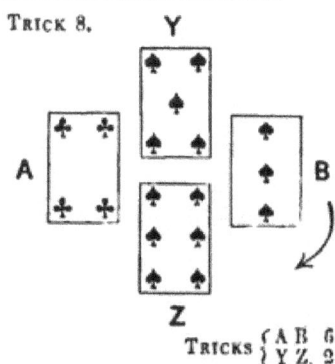

TRICKS $\begin{cases} A B, 6 \\ Y Z, 2 \end{cases}$

REMARK (Trick 7).—It is clear from Y's putting the king on the two of hearts that A has all the remaining hearts. He has one other card, which, if there has been no false card played in clubs, must be the four of clubs (*see* fall of the club suit in Tricks 5 and 6). If Z parts with the queen of clubs while the four remains in A's hand, A will bring in the hearts, and make four by cards. Z very properly, therefore, refuses to overtrump.

TRICKS 9 to 13.—A leads a heart; Z trumps it, and makes three tricks in diamonds; his partner makes the last trick with the ace of spades (*see* Y's hand below); and

Y Z win the odd trick.

THE HANDS.

(Z's hand is given above.)

A's HAND.	Y's HAND.	B's HAND.
7 . ♠ 3 . ♦	A, Kg, Kv, 8, 5 ♠	Qn, 9, 4, 3 . . ♠
Ace, Knv, 10, 9, 6,	Kg, Qn, 5 . . ♥	7 . . . . . ♥
4, 3, 2 . . ♥	Knv, 10 . . ♣	8, 7, 6, 3 . . ♣
Ace, Kg, 4 . ♣	9, 4, 2 . . . ♦	Kg, 8, 7, 6 . . ♦

At Trick 6, A should not return the trump. The eight is certainly B's best trump if he leads by rule, for he has neither the nine (turned up by Z), nor the ten (dropped by Y), and he cannot have led from queen, knave, eight, or he would have commenced with the queen. The best heart and best diamond being still against him, A should lead the heart in hopes of forcing his partner. If he does so, and B is overtrumped, A B win four by cards. If Z refuses to overtrump, and B continues with another round of trumps, A B equally win four by cards, as will clearly appear by so playing the hand.

HAND XXIII.

Refusing to overtrump.

Y's HAND.

Score: Four-all.

————

Five of spades turned up.

THE PLAY.

TRICK 1.　Z

B　A

Y

TRICKS $\begin{cases} A B, 1 \\ Y Z, 0 \end{cases}$

TRICK 2.　Z

B　A

Y

TRICKS $\begin{cases} A B, 2 \\ Y Z, 0 \end{cases}$

TRICK 3. Z

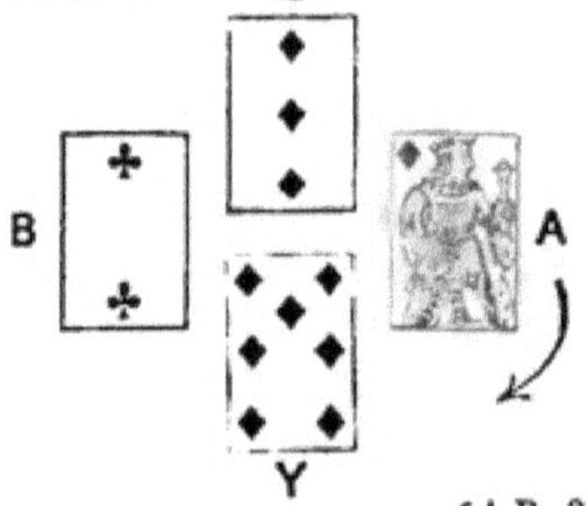

B A

Y

TRICKS $\begin{cases} A\ B,\ 3 \\ Y\ Z,\ 0 \end{cases}$

TRICK 4. Z

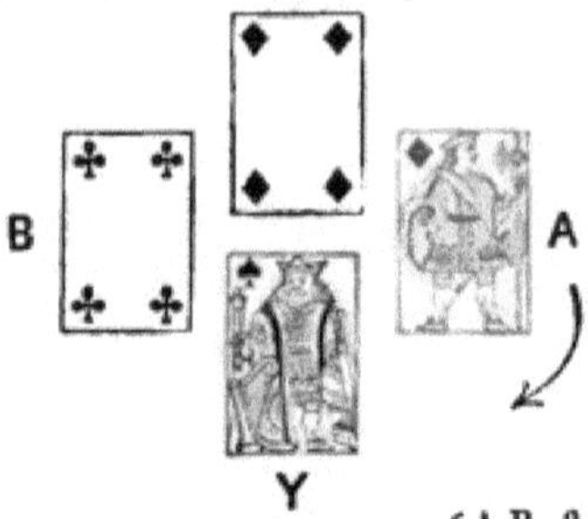

B A

Y

TRICKS $\begin{cases} A\ B,\ 3 \\ Y\ Z,\ 1 \end{cases}$

TRICK 5. Z

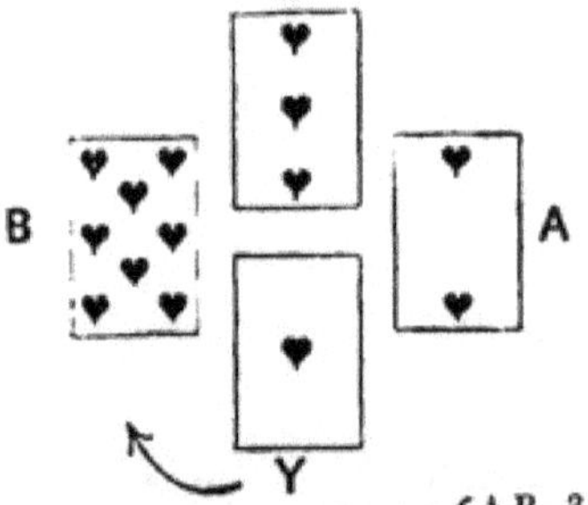

B A

Y

TRICKS $\begin{cases} A\ B,\ 3 \\ Y\ Z,\ 2 \end{cases}$

TRICK 6. Z

B A

Y

TRICKS $\begin{cases} A\ B,\ 4 \\ Y\ Z,\ 2 \end{cases}$

REMARK.—From actual
play; but should not Y
lead a trump?

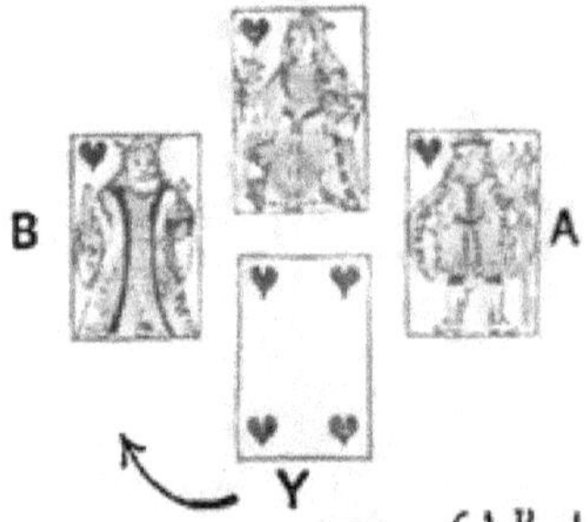

TRICK 7. Z

B A

Y

TRICKS $\begin{cases} A\ B,\ 4 \\ Y\ Z,\ 3 \end{cases}$

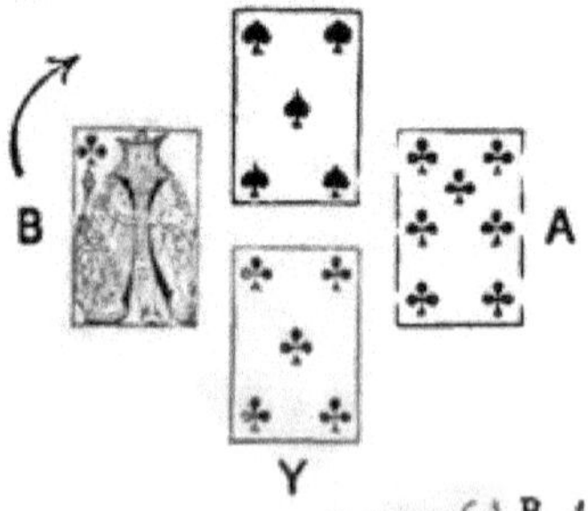

TRICK 8. Z

B A

Y

TRICKS $\begin{cases} A\ B,\ 5 \\ Y\ Z,\ 3 \end{cases}$

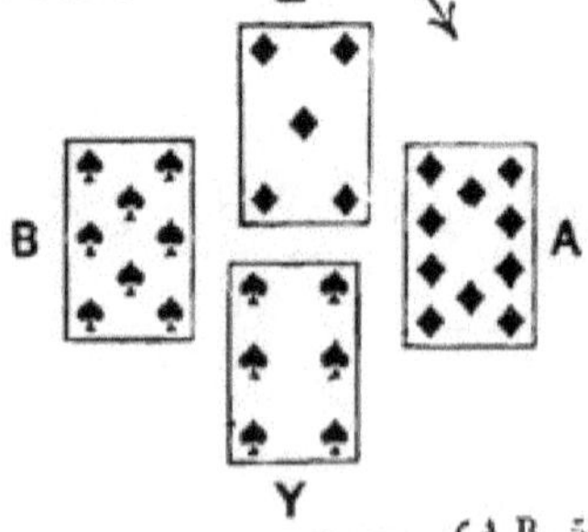

TRICK 9.

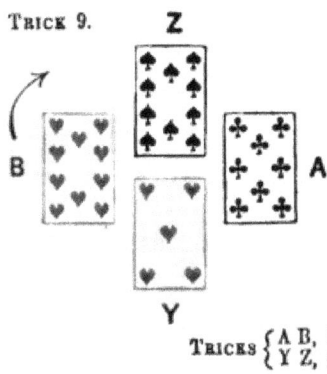

TRICKS { A B, 5
         Y Z, 4

TRICK 10.

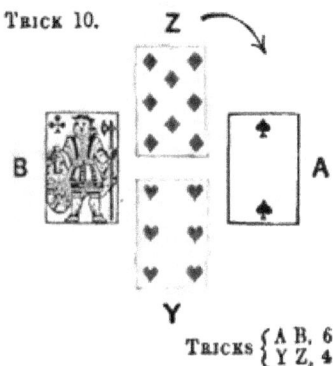

TRICKS { A B, 6
         Y Z, 4

REMARK (Trick 10).—Y's play in not overtrumping is very good. He counts the hand thus: to save the game Z must hold ace, queen, or ace, knave of spades; his third card is evidently the remaining diamond. A has the nine of clubs (see fall of the club suit in Tricks 2, 7, and 9), and two trumps. B has two trumps, one being queen or knave (see Trick 9), and queen, knave of clubs. If the cards remaining in each hand are placed face upwards on the table, and the uncertain cards, viz., the nine, four, and three of trumps are given two to A, and one to B, it will be seen that, if Y overtrumps with the seven, he cannot make the requisite three tricks; but that, if he leaves the lead with A, Y Z make the remaining tricks.

It may be added, that if at Trick 10 A discards his club, and keeps his three little trumps together, leaving the trick to B, A B must win the odd trick if B leads a trump at Trick 11 after trumping. This A might have reckoned.

THE HANDS.

(Y's hand is given above.)

A's HAND.	B's HAND.	Z's HAND.
4, 3, 2 . . . ♠	Qn, 9, 8 . . . ♠	Ace, Knv, 10, 5 ♠
Knv, 2 . . . ♥	Kg, 10, 8 . . ♥	Qn, 3 . . . . ♥
Ace, 9, 8, 7 . ♣	Kg, Q, Kv, 10, 4, 2 ♣	6 . . . . . ♣
Kg, Knv, 10, 9 ♦	Ace . . . . ♦	8, 6, 5, 4, 3, 2 . ♦

HAND XXIV.

Counting the hands, and consequent departure from rule.

Y's HAND.

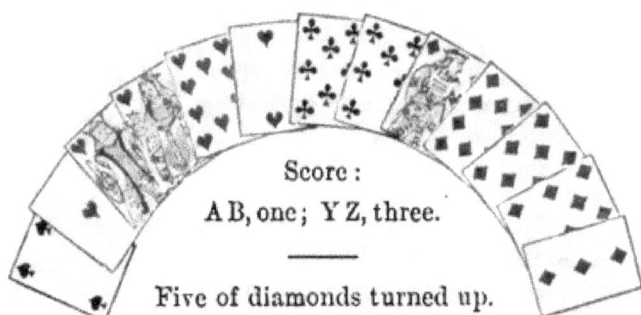

Score :
A B, one; Y Z, three.

———

Five of diamonds turned up.

THE PLAY.

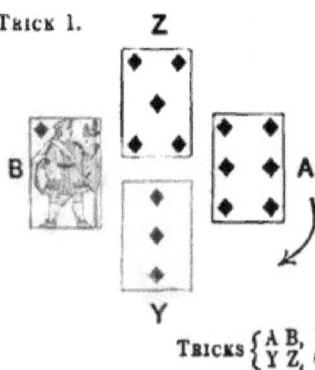

TRICK 1.

TRICKS { A B, 1
         Y Z, 0

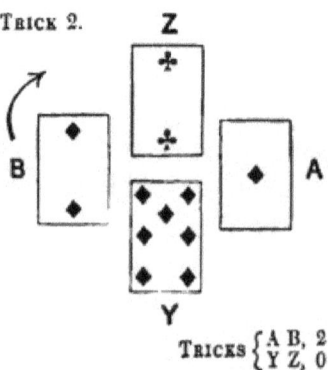

TRICK 2.

TRICKS { A B, 2
         Y Z, 0

P

TRICK 3.

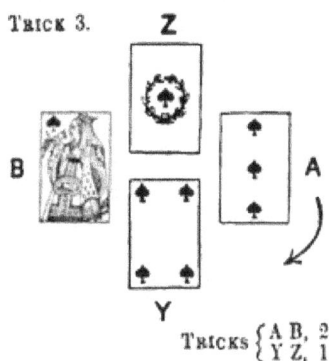

TRICKS $\begin{cases} A\,B, & 2 \\ Y\,Z, & 1 \end{cases}$

TRICK 4.

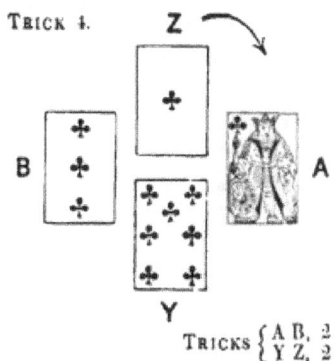

TRICKS $\begin{cases} A\,B, & 2 \\ Y\,Z, & 2 \end{cases}$

TRICK 5.

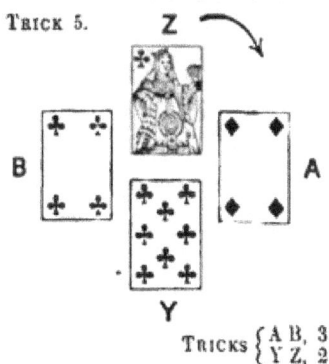

TRICKS $\begin{cases} A\,B, & 3 \\ Y\,Z, & 2 \end{cases}$

TRICK 6.

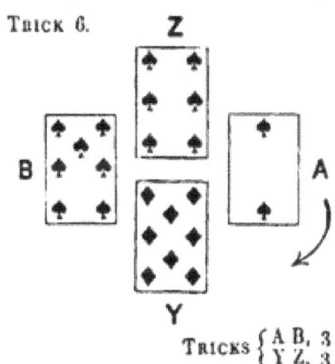

TRICKS $\begin{cases} A\,B, & 3 \\ Y\,Z, & 3 \end{cases}$

TRICK 7.

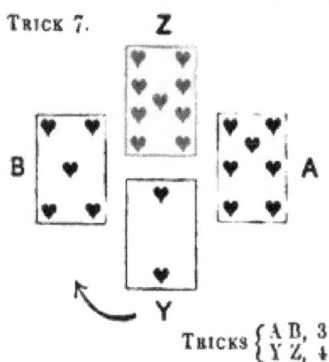

TRICKS $\begin{cases} A\,B, & 3 \\ Y\,Z, & 4 \end{cases}$

TRICK 8.

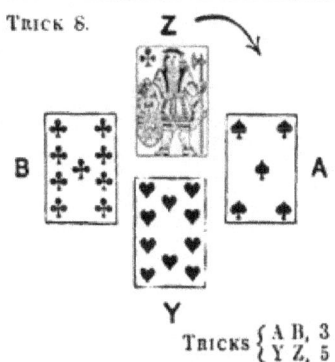

TRICKS $\begin{cases} A\,B, & 3 \\ Y\,Z, & 5 \end{cases}$

REMARK (Trick 7).—This is strong illustration of a case for departing from rule. Y can count two more trumps and at least three more spades in A's hand (*see* A's lead and the card he afterwards plays, Tricks 3 and 6, and refer to Appendix A). It is clear that A can have at most two hearts; consequently, if Y leads his tierce major in hearts, he must lose the game, as the opponents have two by honours. But, if Y can give his partner the lead, and Z has the entire command of clubs, or the winning club, and A makes the mistake of trumping it, Y Z may make every trick, and win the game.

Y would be right to play as he does even if A had led from only four spades, but the hand is given as it was played.

TRICKS 9 to 13.—Z continues to lead clubs (*see* his hand below), and, whether A passes or trumps,

Y Z score four by cards.

THE HANDS.

(Y's hand is given above.)

A's Hand.	B's Hand.	Z's Hand.
Knv, 9, 5, 3, 2 ♠	Kg, Qn, 10, 8, 7 ♠	Ace, 6 . . . ♠
8, 7 . . . . ♥	Knv, 6, 5 . . ♥	9, 4, 3 . . . ♥
Kg . . . ♣	9, 4, 3 . . . ♣	A, Q, Kv, 10, 6, 5, 2 ♣
Ace, Qn, 9, 6, 4 ♦	Knv, 2 . . . ♦	5 . . . . . ♦

HAND XXV.

See Leading from weakest suit, p. 119.

Z's HAND.

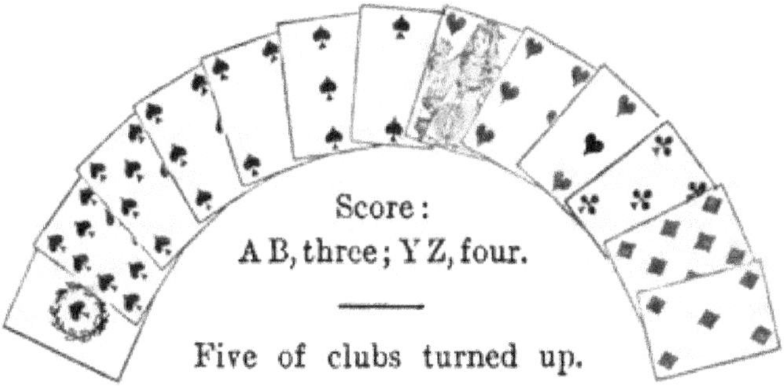

Score:
A B, three; Y Z, four.

———

Five of clubs turned up.

THE PLAY.

TRICK 1.

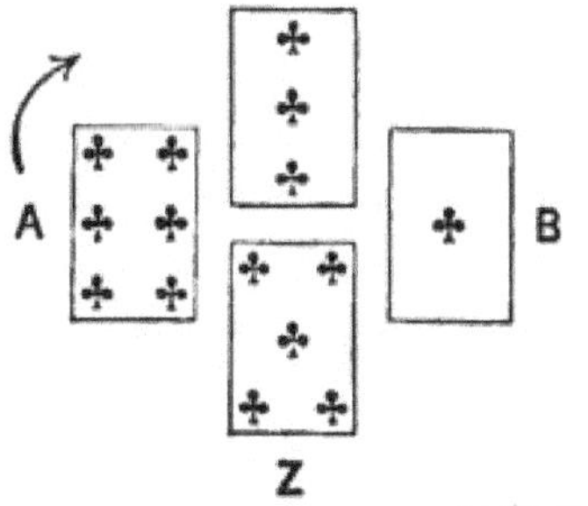

Y

A

B

Z

TRICKS { A B, 1
Y Z, 0

TRICK 2.

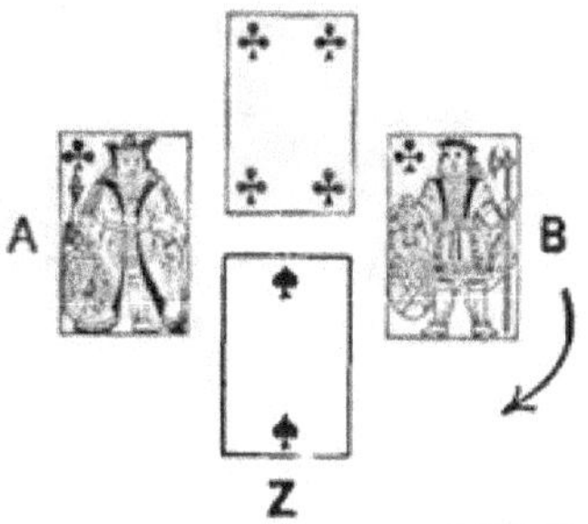

Y

A

B

Z

TRICKS { A B, 2
Y Z, 0

TRICK 3. Y

A B

Z

TRICKS $\begin{cases} \text{A B, 2} \\ \text{Y Z, 1} \end{cases}$

TRICK 4. Y

A B

Z

TRICKS $\begin{cases} \text{A B, 2} \\ \text{Y Z, 2} \end{cases}$

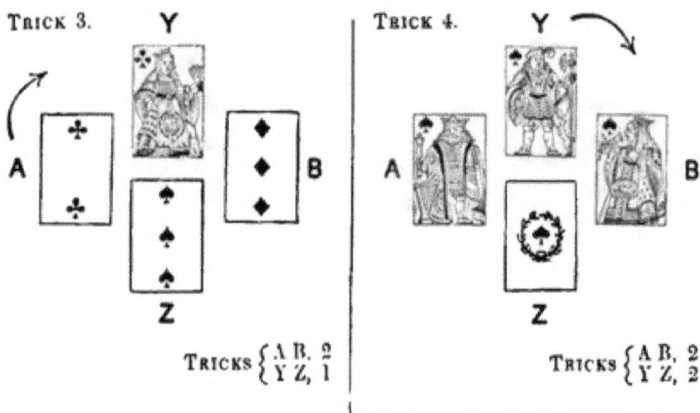

REMARK (Trick 3).—By the first discard Z shows his strong suit to be spades. In an ordinary hand Z might afterwards throw a diamond. But here Y must be strong in diamonds in order to save the game, and it is important to Z to keep the power of leading that suit more than once.

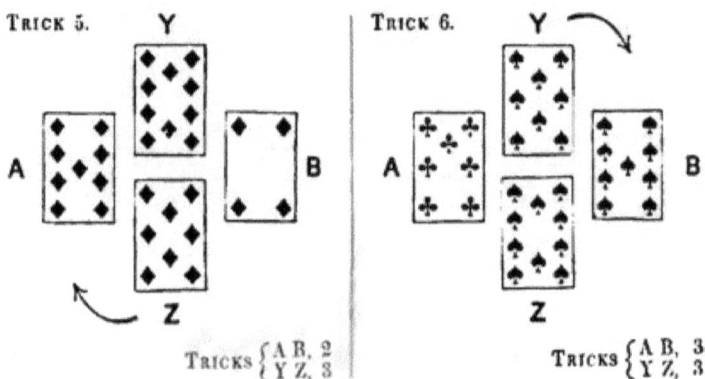

TRICK 5. Y

A B

Z

TRICKS $\begin{cases} \text{A B, 2} \\ \text{Y Z, 3} \end{cases}$

TRICK 6. Y

A B

Z

TRICKS $\begin{cases} \text{A B, 3} \\ \text{Y Z, 3} \end{cases}$

TRICK 7.

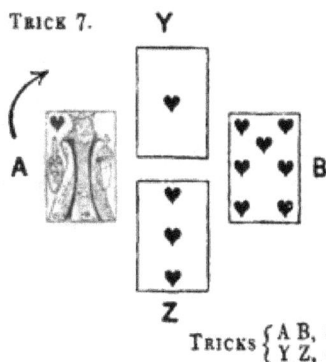

TRICKS { A B, 3
        { Y Z, 4

TRICK 8.

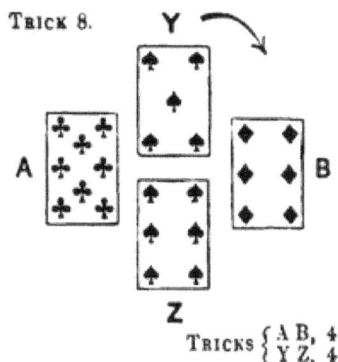

TRICKS { A B, 4
        { Y Z, 4

TRICK 9.

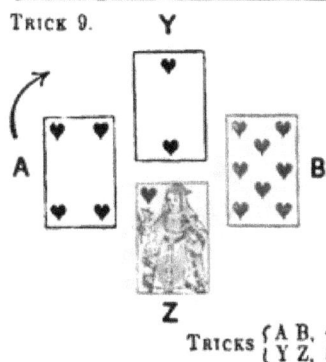

TRICKS { A B, 4
        { Y Z, 5

TRICK 10.

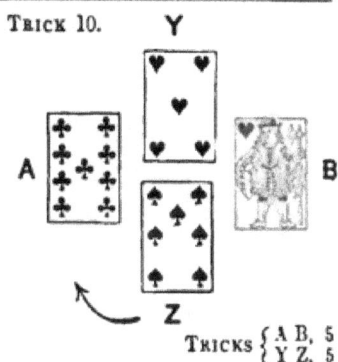

TRICKS { A B, 5
        { Y Z, 5

TRICKS 11 to 13.—A, with the lead, remains with the last trump and king, knave of diamonds. He (Trick 11) leads the trump; but, whatever he plays,

YZ win the odd trick.

THE HANDS.

(Z's hand is given above.)

A's HAND.	Y's HAND.	B's HAND.
Kg . . . . ♠	Knv, 8, 5 . . ♠	Qn, 9 . . . ♠
Kg, 4 . . . ♥	Ace, 5, 2 . . ♥	Knv, 10, 9, 8, 7 ♥
Kg,10.9.8,7,6.2 ♣	Qn, 4, 3 . . ♣	Ace, Knv . . ♣
Kg, Knv, 9 . ♦	Ace, Qn, 10, 2 . ♦	7, 6, 4, 3 . . ♦

A plays well throughout, but he cannot prevent the result. His lead of the trump at Trick 3 to show his strength, and to tell his partner to make one trick certain if he has the chance, is unlucky, as it puts the adversaries on the only tack for saving the game.

HAND XXVI.

See Treating long suits like short ones, pp. 120-122.

B's HAND.

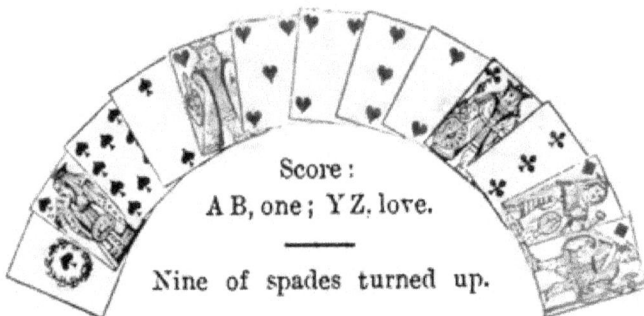

Score :
A B, one ; Y Z, love.

Nine of spades turned up.

THE PLAY.

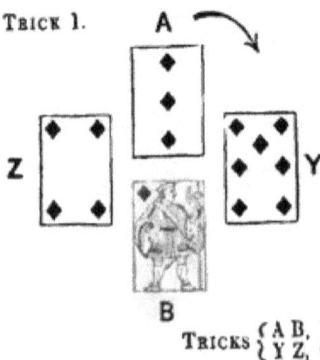

TRICK 1.

TRICKS { A B, 1 / Y Z, 0

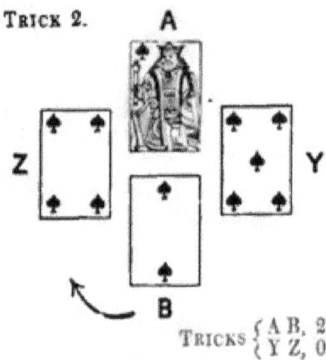

TRICK 2.

TRICKS { A B, 2 / Y Z, 0

TRICK 3.

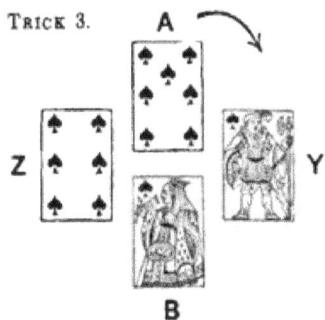

TRICKS { A B, 3
        { Y Z, 0

TRICK 4.

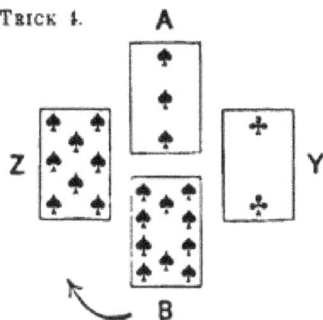

TRICKS { A B, 4
        { Y Z, 0

TRICK 5.

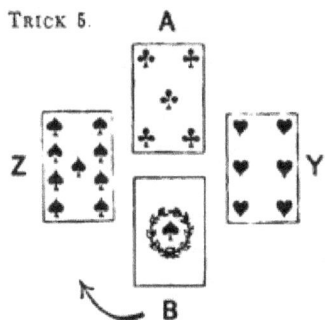

TRICKS { A B, 5
        { Y Z, 0

TRICK 6.

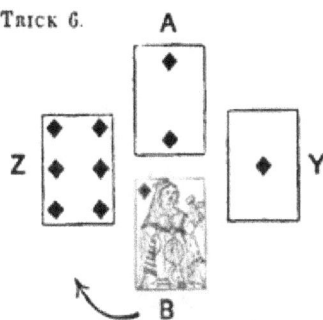

TRICKS { A B, 5
        { Y Z, 1

TRICK 7.

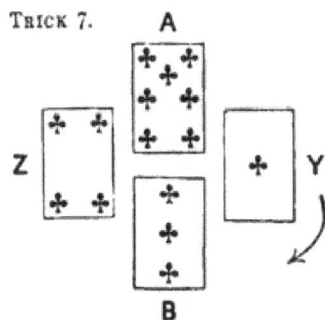

TRICKS { A B, 5
        { Y Z, 2

TRICK 8.

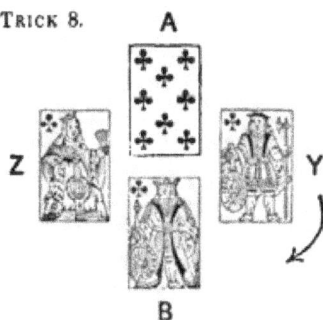

TRICKS { A B, 6
        { Y Z, 2

TRICK 9.

Z   A   Y

B

TRICKS $\begin{cases} A\ B,\ 6 \\ Y\ Z,\ 3 \end{cases}$.

TRICK 10.

Z   A   Y

B

TRICKS $\begin{cases} A\ B,\ 6 \\ Y\ Z,\ 4 \end{cases}$

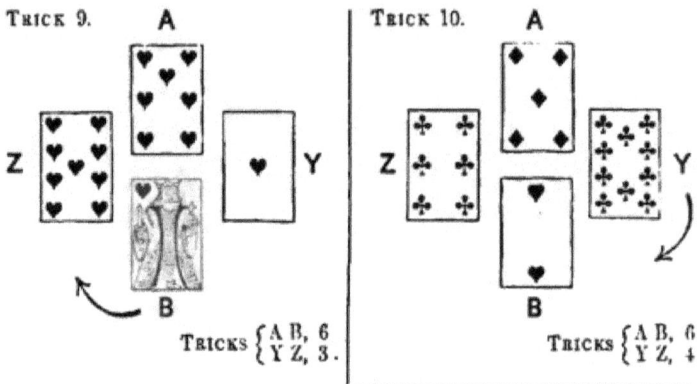

REMARK (Trick 9).—Deschapelles' Coup. B can count A's hand, three diamonds and two hearts, for the ten, nine of clubs are clearly with Y (*see* Tricks 7 and 8). B, therefore, leads the king of hearts (*see* p. 121). If he makes the usual lead of a small heart, he makes a trick less as the cards happen to lie.

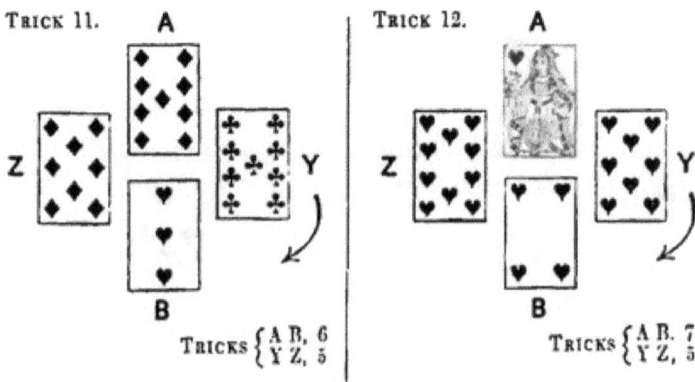

TRICK 11.

Z   A   Y

B

TRICKS $\begin{cases} A\ B,\ 6 \\ Y\ Z,\ 5 \end{cases}$

TRICK 12.

Z   A   Y

B

TRICKS $\begin{cases} A\ B,\ 7 \\ Y\ Z,\ 5 \end{cases}$

TRICK 13.—A makes the king of diamonds; and

A B score two by cards and two by honours.

If Y, at Trick 4, discards a heart, he saves the game. Nevertheless, his proper discard is the club (*see* pp. 93, 94).

THE HANDS.

(B's hand is given above.)

A's HAND.	Y's HAND.	Z's HAND.
Kg, 7, 3 . . ♠	Knv, 5 . . . ♠	9, 8, 6, 4 . . ♠
Qn, 7 . . . ♥	Ace, 8, 6 . . ♥	Knv, 10, 9. . ♥
8, 7, 5 . . . ♣	Ace, Kv, 10,9,2 ♣	Qn, 6, 4. . . ♣
Kg, 9, 5, 3, 2 . ♦	Ace, 10, 7. . ♦	8, 6, 4 . . . ♦

HAND XXVII.

See Refusing to win the second round of a suit, p. 122.

Z's HAND.

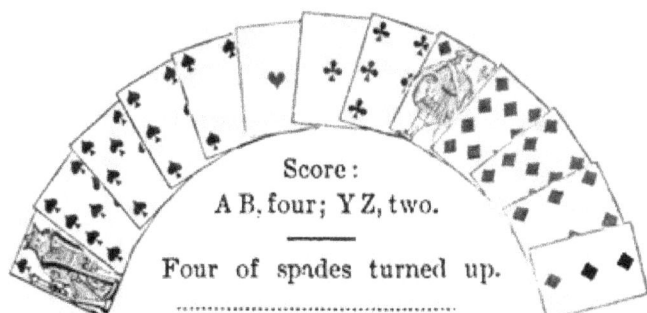

Score :
A B, four; Y Z, two.

Four of spades turned up.

THE PLAY.

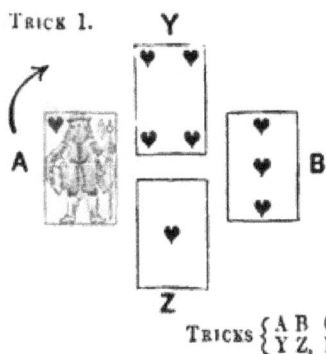

TRICK 1.

TRICKS { A B, 0 ; Y Z, 1

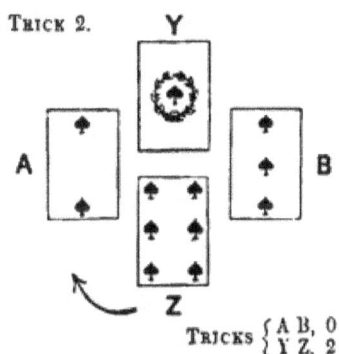

TRICK 2.

TRICKS { A B, 0 ; Y Z, 2

TRICK 3.

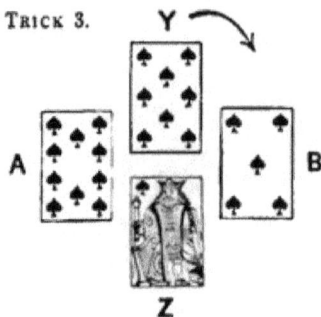

TRICKS { A B, 0
        { Y Z, 3

TRICK 4.

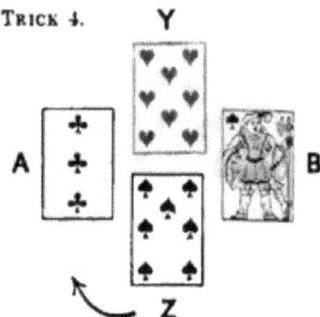

TRICKS { A B, 1
        { Y Z, 3

TRICK 5.

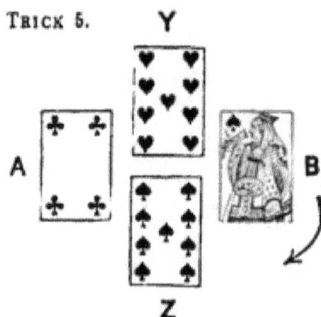

TRICKS { A B, 2
        { Y Z, 3

TRICK 6.

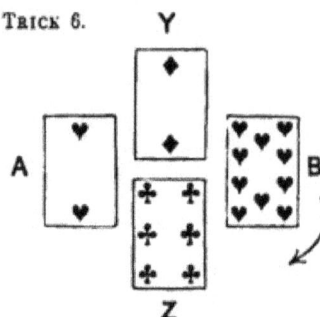

TRICKS { A B, 3
        { Y Z, 3

TRICK 7.

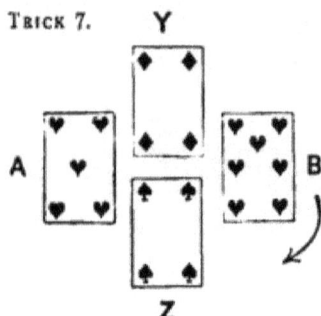

TRICKS { A B, 3
        { Y Z, 4

TRICK 8.

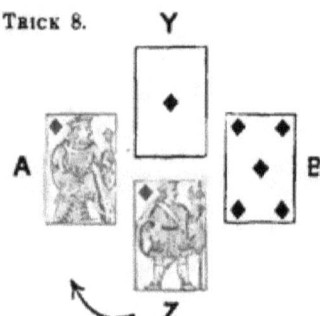

TRICKS { A B, 3
        { Y Z, 5

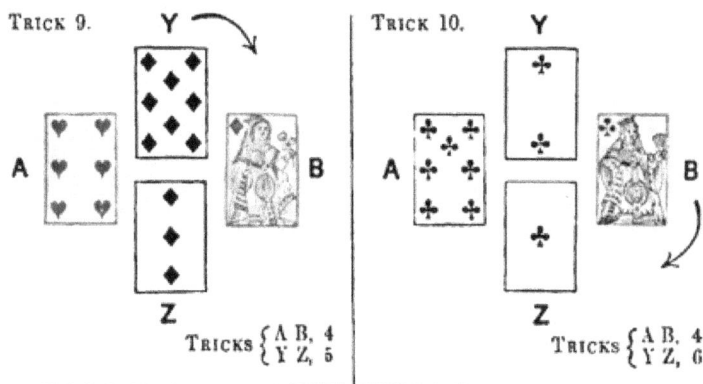

TRICK 9.

TRICKS { A B, 4
        { Y Z, 5

TRICK 10.

TRICKS { A B, 4
        { Y Z, 6

TRICKS 10 to 13.—Z brings in the diamonds; and

Y Z win three by cards.

THE HANDS.

(Z's hand is given above.)

A's HAND.	Y's HAND.	B's HAND.
10, 2 . . . ♠	Ace, 8 . . . ♠	Qn, Knv, 5, 3 . ♠
Kg, Q, Kv, 6, 5, 2 ♥	9, 8, 4 . . . ♥	10, 7, 3 . . . ♥
Kg, 7, 4, 3 . . ♣	10, 9, 8, 2 . . ♣	Qn, Knv, 5 . ♣
Kg . . . . ♦	Ace, 8, 4, 2 . ♦	Qn, 7, 5 . . ♦

At Trick 4, A having already shown his suit does not
discard from it, as there is still a possibility of bringing
it in (*see* pp. 93, 94), and his king of clubs is sufficiently
protected even after the discard.

If Z parts with the last trump at Trick 6, and leads
diamonds, A. on the second round of diamonds, will
unguard his king of clubs (knowing his partner to have
a heart to lead him—*see* fall of the heart suit, Tricks
1, 4, and 5), will bring in all the hearts, and win the
odd trick.

HAND XXVIII.

See Refusing to win the second round of a suit,
p. 122.

B's HAND.

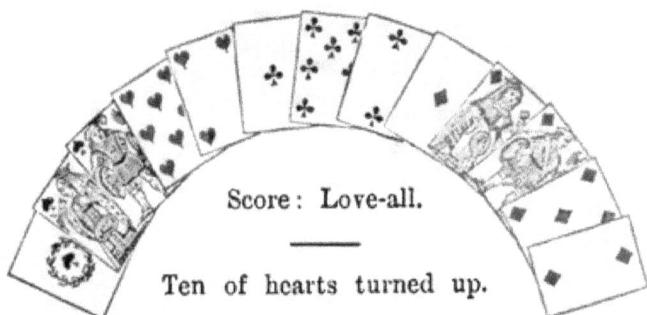

Score : Love-all.

———

Ten of hearts turned up.

....

THE PLAY.

TRICK 1.

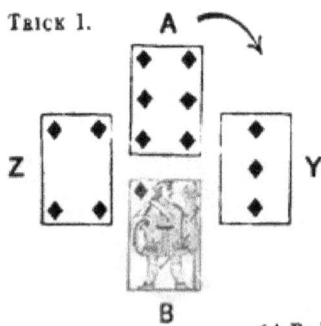

TRICKS $\begin{cases} A B, 1 \\ Y Z, 0 \end{cases}$

TRICK 2.

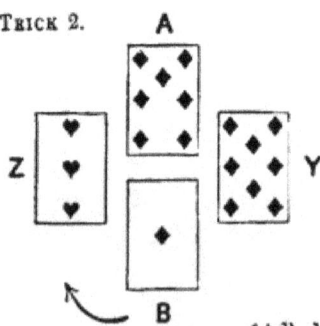

TRICKS $\begin{cases} A B, 1 \\ Y Z, 1 \end{cases}$

TRICK 3.

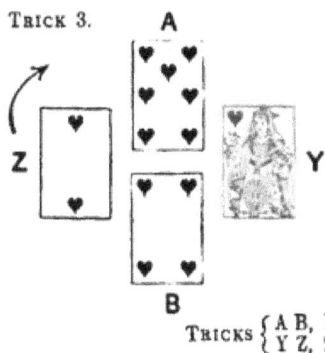

TRICKS $\begin{cases} A\,B, & 1 \\ Y\,Z, & 2 \end{cases}$

TRICK 4.

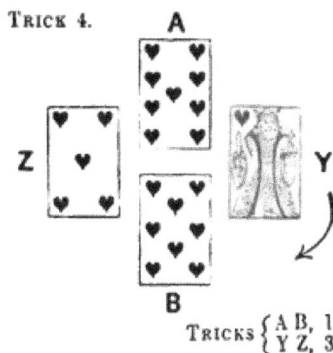

TRICKS $\begin{cases} A\,B, & 1 \\ Y\,Z, & 3 \end{cases}$

TRICK 5.

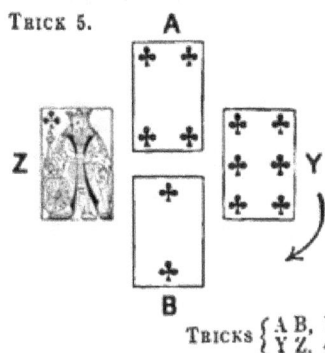

TRICKS $\begin{cases} A\,B, & 1 \\ Y\,Z, & 4 \end{cases}$

TRICK 6.

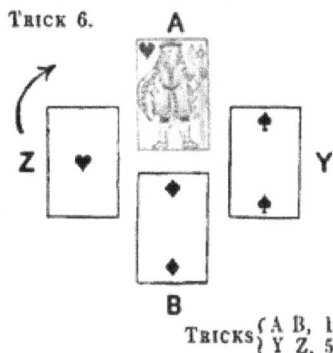

TRICKS $\begin{cases} A\,B, & 1 \\ Y\,Z, & 5 \end{cases}$

REMARK (Trick 6).—B has next to no chance of bringing in the diamonds. He therefore plays to protect his short suits (*see* pp. 93, 94).

TRICK 7.

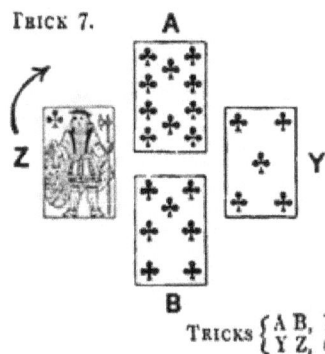

TRICKS $\begin{cases} A\,B, & 1 \\ Y\,Z, & 6 \end{cases}$

TRICK 8.

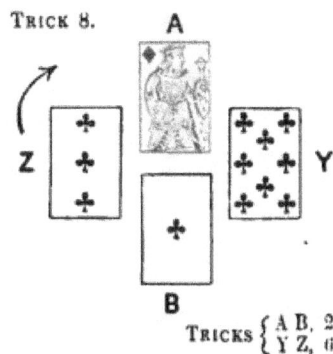

TRICKS $\begin{cases} A\,B, & 2 \\ Y\,Z, & 6 \end{cases}$

REMARK (Trick 7).—B refuses to win this trick. The three of clubs is clearly in Z's hand (*see* fall of the club suit, Tricks 5 and 7), and the two long trumps. The remaining clubs are evidently in Y's hand. If, therefore, B parts with the ace of clubs while Z has a club to lead, A B lose the game, unless A has the king of spades; and if A has that card, B loses nothing by passing this trick, as Z, having only one more club, must hold three spades.

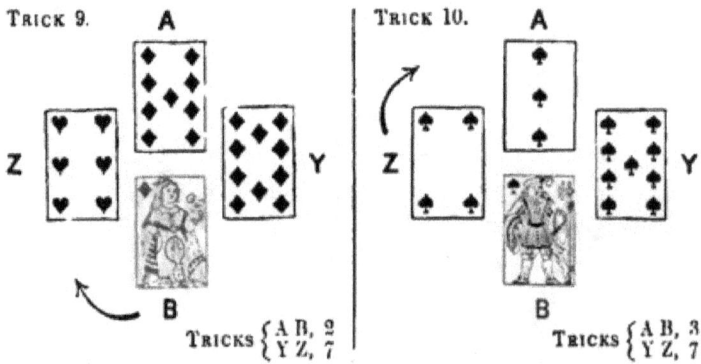

TRICK 9.

A

Z

Y

B

TRICKS { A B, 2
        { Y Z, 7

TRICK 10.

A

Z

Y

B

TRICKS { A B, 3
        { Y Z, 7

TRICKS 11 to 13.—B (Trick 11) leads the last diamond. and forces Z. Z (Trick 12) has only spades to lead; B makes ace, queen of spades; and

A B score two by cards and two by honours.

THE HANDS.

(B's hand is given above.)

A's HAND.		Y's HAND.		Z's HAND.	
10, 8, 7, 3 . . ♠		9, 5, 2 . . . ♠		Kg, 6, 4 . . ♠	
Knv, 9, 7 . . ♥		Kg, Qn . . . ♥		Ace, 10, 6, 5, 3, 2 ♥	
10, 4 . . . . ♣		Qn, 9, 8, 6, 5 . ♣		Kg, Knv, 3 . ♣	
Kg, 9, 7, 6 . . ♦		10, 8, 3 . . . ♦		4 . . . . . ♦	

HAND XXIX.

See Declining to draw the losing trump,
pp. 123, 124.

A's HAND.

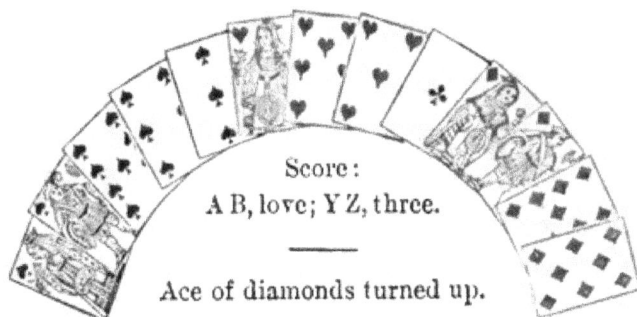

Score:
A B, love; Y Z, three.

———

Ace of diamonds turned up.

THE PLAY.

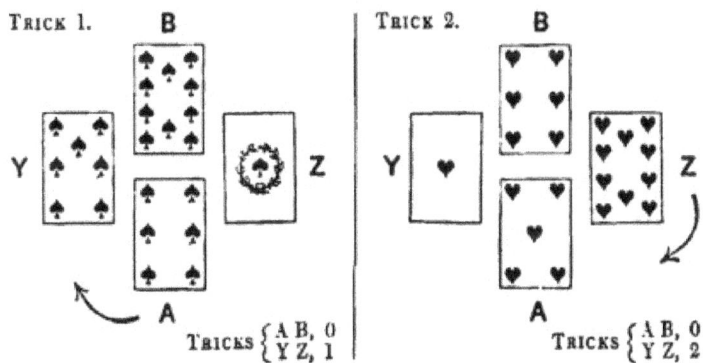

TRICK 1.

TRICK 2.

TRICKS { A B, 0
{ Y Z, 1

TRICKS { A B, 0
{ Y Z, 2

TRICK 3.

B

Y   Z

A

TRICKS $\left\{ \begin{array}{l} \text{A B, 0} \\ \text{Y Z, 3} \end{array} \right.$

TRICK 4.

B

Y   Z

A

TRICKS $\left\{ \begin{array}{l} \text{A B, 0} \\ \text{Y Z, 4} \end{array} \right.$

TRICK 5.

B

Y   Z

A

TRICKS $\left\{ \begin{array}{l} \text{A B, 1} \\ \text{Y Z, 4} \end{array} \right.$

TRICK 6.

B

Y   Z

A

TRICKS $\left\{ \begin{array}{l} \text{A B, 2} \\ \text{Y Z, 4} \end{array} \right.$

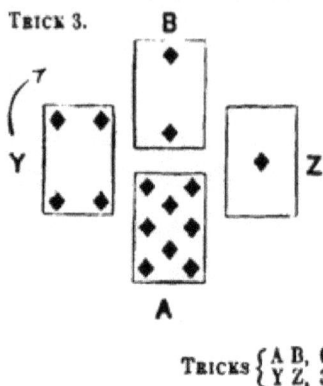

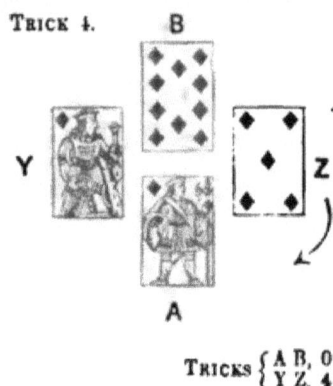

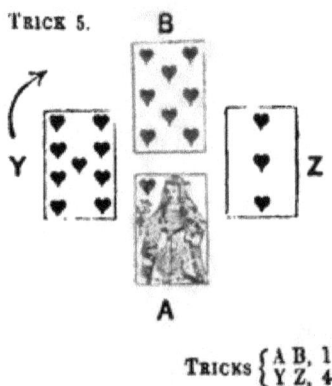

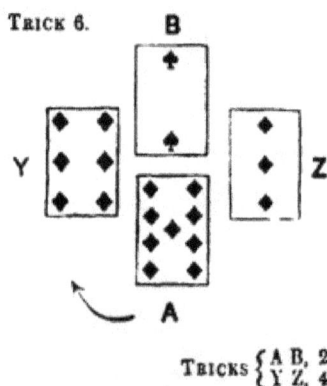

REMARK.—It is evident that Z's lead was from king, knave, ten, &c., and that B has no more hearts. Y returning the nine, and the two not falling, must have the two single, and the other hearts are with Z.

REMARK.—The case now arises contemplated at p.124. A has the best trump and the lead; Y the losing trump. Y also has one card of his partner's established suit (*see* Remark, Trick 5). A therefore (Trick 7) does not draw the trump.

Q

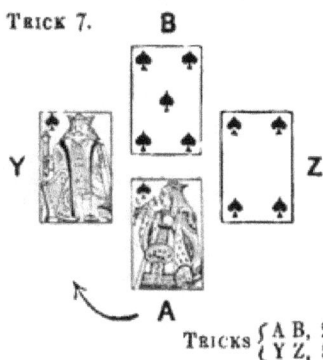

TRICK 7.

TRICKS $\begin{cases} \text{A B, 2} \\ \text{Y Z, 5} \end{cases}$

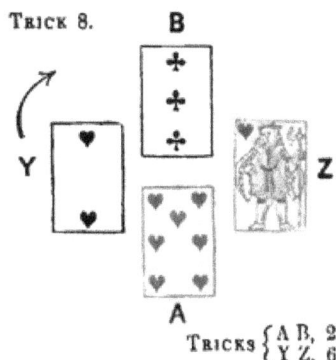

TRICK 8.

TRICKS $\begin{cases} \text{A B, 2} \\ \text{Y Z, 6} \end{cases}$

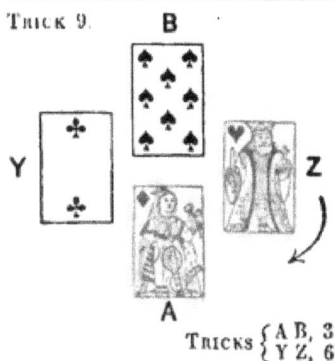

TRICK 9.

TRICKS $\begin{cases} \text{A B, 3} \\ \text{Y Z, 6} \end{cases}$

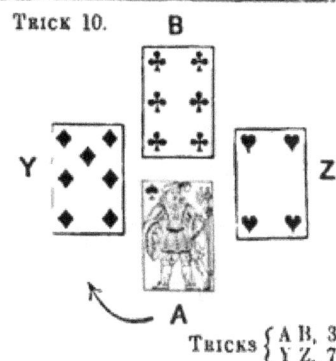

TRICK 10.

TRICKS $\begin{cases} \text{A B, 3} \\ \text{Y Z, 7} \end{cases}$

TRICKS 11 to 13.—Y has nothing but clubs to lead. A wins the three tricks; and

YZ win the odd trick.

If, at Trick 7, A draws the trump, Y Z win two by cards.

THE HANDS.

(A's hand is given above.)

Y's HAND.	B's HAND.	Z's HAND.
Kg, 7 . . . ♠	10, 8, 5, 2 . . ♠	Ace, 4 . . . ♠
Ace, 9, 2 . . ♥	8, 6 . . . . ♥	Kg, Kv, 10, 4, 3 ♥
Kg, Qn, 4, 2 . ♣	Knv, 9, 8, 6, 3 ♣	10, 7, 5 . . . ♣
Kg, 7, 6, 4 . . ♦	10, 2 . . . . ♦	Ace, 5, 3 . . . ♦

HAND XXX.

See Refusing to overtrump, pp. 125, 126.

B's HAND.

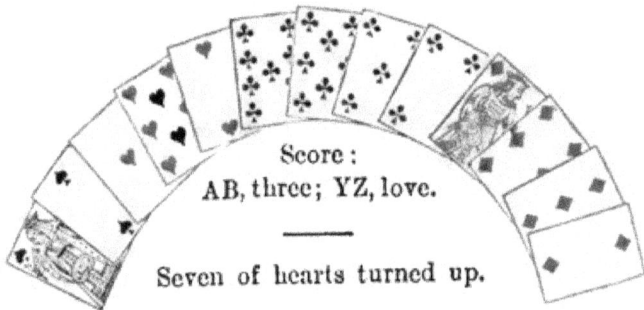

Score :
AB, three; YZ, love.

———

Seven of hearts turned up.

THE PLAY.

TRICK 1.

TRICK 2.

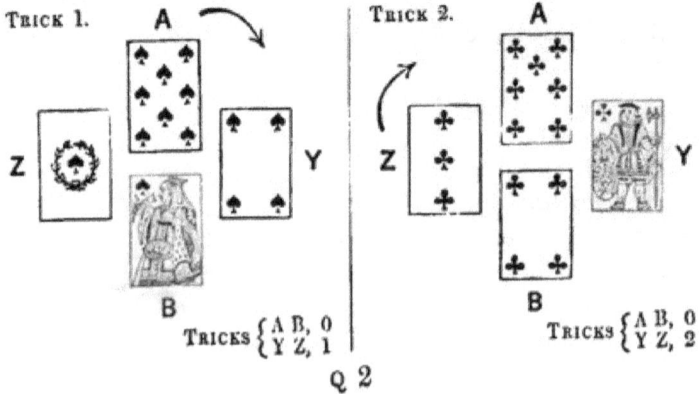

TRICKS { A B, 0
{ Y Z, 1

TRICKS { A B, 0
{ Y Z, 2

Q 2

TRICK 3.

A

Z   Y

B

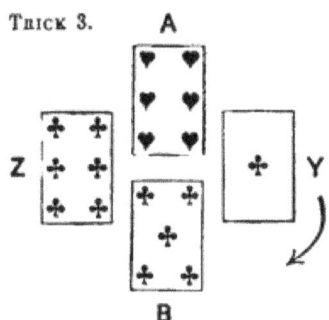

TRICKS $\begin{cases} A\ B, & 1 \\ Y\ Z, & 2 \end{cases}$

TRICK 4.

A

Z   Y

B

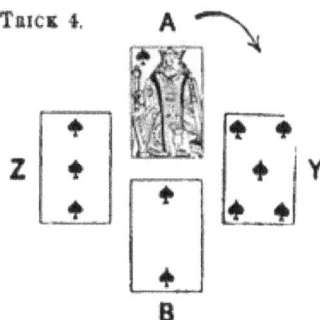

TRICKS $\begin{cases} A\ B, & 2 \\ Y\ Z, & 2 \end{cases}$

TRICK 5.

A

Z   Y

B

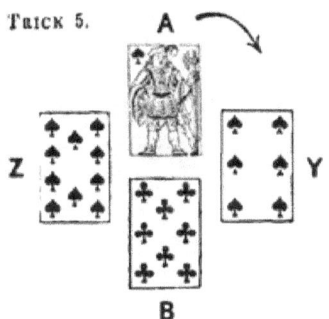

TRICKS $\begin{cases} A\ B, & 3 \\ Y\ Z, & 2 \end{cases}$

TRICK 6.

A

Z   Y

B

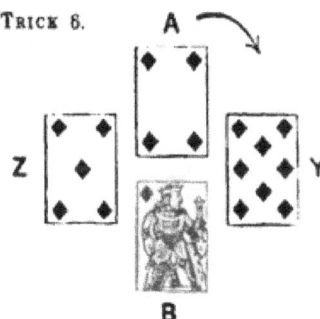

TRICKS $\begin{cases} A\ B, & 4 \\ Y\ Z, & 2 \end{cases}$

TRICK 7.

A

Z   Y

B

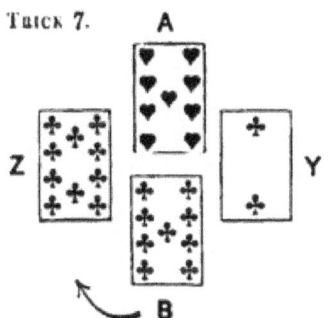

TRICKS $\begin{cases} A\ B, & 5 \\ Y\ Z, & 2 \end{cases}$

TRICK 8.

A

Z   Y

B

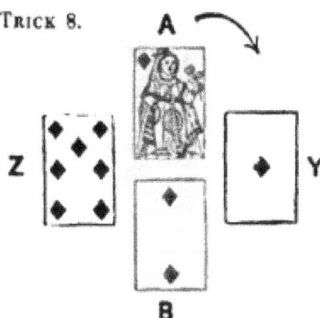

TRICKS $\begin{cases} A\ B, & 5 \\ Y\ Z, & 3 \end{cases}$

TRICK 9.

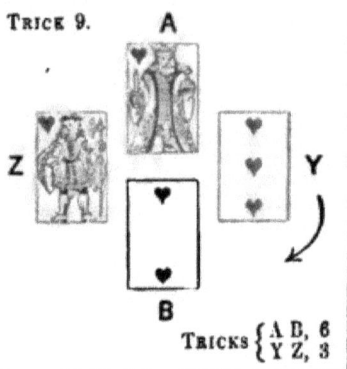

TRICK 10.

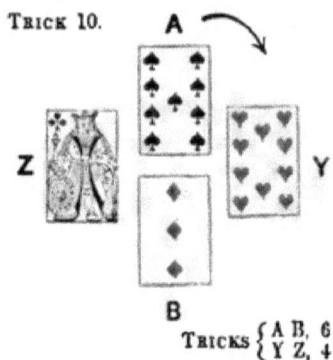

TRICKS $\{$ A B, 6 / Y Z, 3

TRICKS $\{$ A B, 6 / Y Z, 4

REMARK (Trick 10).—A should probably have played the winning diamond here (*see* his hand below). However, he luckily leads the spade.

B does not overtrump for this reason: he can count A's hand to consist of the other spade and knave and another diamond (as, if A had led from queen, knave, and only one small diamond, he would have commenced with the queen instead of the small one—*see* Trick 6), A, therefore, having no more trumps, B cannot possibly win two more tricks unless the queen of hearts is to his right.

TRICK 11.

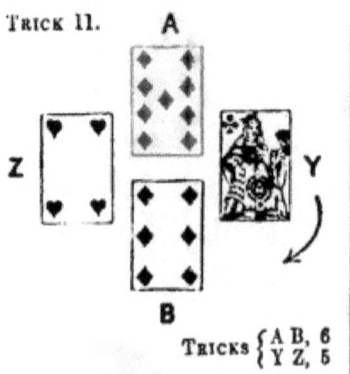

TRICKS 12 and 13.—Z leads a trump (he has only trumps in hand), and B makes ace and eight.

TRICKS $\{$ A B, 6 / Y Z, 5

A B win two by cards.

THE HANDS.

(B's hand is given above.)

A's Hand.	Y's Hand.	Z's Hand.
Kg, Knv, 9, 8, 7 ♠	6, 5, 4 . . . ♠	Ace, 10, 3 . . ♠
Kg, 9, 6 . . ♥	Qn, 10, 3 . . ♥	Knv, 7, 5, 4 . ♥
7 . . . . . ♣	Ace, Qn, Knv, 2 ♣	Kg, 10, 6, 3 . ♣
Qn, Knv, 9, 4 ♦	Ace, 10, 8 . . ♦	7, 5 . . . . . ♦

HAND XXXI.

See Throwing high cards to place the lead, pp. 126-130.

A's Hand.

Score: Love-all.

———

Five of clubs turned up.

THE PLAY.

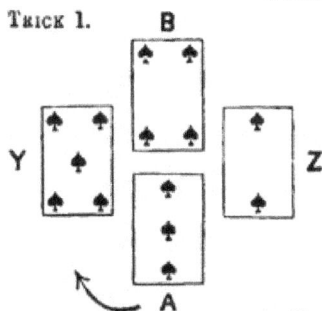

TRICK 1.

TRICKS { A B, 0 / Y Z, 1

REMARK.—B has no more spades.

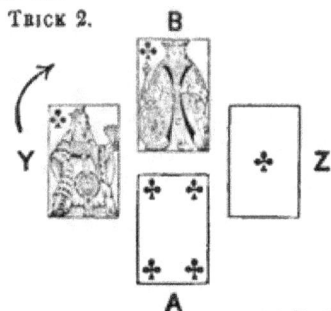

TRICK 2.

TRICKS { A B, 0 / Y Z, 2

TRICK 3.

B

Y

Z

A

TRICKS $\begin{cases} A B, & 0 \\ Y Z, & 3 \end{cases}$

TRICK 4.

B

Y

Z

A

TRICKS $\begin{cases} A B, & 0 \\ Y Z, & 4 \end{cases}$

TRICK 5.

B

Y

Z

A

TRICKS $\begin{cases} A B, & 1 \\ Y Z, & 4 \end{cases}$

TRICK 6.

B

Y

Z

A

TRICKS $\begin{cases} A B, & 2 \\ Y Z, & 4 \end{cases}$

TRICK 7.

B

Y

Z

A

TRICKS $\begin{cases} A B, & 2 \\ Y Z, & 5 \end{cases}$

TRICK 8.

B

Y

Z

A

TRICKS $\begin{cases} A B, & 2 \\ Y Z, & 6 \end{cases}$

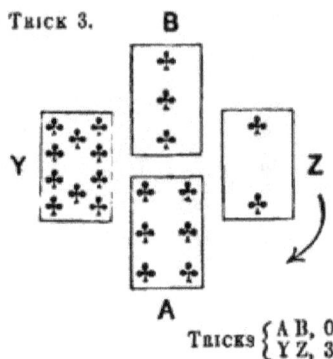

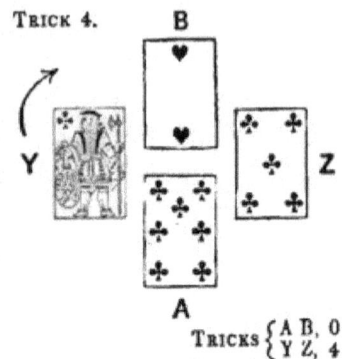

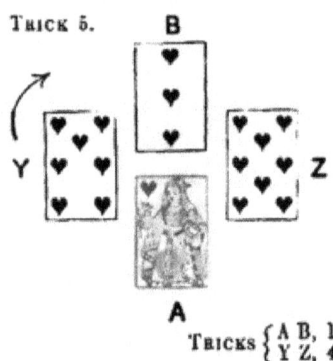

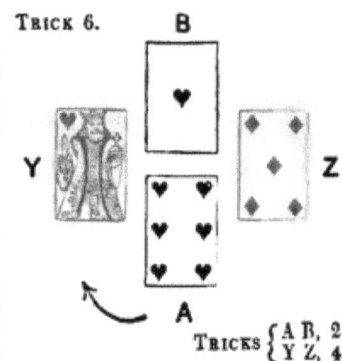

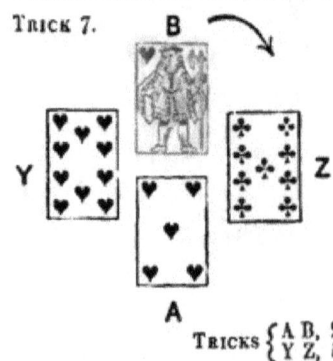

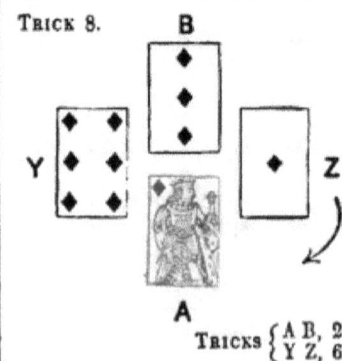

REMARK (Trick 8).—Well played by A. He sees that if
he obtains the lead on the second round of diamonds

he must continue the spade suit, a course demonstrably
fatal to him, unless his partner has the queen of diamonds
together with the long hearts (*see* fall of hearts, Trick 7).
By throwing the king to the ace A avoids the lead, and
saves the game if his partner has either queen or knave of
diamonds (as may be seen by placing the cards), unless
the adversaries continue the spade suit, when the game
cannot be saved by any course of play.   This clever *coup*
occurred in actual play.

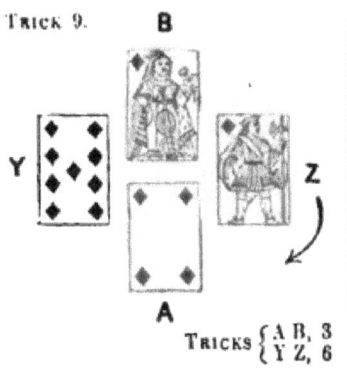

TRICK 9.

TRICKS 10 to 13.—B
brings in the hearts, winning two more tricks; A
makes his trump; and

TRICKS { A B, 3
         { Y Z, 6

Y Z score the odd trick and two by honours.

THE HANDS.

(A's hand is given above.)

Y's HAND.	B's HAND.	Z's HAND.
Kg, 10, 8, 6, 5 ♠	4 . . . . . ♠	Ace, Qn, 2 . . ♠
Kg, 10, 7 . . ♥	Ace,Kv,9,4,3,2 ♥	8 . . . . . ♥
Qn, Knv, 10 . ♣	Kg, 3 . . . ♣	Ace, 9, 5, 2 . ♣
9, 6 . . . . ♦	Qn, 8, 3, 2 . . ♦	Ace, Kv, 10,7,5 ♦

HAND XXXII.

See Throwing high cards to place the lead, pp. 126-130.

A's HAND.

Score: Love-all.

———

Ace of clubs turned up.

THE PLAY.

TRICK 1.

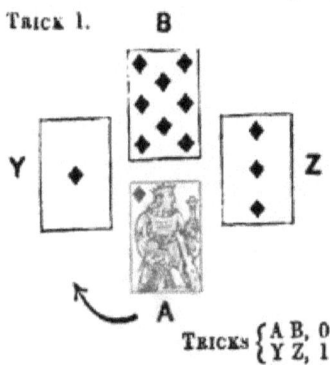

TRICKS { A B, 0
Y Z, 1

TRICK 2.

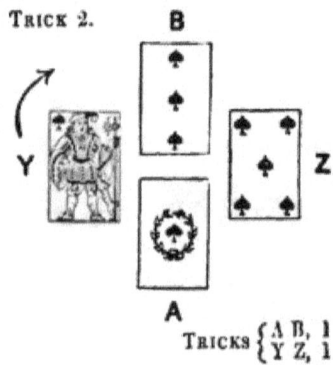

TRICKS { A B, 1
Y Z, 1

234   WHIST.

TRICK 3. B

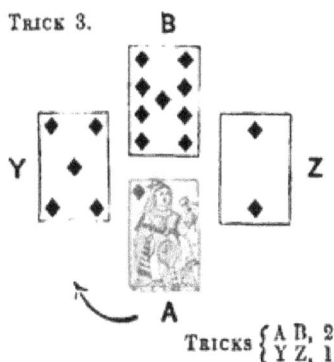

Y   Z

A

TRICKS { A B, 2
         Y Z, 1

TRICK 4. B

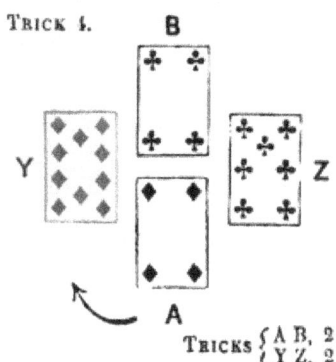

Y   Z

A

TRICKS { A B, 2
         Y Z, 2

REMARK.—Y has the knave
of diamonds.

TRICK 5. B

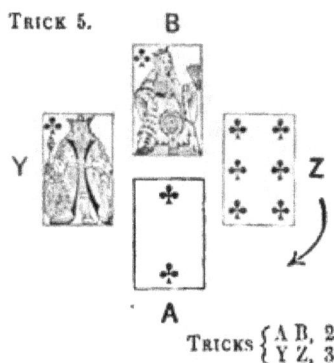

Y   Z

A

TRICKS { A B, 2
         Y Z, 3

TRICK 6. B

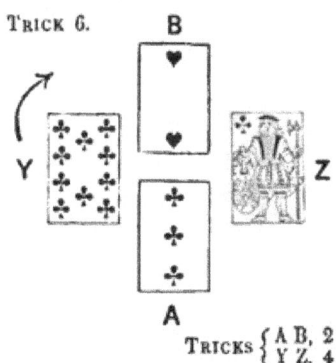

Y   Z

A

TRICKS { A B, 2
         Y Z, 4

TRICK 7. B

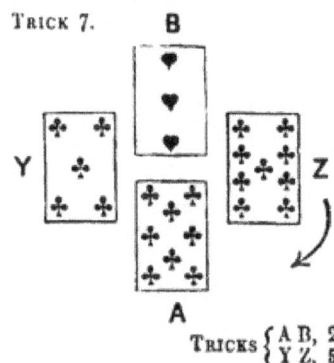

Y   Z

A

TRICKS { A B, 2
         Y Z, 5

TRICK 8. B

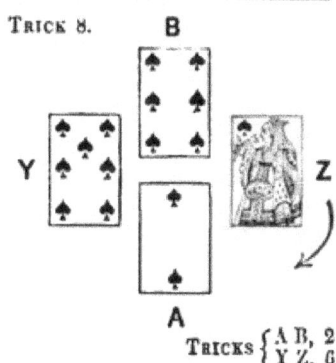

Y   Z

A

TRICKS { A B, 2
         Y Z, 6

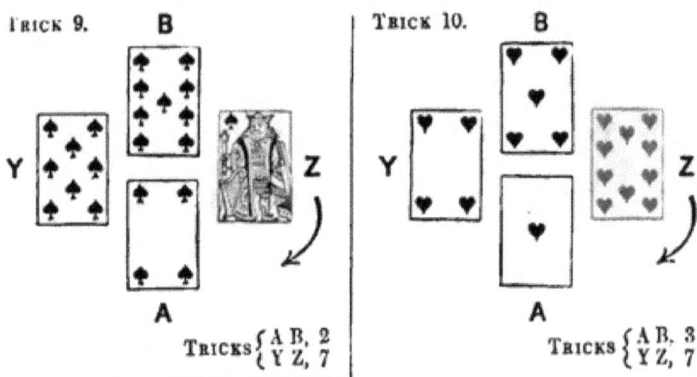

TRICK 9. B
Y · · · Z
A
TRICKS { A B, 2 / Y Z, 7

TRICK 10. B
Y · · · Z
A
TRICKS { A B, 3 / Y Z, 7

REMARK (Trick 10).—A plays very well in putting on the ace. He wants two more tricks besides his ace of hearts to save the game. The last trump and best diamond are against him. It is clear, therefore, if A has the lead after the second round of hearts (when he must lead a diamond), he loses the game. It is also clear that unless B has king, knave, and a small heart, the game is gone.

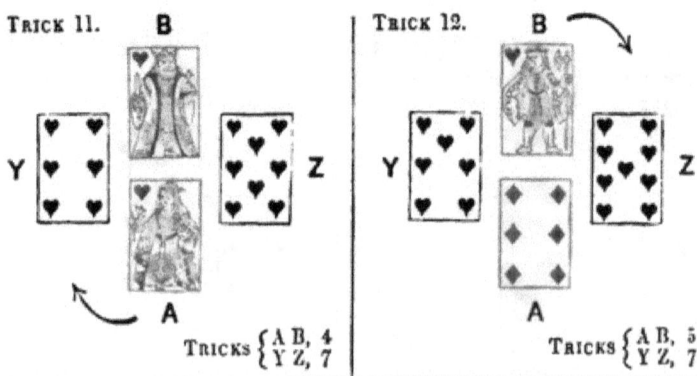

TRICK 11. B
Y · · · Z
A
TRICKS { A B, 4 / Y Z, 7

TRICK 12. B
Y · · · Z
A
TRICKS { A B, 5 / Y Z, 7

YZ score two by cards and two by honours.

THE HANDS.

(A's hand is given above.)

Y's Hand.	B's Hand.	Z's Hand.
Knv, 8, 7 . . ♠	10, 9, 6, 3 . . ♠	Kg, Qn, 5 . . ♠
7, 6, 4 . . . ♥	Kg, Knv, 5, 3, 2 ♥	10, 9, 8 . . . ♥
Kg, 10, 5 . . ♣	Qn, 4 . . . . ♣	Ace, Knv, 9, 7, 6 ♣
Ace, Knv, 10, 5 ♦	9, 8 . . . . ♦	3, 2 . . . . . ♦

At **Trick 2, Y** is in difficulties. His strong suit has been led by his right-hand adversary. Under these circumstances, his best game (bad as it is) is to lead from his strongest weak suit.

At **Trick 6, Y** is quite right to continue the trump, though the queen fell the previous round. It is a common ruse to play a false card in trumps, in hopes of stopping the lead. Z wins his partner's ten in order to draw all the trumps. It is very bad play, for if Z passes the ten, and Y leads the knave of diamonds, the game is certain. This is an example of the very common error of winning partner's trick. It should seldom be done, and only if a positive advantage can be demonstrated from doing it.

At **Trick 11,** the advantage of winning partner's trick—when judiciously done—is shown. B, seeing A's anxiety to get rid of the lead, rightly conjectures that A has two more diamonds. He therefore takes the only course to save the game, by winning his partner's queen.

HAND XXXIII.

(*See* Appendix A, pp. 257-266.)

Y's HAND.

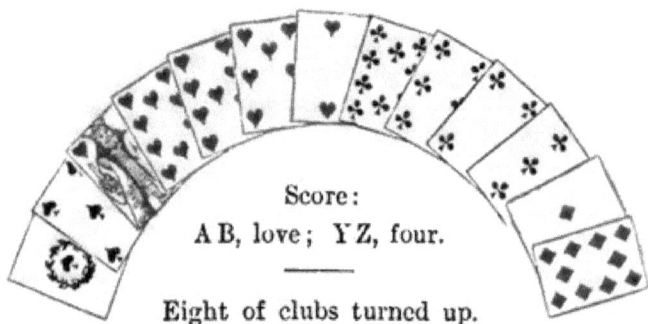

Score:
A B, love; Y Z, four.

———

Eight of clubs turned up.

....

THE PLAY

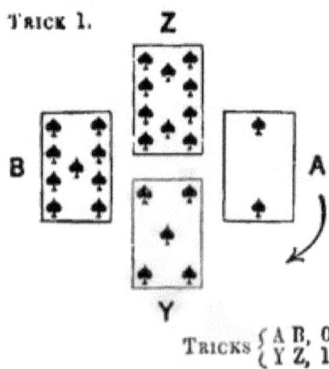

TRICK 1.   Z

B   A

Y

TRICKS { A B, 0
       { Y Z, 1

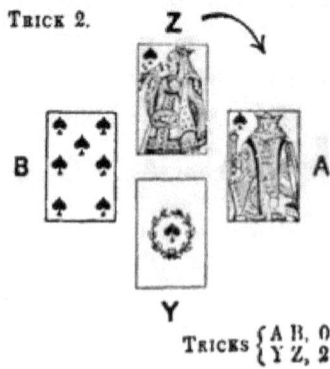

TRICK 2.   Z

B   A

Y

TRICKS { A B, 0
       { Y Z, 2

TRICK 3.

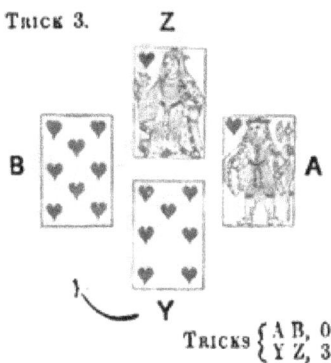

TRICKS $\begin{cases} A B, 0 \\ Y Z, 3 \end{cases}$

REMARK.—*See* Appendix
A, pp. 257-266.

TRICK 4.

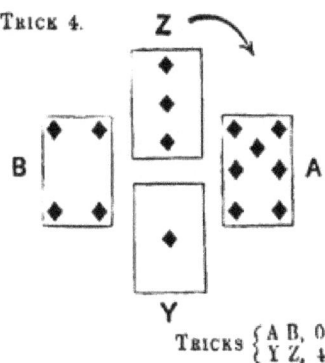

TRICKS $\begin{cases} A B, 0 \\ Y Z, 4 \end{cases}$

TRICK 5.

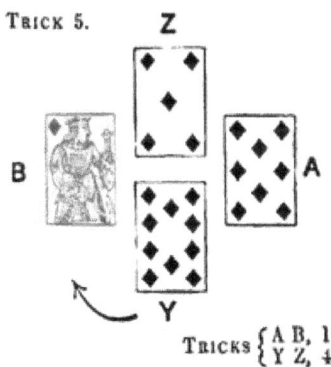

TRICKS $\begin{cases} A B, 1 \\ Y Z, 4 \end{cases}$

TRICK 6.

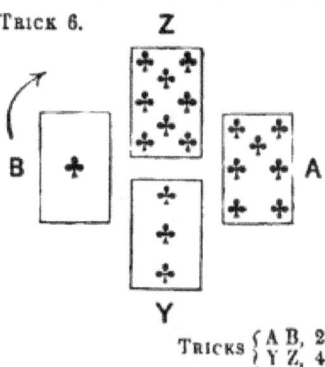

TRICKS $\begin{cases} A B, 2 \\ Y Z, 4 \end{cases}$

TRICK 7.

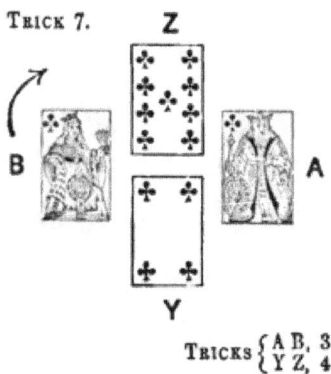

TRICKS $\begin{cases} A B, 3 \\ Y Z, 4 \end{cases}$

TRICK 8.

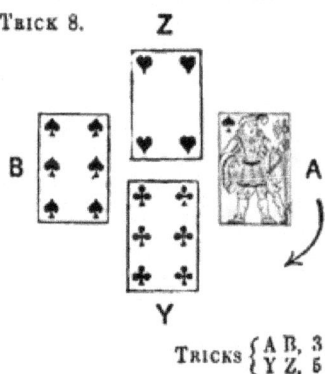

TRICKS $\begin{cases} A B, 3 \\ Y Z, 5 \end{cases}$

TRICK 9.

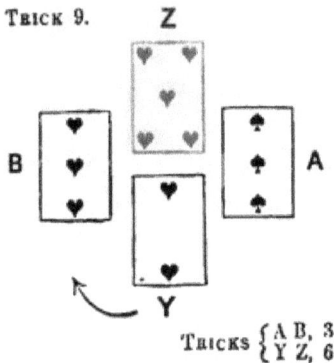

TRICKS $\begin{cases} \text{A B, 3} \\ \text{Y Z, 6} \end{cases}$

TRICK 10.

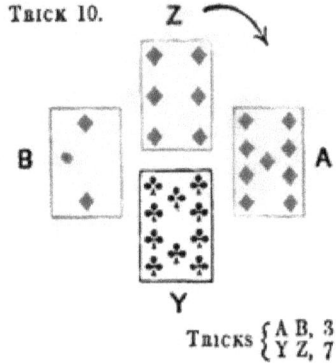

TRICKS $\begin{cases} \text{A B, 3} \\ \text{Y Z, 7} \end{cases}$

REMARK.—It is clear now that Y led from five hearts originally. Consequently, Y Z have all the remaining hearts between them.

REMARK.—Z can count his partner's hand, viz., three more hearts (*see* Remark, Trick 9,) and one other card, either the deuce of diamonds (*see* the fall of the diamonds, Tricks 4 and 5,) or a trump. If Y has the diamond, it matters not what Z leads, as B must then hold four trumps. Z therefore assumes that his partner has another trump, and plays to force him.

But if Z could not tell that Y has three hearts, or, rather, could tell that he has only two (*see* Appendix A, p. 257), Z's proper lead at Trick 10 would be the ace of hearts. For then B must have a heart, and if Z leads a losing diamond, B discards his heart on it, and wins the game.

THE HANDS.

(Y's hand is given above.)

A's HAND.	B's HAND.	Z's HAND.
Kg, Kv, 8,4,3,2 ♠	9, 7, 6 . . . ♠	Qn, 10 . . . ♠
Knv . . . ♥	8, 3 . . . . ♥	Ace, Qn, 6, 5, 4 ♥
Kg, 7 . . . ♣	Ace,Qn,Kv,5,2 ♣	9, 8 . . . . ♣
Qn, 9, 8, 7 . . ♦	Kg, 4, 2 . . ♦	Knv, 6, 5, 3 . ♦

At Trick 2, Z's better play would be to open the heart suit.

At Trick 6, B should play to force his partner in hearts, instead of leading trumps.

HAND XXXIV.

(Echo of the Call, *see* Appendix B, pp. 267, 268.)

Z's HAND.

Score : Love-all.

Eight of hearts turned up.

THE PLAY.

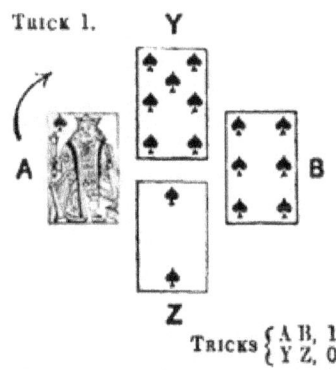

TRICK 1.

TRICKS { A B, 1
{ Y Z, 0

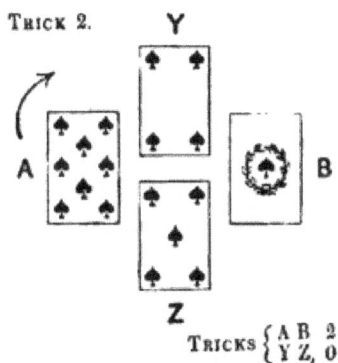

TRICK 2.

TRICKS { A B 2
{ Y Z, 0

REMARK (Trick 2).—Y has called for trumps. Z, having four trumps himself, commences to echo his partner's call (*see* Appendix B, pp. 267, 268).

TRICK 3.

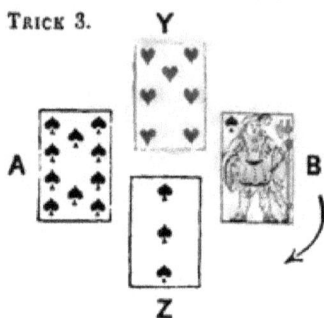

TRICKS $\begin{cases} \text{A B, 2} \\ \text{Y Z, 1} \end{cases}$

REMARK.—Z completes the echo of the call.

TRICK 4.

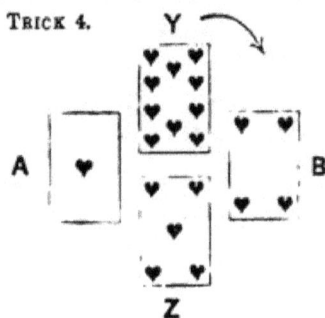

TRICKS $\begin{cases} \text{A B, 3} \\ \text{Y Z, 1} \end{cases}$

REMARK.—Y, perceiving the echo, has no hesitation in trumping and leading trumps.

TRICK 5.

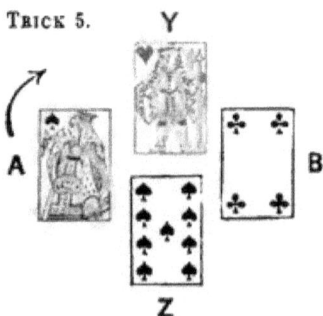

TRICKS $\begin{cases} \text{A B, 3} \\ \text{Y Z, 2} \end{cases}$

TRICK 6.

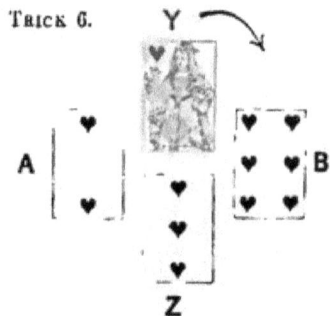

TRICKS $\begin{cases} \text{A B, 3} \\ \text{Y Z, 3} \end{cases}$

REMARK (Trick 6).—Notwithstanding that Y is forced again, he perseveres with the trump, as he knows from Z's echo that he may safely lead another round. After this round Y knows that Z has the remaining trumps.

R

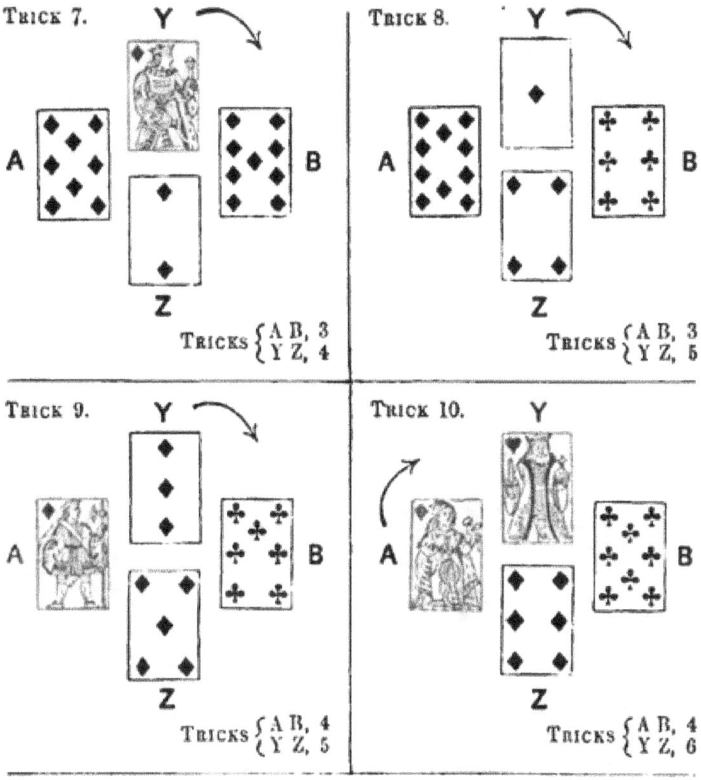

TRICK 7.

Y

A B

Z

TRICKS { A B, 3
Y Z, 4

TRICK 8.

Y

A B

Z

TRICKS { A B, 3
Y Z, 5

TRICK 9.

Y

A B

Z

TRICKS { A B, 4
Y Z, 5

TRICK 10.

Y

A B

Z

TRICKS { A B, 4
Y Z, 6

TRICKS 11 to 13.—Y (Trick 11) leads a club; Z trumps, and makes the remaining tricks; and

YZ score three by cards and two by honours.

But for the echo the game might easily have been missed. At Trick 4. Y might have thought it prudent not to lead a trump after being forced, when, if he tries two rounds of diamonds, B makes a small trump, and the game is saved. A similar remark applies with increased force to Trick 6, after Y has been forced again.

THE HANDS.

(Z's hand is given above.)

A's Hand.	Y's Hand.	B's Hand.
Kg, Qn, 10, 8 . ♠	7, 4 . . . . ♠	Ace, Knv, 6 . ♠
Ace, 2 . . . ♥	Kg, Q, Kv, 10, 7 ♥	6, 4 . . . . ♥
Qn, Knv, 3 . ♣	10, 5, 2 . . ♣	A, Kg, 9,8,7,6,4 ♣
Qn, Knv, 10, 8 ♦	Ace, Kg, 3 . ♦	9 . . . . . ♦

HAND XXXV.

Leading losing trump, and Echo of the Call
(*see* pp. 267, 268).

Y's Hand.

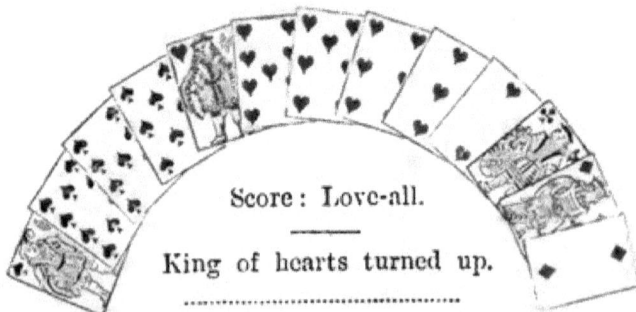

Score : Love-all.

King of hearts turned up.

THE PLAY.

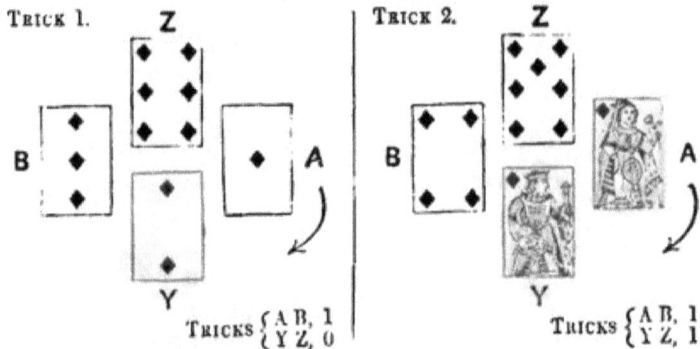

Trick 1.		
	Z	
B		A
	Y	

Tricks { A B, 1
{ Y Z, 0

Trick 2.		
	Z	
B		A
	Y	

Tricks { A B, 1
{ Y Z, 1

TRICK 3.

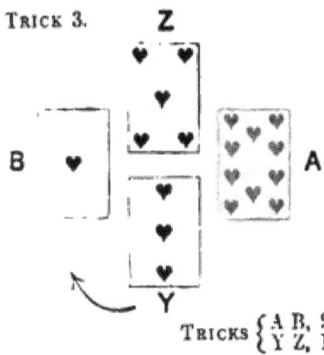

B

Z

A

Y

TRICKS { A B, 2
Y Z, 1

TRICK 4.

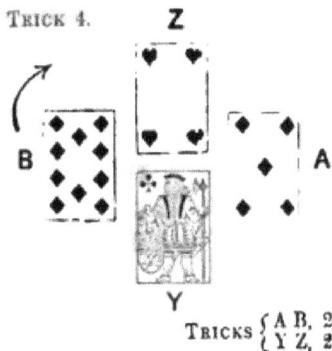

B

Z

A

Y

TRICKS { A B, 2
Y Z, 2

REMARK (Trick 4).—Z, at Trick 3, played the five of hearts, and now trumps with the four. He had therefore at least four trumps originally (*see* Appendix B, pp. 267, 268.)

TRICK 5.

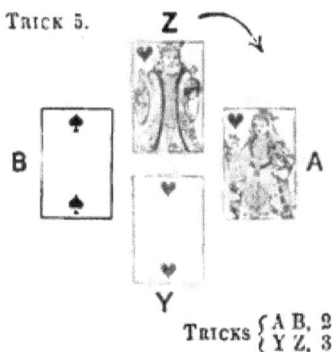

B

Z

A

Y

TRICKS { A B, 2
Y Z, 3

TRICK 6.

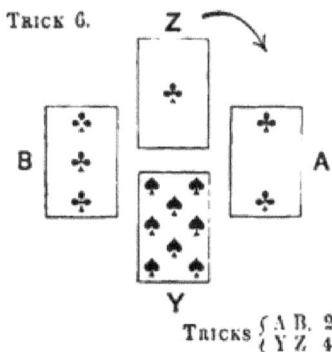

B

Z

A

Y

TRICKS { A B, 2
Y Z, 4

TRICK 7.

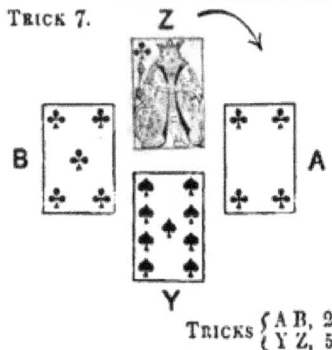

B

Z

A

Y

TRICKS { A B, 2
Y Z, 5

TRICK 8.

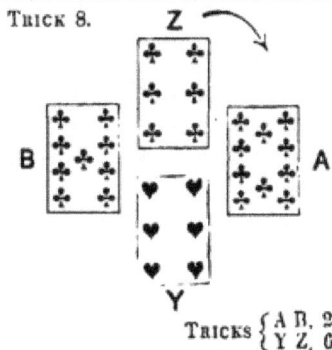

B

Z

A

Y

TRICKS { A B, 2
Y Z, 6

TRICK 9.

TRICK 10.

TRICKS { A B, 2
{ Y Z, 7

TRICKS { A B, 2
{ Y Z, 8

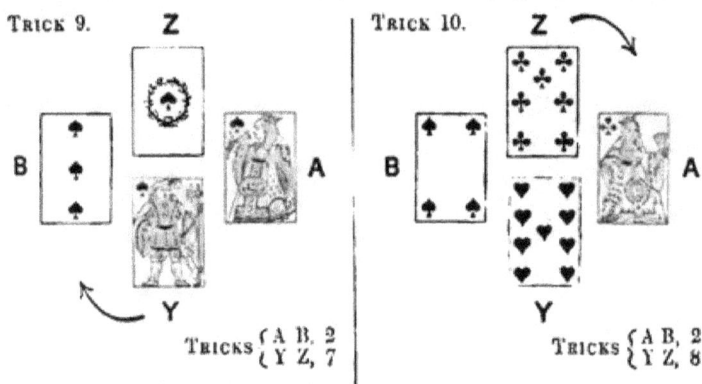

REMARK (Trick 10).—Well played by Y. He can count his partner's hand, viz., the eight of trumps (*see* Remark, Trick 4. and the fall of the hearts, Tricks 3, 4, and 5), the last club, and a losing spade, as Z, having put on the ace of spades (Trick 9), cannot have the king. Y therefore trumps with the nine, and (Trick 11) leads the seven of hearts to put the lead in Z's hand. Z (Trick 12) leads the club, to which Y discards the ten of spades; and

Y Z win five by cards.

THE HANDS.

(Y's hand is given above.)

A's HAND.	B's HAND.	Z's HAND.
Qn . . . . ♠	Kg, 7, 5, 4, 3, 2 ♠	Ace, 6 . . . ♠
Qn, 10 . . . ♥	Ace . . . ♥	Kg, 8, 5, 4 . . ♥
Qn, 10, 4, 2 . ♣	9, 5, 3 . . . ♣	Ace, Kg, 8, 7, 6 ♣
A, Qn, Kv, 9, 8, 5 ♦	10, 4, 3 . . . ♦	7, 6 . . . . . ♦

HAND XXXVI.

Coup of compelling a discard, same in principle as
the Vienna Coup.

Y's HAND.

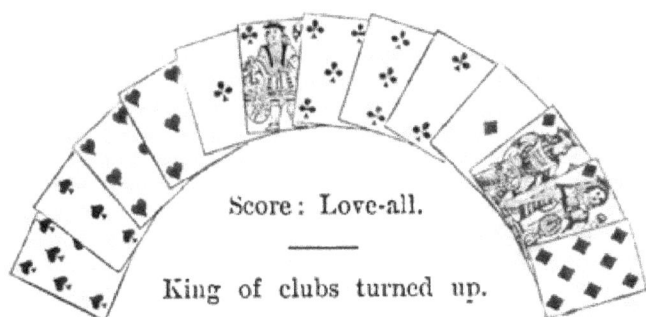

Score : Love-all.

———

King of clubs turned up.

THE PLAY.

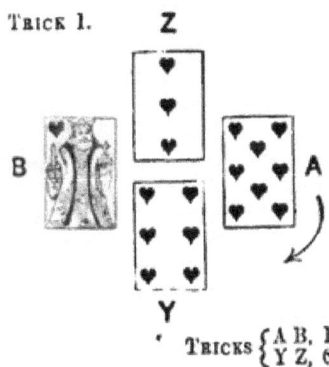

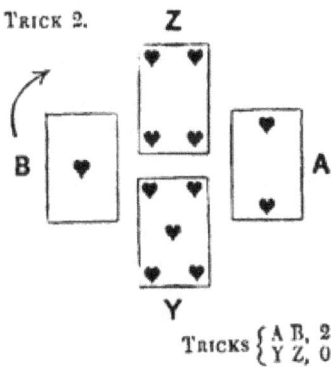

TRICK 3.

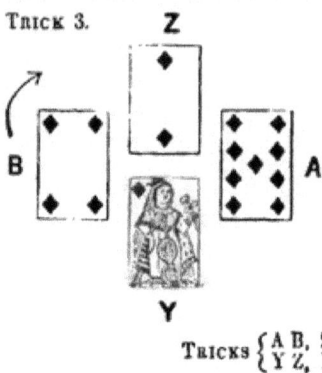

TRICKS { A B, 2
        { Y Z, 1

TRICK 4.

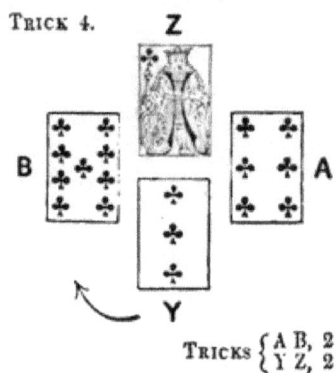

TRICKS { A B, 2
        { Y Z, 2

TRICK 5.

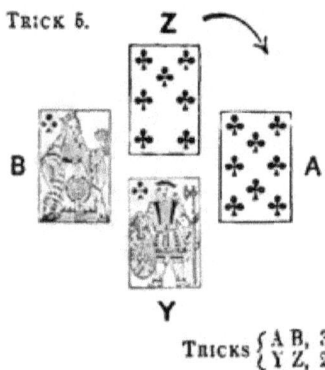

TRICKS { A B, 3
        { Y Z, 2

TRICK 6.

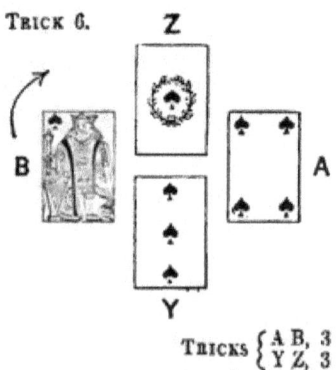

TRICKS { A B, 3
        { Y Z, 3

TRICK 7.

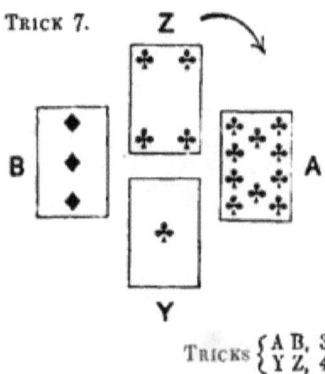

TRICKS { A B, 3
        { Y Z, 4

TRICK 8.

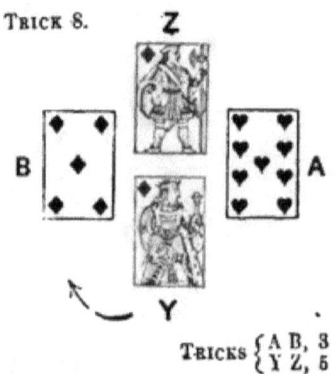

TRICKS { A B, 3
        { Y Z, 5

TRICK 9.

TRICK 10.

TRICKS $\begin{cases} \text{A B, 3} \\ \text{Y Z, 6} \end{cases}$ 　　　　TRICKS $\begin{cases} \text{A B, 3} \\ \text{Y Z, 7} \end{cases}$

REMARK (Trick 9).—Well played by Y. He can count B's hand as follows: ten and two small diamonds (for Z dropped the knave, Trick 8, and A renounced); queen of spades (*see* Trick 6—the lead of the king could only be from king, queen); and one other card, probably a small spade, for had B another heart he would most likely have continued his partner's original lead, instead of changing the suit. Y now leads a trump in hopes that B will discard the small spade, when Y will lead the seven of spades to throw the lead into B's hand, and B will be obliged to lead a diamond up to Y's tenace.

B, however, discards a diamond. Y continues his tactics (*see* Trick 10), leading another trump. This compels another discard from B. If B discards the small spade, Y leads the losing spade; if B discards another diamond, Y establishes the diamonds, and in either case wins the game. This fine *coup* occurred in actual play.

TRICKS 11 to 13.—Y (Trick 11) leads the spade. B is obliged (Trick 12) to lead a diamond; and

Y Z score three by cards and two by honours.

THE HANDS.

(Y's hand is given above.)

A's Hand.	B's Hand.	Z's Hand.
Knv, 9, 8, 4 . ♠	Kg, Qn, 2 . . ♠	Ace, 10, 6, 5 . ♠
Qn, 10, 9, 8, 2 ♥	Ace, Kg . . ♥	Knv, 7, 4, 3 . ♥
10, 8, 6 . . . ♣	Qn, 9 . . . ♣	Kg, 7, 4 . . ♣
9 . . . . . ♦	10, 7, 6, 5, 4, 3 . ♦	Knv, 2 . . . ♦

At Trick 10, B should notice that he must lose the game if he retains the queen of spades. His only chance of saving the game here is to discard the queen of spades, in hopes of finding his partner with two tricks in spades, or with a trick in spades and hearts. If A has not these cards, the game is lost.

HAND XXXVII.

Grand Coup (*see* pp. 130-134).

B's Hand.

Score: Love-all.

———

Ace of clubs turned up.

....

THE PLAY.

Trick 1.

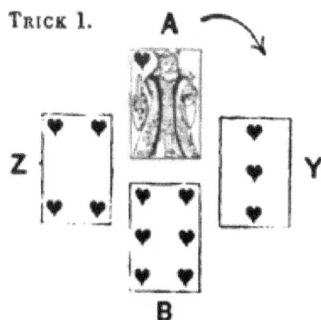

TRICKS $\begin{cases} A B, 1 \\ Y Z, 0 \end{cases}$

Trick 2.

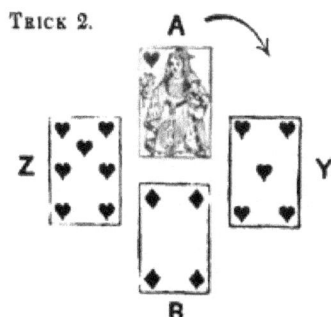

TRICKS $\begin{cases} A B, 2 \\ Y Z, 0 \end{cases}$

TRICK 3.

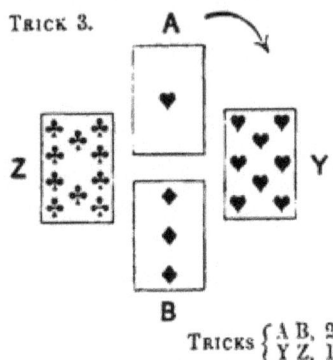

TRICKS $\left\{\begin{array}{l} A\,B,\ 2 \\ Y\,Z,\ 1 \end{array}\right.$

TRICK 4.

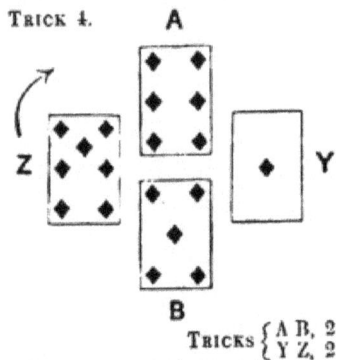

TRICKS $\left\{\begin{array}{l} A\,B,\ 2 \\ Y\,Z,\ 2 \end{array}\right.$

TRICK 5.

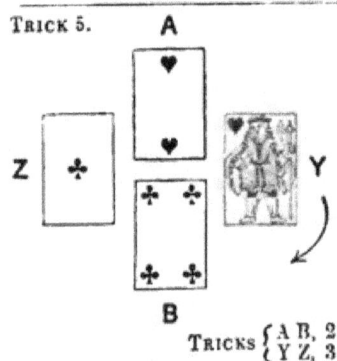

TRICKS $\left\{\begin{array}{l} A\,B,\ 2 \\ Y\,Z,\ 3 \end{array}\right.$

TRICK 6.

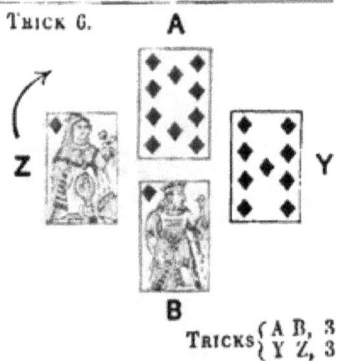

TRICKS $\left\{\begin{array}{l} A\,B,\ 3 \\ Y\,Z,\ 3 \end{array}\right.$

TRICK 7.

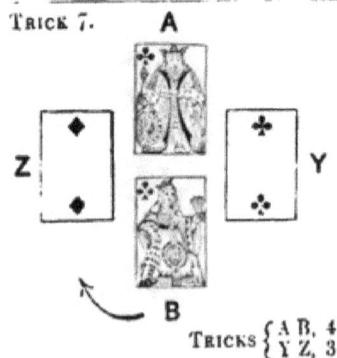

TRICKS $\left\{\begin{array}{l} A\,B,\ 4 \\ Y\,Z,\ 3 \end{array}\right.$

TRICK 8.

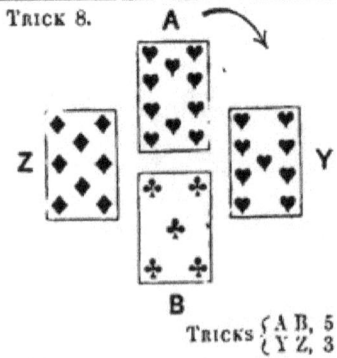

TRICKS $\left\{\begin{array}{l} A\,B,\ 5 \\ Y\,Z,\ 3 \end{array}\right.$

REMARK.—The fall of the king shows that the remaining clubs are in Y's hand.

REMARK.—Well played by B. All the hearts are out; the remaining diamonds are in Z's hand (*see* fall of the

diamonds, Tricks 2. 3, 4, 6, and 7), and all the clubs are
in Y's hand. Y must therefore have three trumps and
two spades. If B discards a spade to this trick, he cannot
avoid leading trumps twice up to Y. In that case, Y will
make two tricks in trumps, saving the game, as will be
apparent by so playing the cards. The result is otherwise
if B trumps his partner's best heart. He can then lead
out ace and king of spades, to which Y must follow suit ;
and by continuing with the six of clubs (the nine, eight,
and three are in against him), B secures the tenace, and
wins the game.

TRICKS 9 to 13.—B (Tricks 9 and 10) leads spades, and
(Trick 11) the six of clubs. B makes the last two tricks,
and

A B score three by cards and two by honours.

THE HANDS.

(B's hand is given above.)

A's HAND.	Y's HAND.	Z's HAND.
9, 5. 4, 3, 2 . ♠	Qn, 6 . . . ♠	Knv, 10, 8, 7 . ♠
Ace,Kg,Q,10,2 ♥	Knv, 9, 8, 5, 3 ♥	7, 4 . . . . ♥
Kg . . . . ♣	9, 8, 3, 2 . ♣	Ace, 10 . . . ♣
10, 6 . . . . ♦	Ace, 9 . . ♦	Qn, Knv, 8, 7, 2 ♦

HAND XXXVIII.

Grand Coup (*see* pp. 130-134).

Z's HAND.

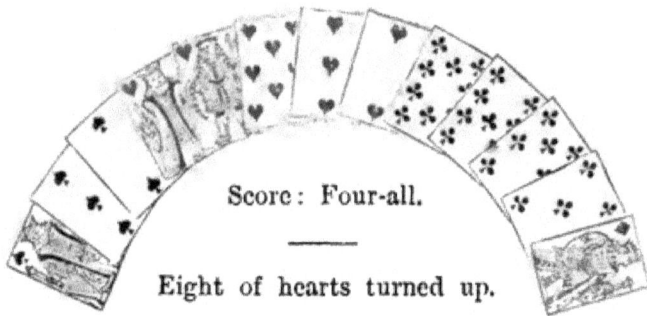

Score: Four-all.

———

Eight of hearts turned up.

THE PLAY.

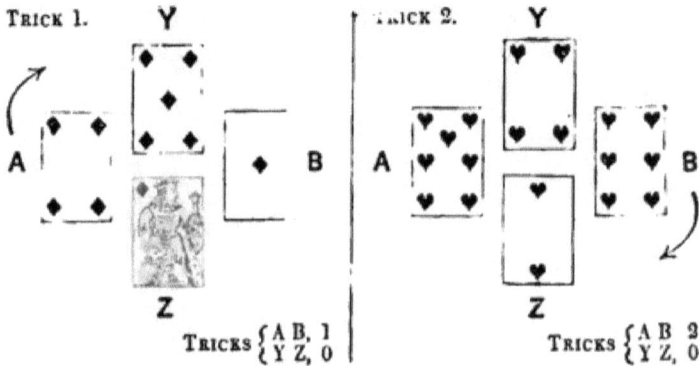

TRICK 1.

Y

A   B

Z

TRICKS $\begin{cases} \text{A B, } 1 \\ \text{Y Z, } 0 \end{cases}$

TRICK 2.

Y

A   B

Z

TRICKS $\begin{cases} \text{A B, } 2 \\ \text{Y Z, } 0 \end{cases}$

TRICK 3.

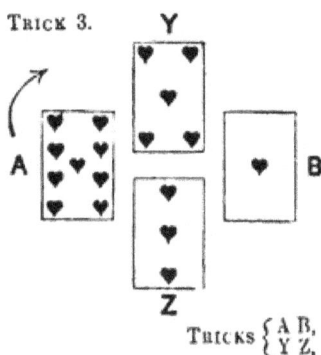

TRICK 4.

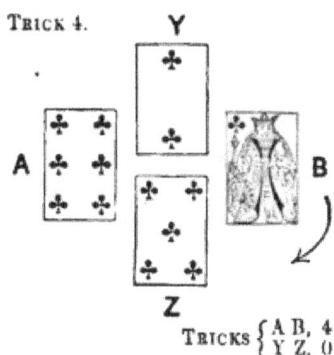

Tricks { A B, 3
         { Y Z, 0

Tricks { A B, 4
         { Y Z, 0

REMARK (Trick 3).—A and Y have no more trumps, and
Z knows that the queen, ten are in B's hand.

TRICK 5.

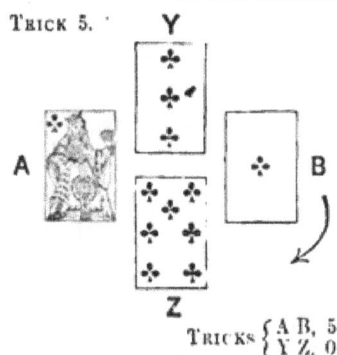

TRICK 6.

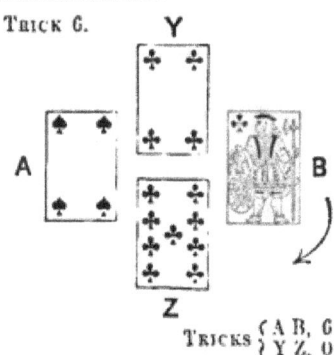

Tricks { A B, 5
         { Y Z, 0

Tricks { A B, 6
         { Y Z, 0

TRICK 7.

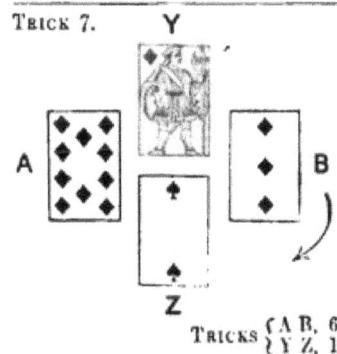

TRICK 8.

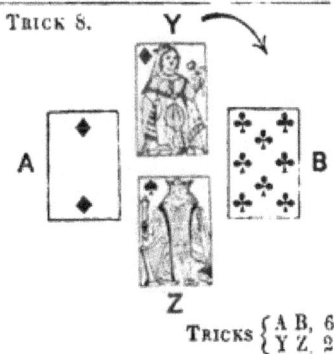

Tricks { A B, 6
         { Y Z, 1

Tricks { A B, 6
         { Y Z, 2

REMARK (Trick 8).—Z throws the king of spades

instead of the two.for this reason. If Z has the lead at
the tenth trick, he must lose a trick in trumps, and the
game. The king of spades is useless to Z. as he must lose
the game unless Y has the ace of spades; and Z fears, if
he retains the king, that his partner may refrain from
winning the tenth trick.

Of course, if Z had the ace of spades instead of the
king, he would similarly throw the ace at Trick 8, as
it is evident that in that case the game is lost unless
Y has the king of spades.

TRICK 9.

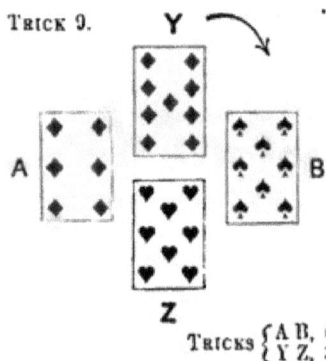

TRICKS { A B, 6
        { Y Z, 3

REMARK.—The *Grand Coup.*

TRICK 10.

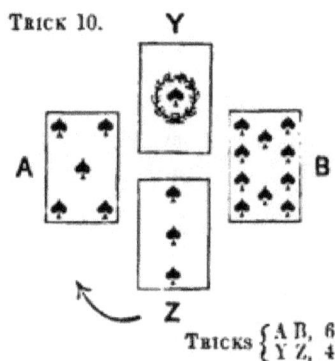

TRICKS { A B, 6
        { Y Z, 4

TRICK 11.

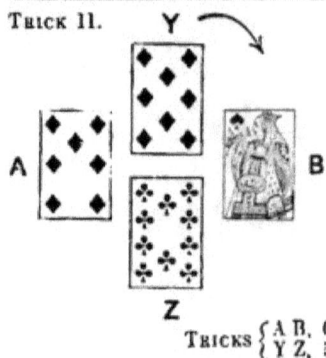

TRICKS { A B, 6
        { Y Z, 5

TRICKS 12 and 13.—Z
makes his two trumps; and

Y Z win the odd trick.

THE HANDS.

(Z's hand is given above.)

A's HAND.	Y's HAND.	B's HAND.
9, 7, 5, 4 . . ♠	Ace, Knv, 6 . ♠	Qn, 10, 8 . . ♠
9, 7 . . . . ♥	5, 4 . . . . ♥	Ace, Qn, 10, 6 ♥
Qn, 6 . . . ♣	4, 3, 2 . . . ♣	Ace, Kg, Knv, 8 ♣
10, 7, 6, 4, 2 . ♦	Qn, Knv, 9, 8, 5 ♦	Ace, 3 . . . ♦

It may be remarked that B refuses to trump several winning cards. He refrains advisedly. Knowing his left-hand adversary to have three more trumps, he expects that a trump must be led up to the queen, ten at Trick 11, and that he must then make the odd trick.

APPENDIX A.

ON THE CARD TO LEAD FROM SUITS OF FIVE OR MORE.

All Whist players are aware of the importance of affording information as to the unplayed cards they hold by following certain rules of play. Some of these rules are purely conventional—*i.e.*, it matters not which of several cards is played, so far as trick-making is concerned; but one card is frequently selected in preference to another for the simple purpose of giving information. The selection, however, is not an arbitrary one; it is made in conformity with the rules of play that in similar cases might affect trick-making, and, by analogy, the principle is extended to other cases (*see* p. 98, last paragraph).

A familiar instance of extension of principle is in the case of returned leads. All players know that, with only two cards remaining of a suit previously led once, the player returning the lead selects the highest of the two remaining cards. The original reason for this is that, inasmuch as three cards in a suit are less than the average, the suit is weak; and the weak suit is sacrificed in the endeavour to strengthen partner.

s

If you have two small cards remaining—say the trey and the deuce—it is not pretended that the return of the trey strengthens your partner in the least. But by adhering to the rule, by extending the principle to all cards, high or low, you enable a good partner to calculate how many you have left of the suit. The original reason for returning the high card is lost sight of, and, in such a case, the return of the trey is a mere convention.

The Author feels bound to go thus far into conventional rules because he is about to propose a conventional method of leading from suits containing five or more cards; and he wishes to show how far conventions are allowable at Whist, so as not to be met with the objection that his proposed method of leading is a mere arbitrary signal. In order to explain whence it is deduced, it will be necessary to enter at length into leads from inter-mediate sequences (*see* p. 62).

The general rule for leading from suits which contain no cards in sequence is to lead the lowest card, with the exception of ace and four or more small ones. From suits containing cards in sequence heading the suit, such as ace, king; king, queen; queen, knave, ten, the rule is to lead one of the sequence.

From suits containing a sequence that does not head the suit, the lowest card is led. The only generally admitted exception is in the case of king, knave, ten, and a small card or cards, from which the ten, the lowest of the intermediate cards in sequence, is led. So also from king, knave, ten, nine, &c., the nine is led; and from king, knave, ten, nine, eight, &c., the eight.

It has always surprised the writer to find that this mode of leading is confined to this particular sequence, instead of being extended to lower intermediate sequences. Thus, from king, ten, nine, eight, deuce, or from queen, ten, nine, eight, deuce, the eight seems the best card to lead, but the deuce is generally led. And, as no line can be drawn which will tell us where the trick-making advantage of leading from the sequence is to stop, the principle should be extended to *all* intermediate sequences when the suit contains at least five cards. This proviso is necessary, as, with the exception of the king, knave, ten, and one small card, there is no advantage in leading a middle card from suits of four cards only.

It has already been seen that extensions of principle obtain in similar cases, notoriously in the case of returned leads; therefore there can be no theoretical objection to pursuing the plan here advocated. But some players say there is a practical disadvantage. By leading the intermediate card you simulate a lead from a weak suit (*see* p. 67); and the disadvantage of concealing your strength for the moment, more than counterbalances the advantage your partner may subsequently derive when the true nature of the lead becomes evident.

But why, it may be asked, if your partner is not deceived by the lead of eight, from king, knave, ten, nine, eight, and a small one, should he be deceived by the lead of the eight from king, ten, nine, eight, and a small one?

The reply is on the surface. Whist players are accustomed to the one lead, and not to the other; and it is by no means easy to get people out of a groove in which they and their predecessors have run for over a hundred years.

Now there is a very good reason why the lead of the intermediate card ought not to deceive anyone who has confidence in his partner. It is this : The *original* lead of a good player is from his strongest suit.

If, then, this good player commences with an eight, and in the second round drops a smaller card, the eight cannot by the hypothesis be the best card of his suit, for he never chose such a suit to lead from originally during his career as a Whist player. What, then, can be the meaning of his lead? It may be (and would now be understood to be) from king, knave, ten, nine, eight, and a small card. It might equally be, if Whist players were less conservative, from king, ten, nine, eight, and a small card, or from queen, ten, nine, eight, and a small card; a protective card, lest the leader's partner should turn out to be very weak in the suit.

It is objected to this argument that the advantage, *quoad* trick-making, when you lead from a small intermediate card is next to nothing. This is true; but the lead of the intermediate card gives a great advantage to players who practise and understand it, inasmuch as, with the exception of the recognised king, knave, ten lead, *such a lead can only be made from a suit of five cards at least.* **Your** partner is thus informed, probably on the second round, of the number of cards of that suit remaining in your hand. The original reason of the rule—to prevent a very small card from winning the first trick—is lost sight of; and the rule is extended to all sequences, whether it improves the chance of trick-making or not, in order to enable your partner to count your hand. It need not be argued here that this is an admissible convention, as the subject has already been fully debated.

Every player (in the philosophical sense of the word) knows the advantages that accrue from being able to count the three cards in hand after an original lead of ace and a small one (an original lead be it observed, not a forced lead); and also the advantages derived from leading the knave from king, queen, knave, and more than one small one; the king from king, queen, knave, and only one small one. Indeed, no one will deny the importance of being able to tell his partner the number of cards he holds in a given suit, especially in a strong suit. This can be done by extending the original lead of the lowest card but one to *all suits of more than four cards, irrespective of their containing an intermediate sequence.*

Holding an intermediate sequence, as, for instance, knave, seven, six, five, two, it has already been argued that the five is the most advantageous card to lead. Now, suppose the suit to be knave, seven, six, five, four, the five is equally the card that conveys the most information, although not the lowest of an intermediate sequence; so with knave, seven, six, three, two, the three is similarly the card that conveys the most information. There is no sequence here, but by first leading the three (it being an original lead), and then dropping the two, you tell your partner that you have at least three more cards in the suit. This seems to be a legitimate extension of principle.

But, as this may be disputed, it may be as well to re-state the argument. In the parallel case of returned leads the card chosen is the one which enables your partner to count your hand. The original rule applied only to strengthening cards; but as in practice it has been found that adhering to the rule—even though the original reason for it is lost—enables a good player to count the remaining cards, a uniform method has been adopted in all cases, whether the card returned strengthens your partner's hand or not.

Now, if a player, when he holds a strong suit containing an intermediate sequence of three cards, leads the lowest but one of the suit, and, in other cases, the lowest, players would soon perceive that the former lead informs them that their partner held at least five of the suit originally; the latter lead that he held but four. By a train of reasoning, similar to that which has already settled the right card to lead in the case of returned leads, players, in order to enable their partners to count their hands, would naturally extend the rule to all suits of five or more cards, whether containing a sequence or not. The original reason for the rule (as in the parallel case of returned leads) no longer applies; and the lowest card but one is

selected *for the sole purpose of conveying information*.
It would be absurd to stop at small intermediate
sequences, and to say, for example, that from ten, six,
five, four, two, the **four may** legitimately be led to
convey information ; but that from ten, six, five, three,
two, the three may not be led for the same **purpose,**
because in the latter case there is no sequence.

It should not be overlooked that the negative advantage to be derived from this system of leading is
almost as great as the positive advantage. **If it is**
admitted that when you lead the lowest but one of
your strong suit you have at least five, and that when
you lead the lowest you have not five **of it, it is a**
moral certainty when you lead the **lowest** that you
have led from a suit of four exactly. Thus your hand
can be counted in another way.

The rule, then, that the Author proposes **as** the
result of the previous arguments is : *begin with the
lowest but one of the suit you lead originally if it
contains more than four cards.* Suits of ace and four
small ones; ace, king, and small ones; king, queen,
and small ones; king, knave, ten, and one or more
small ones **not in sequence** with the ten; and one
or two other well-known leads from commanding
strength—being of course excepted. There is also
another exception, viz., **in the case of six-card** suits.
From such a suit as queen, ten, **nine, eight, three,**
two, the eight is the best card to lead *quoad* trick-
making, and not **the small one.** Here the lowest but
two is led. This card, however, would be led in the
same way as the ten from king, knave, ten, &c., **by**

anyone who adopts the intermediate sequence lead ; and it would inform partner just as much as the lead of the three that the suit led from contains five cards at least.

Information as to the number of trumps you hold can be similarly communicated by trumping with the lowest but one, and then leading the lowest. Thus, you have ace, queen, eight, six, three of trumps, and **are forced.** You **trump** with the six, and lead the three, when your partner knows that you hold at least three more trumps.

The rule is so simple that anyone **can** practise it. It must be borne in mind that the rule only applies to *original* and not to *forced* leads ; and that it can only be advantageously practised **by** players who **have** confidence in each other, so far as to feel certain that the original lead of each partner is from his strongest suit.

Frequent practice for some two years with good players, who have adopted this mode of leading from five-card suits, has fully convinced the Author of the soundness of the propositions contained in this Appendix, **and of** the advantage of.adopting the practice here recommended.

The only case in **which a** mistake **is** possible is **when** trumps are led originally from numerically weak trumps, with very strong cards in all the plain suits, **or** in desperation. But as in both these cases partner's game is nearly always to go on with trumps at all hazards, his uncertainty as to **the real character of** the lead is of but small consequence.

Mr. Clay, in his "Treatise on Whist," has devoted

a chapter to advocating a contrary view of leads from intermediate sequences. As the opinions of that great player are certain to influence a very large number of persons, the Author has obtained permission to state that Mr. Clay, on reading the foregoing pages (printed for private circulation among members of the Portland and other Clubs), said to the Author, " You have convinced me. When I play with you at the Portland, I shall adopt your system." And Mr. Clay did afterwards at the Portland, to the Author's certain knowledge, use this mode of leading from suits of five cards.

RECAPITULATION.

1. One card is often selected in preference to another for the sole purpose of affording information, and especially of enabling your partner to count your hand, provided always that such selection harmonises with the play which would be naturally adopted in similar cases.

2. The card chosen conveys information in these cases in consequence of a conventional understanding between players generally, a rule being adhered to, notwithstanding that the reason for it no longer exists, because, by practising a uniform system, partner is informed as to the contents of your hand.

3. The lead of the lowest of an intermediate sequence being admitted to be correct in some cases.

s *

as conducing to trick-making, the lead of the lowest
of an intermediate sequence is permissible as a conventional rule—whether such lead conduces to trick-
making or not—in order to impart information, and
to enable partner to count your hand.

4. As, by leading the lowest but one of a suit which
contains an intermediate sequence, partner is enabled
to determine whether the original lead is from a suit
of four or of more than four cards, the rule of leading
the lowest but one may be still further extended to all
suits of more than four cards, whether they contain
intermediate sequences or not, for the purpose of conveying information as to the number of cards originally
held in the suit.

For an illustration, *see* Hand **XXXIII.**

APPENDIX B.

———◦◆◦———

THE ECHO OF THE CALL.

The more advanced players of the present day have adopted an extension of the call for trumps (*see* pp. 106-108), which has received the name of the *Echo*. Echoing a call consists in asking for trumps in response to your partner's ask, when, but for his demand, you would not have called.

The strength which is usually regarded as the minimum that justifies an *original call* is four trumps, two being honours; or five trumps, one being an honour. Late in a hand, when you have already had the opportunity of calling and have not called, you would occasionally be justified in asking with less strength, the fall of the cards showing you that a trump lead is imperatively necessary. This subsequent call has not the same force as an original call, and does not necessarily imply such great strength in trumps.

Now, suppose your partner to have called for trumps originally, and that you have had the chance of making an original call and have not availed yourself of it. After perceiving your partner's call, you also call. What does your call mean? It means that, though you were not strong enough to dictate a trump lead *ab initio*, you are strong enough to help your partner, and you would be very glad to see trumps out.

Numerical strength is of more importance in this case than commanding strength. It has therefore

s * 2

been laid down as a rule, that you should not echo a call unless you have at least four trumps. With four trumps, however small, you should echo.

Similarly, if your partner leads trumps, and you have four or more, you should call in the trump suit, or at the first opportunity.

On the same principle you should echo a call or a trump lead, when you hold four trumps, even if you have not previously declined the opportunity of calling. Here your partner cannot tell whether your card is an original or an echoing one; but he is, at all events, informed that you have numerical strength in trumps.

The advantages of the echo are manifold. Your partner being strong in trumps may hesitate to take a force, but your echo enables him to do so without fear, and to persevere with the trump lead. Or, your partner may be in doubt after the second round of trumps as to the policy of playing a third. But if he can count two more trumps in your hand he will be directed. Thus: eight are out, your partner has three more; you have echoed. He will know that the other two are in your hand, and will not draw two for none, as, without the echo, he might do.

The negative advantage of the echo should not be overlooked. Thus: to take the same case of eight trumps being out, and the leader with three more trumps. You (his partner) have had the chance of sounding an echo, but have not done so. The leader knows that you have not two of the remaining trumps, and he will regulate his game accordingly.

For illustrations of these remarks, *see* Hands XXXIV and XXXV.

ADVERTISEMENTS.